BF315 .V399 2010

The hidden brain :how our
unconscious minds elect
presidents, control
33663004632937

P9-DYO-537

DATE DUE

APR 2 5 2011	
JUN 1 9 2012	
JUL 0 5 2012	

BRODART, CO.   Cat. No. 23-221

SPI
EGE
L&G
RAU

THE HIDDEN BRAIN

THE
HIDDEN BRAIN

How Our Unconscious Minds
Elect Presidents, Control Markets,
Wage Wars, and Save Our Lives

Shankar Vedantam

SPIEGEL & GRAU

NEW YORK

2010

Copyright © 2010 by Shankar Vedantam

All rights reserved.

Published in the United States by Spiegel & Grau, an imprint of
The Random House Publishing Group, a division of Random House, Inc., New York.

SPIEGEL & GRAU and Design is a registered trademark
of Random House, Inc.

Library of Congress Cataloging-in-Publication Data
Vedantam, Shankar.
The hidden brain: how our unconscious minds elect presidents,
control markets, wage wars, and save our lives / Shankar Vedantam.
p. cm.
ISBN 978-0-385-52521-3
eBook ISBN 978-1-588-36939-0
1. Subconsciousness.   2. Perception.   3. Motivation (Psychology).
4. Selectivity (Psychology).   5. Discrimination—Psychological aspects.   I. Title.
BF315.V399 2009   154.2—dc22   2009019717

Printed in the United States of America on acid-free paper

www.spiegelandgrau.com

2 4 6 8 9 7 5 3

Book design by Victoria Wong

ACC LIBRARY SERVICES AUSTIN, TX

For my father, Vedantam L. Sastry,
who has braved innumerable obstacles with fortitude,
and for my daughter, Anya,
with love and gratitude

Contents

THE HIDDEN BRAIN

Introduction

n the spring of 2004, *The Washington Post* assigned me to track Ralph Nader in New England as he campaigned for president. When I got to Boston, several of Nader's own aides, mindful of the consumer advocate's role as spoiler in the disputed 2000 election between George W. Bush and Al Gore, told me they were going to vote against him. Since Nader's campaign was going nowhere, I took a break from the political story and called a local psychologist I'd heard about.

Mahzarin Banaji agreed to meet me on short notice. We met in the afternoon at her corner office in Harvard University's psychology department. It was an extraordinary interview: When I left, three hours later, the whole world looked different.

Banaji studied unconscious prejudices—subtle cognitive errors that lay beneath the rim of awareness. Her research disturbed me because it showed that the way we usually think about human behavior is flawed. Volunteers in Banaji's experiments believed they were acting fairly, honorably, and wisely, but their actions were at odds with their intentions. They meant to do one thing but did something else. Strangely, until a psychological test revealed the discrepancy, the volunteers were not aware that they had been subtly biased.

If unconscious forces could influence us when we made swift judgments about other people, could these forces influence us *all the time*? Upon returning to Washington, I quickly found research that showed how hidden tugs caused people to make grave financial errors and misjudgments about risk. Experiments were showing that voters could be manipulated into choosing one candidate over another—without the voters ever realizing they were manipulated. Unconscious traits explained why some married couples drifted apart and why some teams worked well together. Everywhere I looked, I found evidence of hidden cognitive mechanisms. Unconscious biases in the way memory, emotion, and attention work produced misunderstandings and protracted conflicts between people, groups—even nations. Subtle errors of the mind could explain why we have rushed into foolish wars and why we have sat on our hands as genocides unfolded. Banaji was a social psychologist, but streams of intersecting data about a hidden world in our head were flowing in from other branches of psychology, from sociology and political science, from economics and neuroscience. High-tech scans are revealing brain mechanisms that governed everything from our political preferences to our table manners. Sociological experiments explained why people unconsciously made fatal mistakes during disasters. There was even research into the unconscious biases of suicide bombers.

Most people equate the term "unconscious bias" with prejudice or partiality, but the new research was using the term differently: "Unconscious bias" described any situation where people's actions were at odds with their intentions. The devilish thing was that people never felt manipulated. They rationalized their biases away—and even claimed ownership for actions they had not intended. Some unconscious biases were comical, others were innocuous. Many were useful. But the deadly ones conjured a Shakespearean image in my mind: the demonic Iago manipulating the gullible Othello into believing his wife was unfaithful. Like Iago, unconscious bias influenced people subtly, not overtly. It caused them to make serious errors of judgment—and then feel certain about their conclusions. It derived much of its power from the fact that people were unaware of it.

Theories about the unconscious mind went back centuries, but the new research appealed to me because it was based on measurable evidence. It relied on controlled experiments. It produced data. As a science journalist at *The Washington Post,* and before that at *The*

Philadelphia Inquirer, I found myself attracted to research that explored complex social behavior using the tools of rigorous science. Where previous accounts of the unconscious mind often produced dramatic theories with limited impact, the new research was producing modest theories about the mind—but they had dramatic impact. In writing a *Washington Post* column called *Department of Human Behavior* that I launched in 2006, I learned that one reason unconscious biases were difficult to spot is that they were often mundane. When we saw something as monstrous as genocide, we wanted an explanation that was equally dramatic. We demanded Hitlers to explain holocausts. Dramatic explanations didn't just fit better—they allowed us to write off systematic errors in human judgment, perception, and moral reasoning as mere aberrations.

I saw that a vast gulf had grown between what experts were learning about the mind and what most people believed. Important institutions in our society were oblivious to the new research. When disasters trapped thousands, we widened the exits to tall buildings and assumed this would allow people trapped by future disasters to escape. When discrimination reared its head, we passed hate crime laws. When the stock markets acted crazy, we blamed "unreasonable panic." We believed that frightening teenagers about the consequences of drugs and unsafe sex would prompt them to be careful, we assumed that fact-checking the tall claims of politicians would set the record straight, and we were sure that good laws produced good behavior. All these theories were based on an assumption—that human behavior was the product of knowledge and conscious intention. We believed that if you educated people, and provided them with accurate information, and offered them the right incentives, and threatened them with suitable punishments, and appealed to their better natures, and marked the exits clearly, the errors would vanish. Bad outcomes had to be the product of stupidity, ignorance, and bad intentions.

Like many assumptions, this one was impervious to contradictory evidence. When teenagers got drunk and wrecked their cars, when voters believed a politician's lies, and when juries convicted innocent people, we invariably concluded that those particular teens must have been stupid, that those particular voters must have been gullible, and that those particular juries must have been rash. Even when such errors were multiplied hundreds or thousands of times—when large numbers of people failed to flee disasters, when entire ethnic groups subscribed to vicious prejudices, when millions failed to intervene as their neighbors were dragged off to concentration camps—we convinced ourselves that these behaviors were aberrational, not the norm. The new research showed that many errors, mishaps, and tragedies were caused by unconscious forces that acted upon people without their awareness or consent. The irresponsible driver, the apathetic bystander, and the panicked investor were not aberrations. They were us.

Thinking about human behavior in the context of unconscious bias explained many things to me that previously seemed inexplicable. It wasn't just the small stuff—the gifted athlete who choked under pressure, the family feud over something trivial, the misjudgment in risk that produced a fender-bender—it was the big stuff, too. The uncritical decisions of policy makers that led to domestic and foreign policy catastrophes? Check. The stampeding panics that dragged entire economies to ruin? Check. The collective willingness of nations to avert their gaze from oncoming disasters? That, too. Unconscious biases have always dogged us, but multiple factors made them especially dangerous today. Globalization and technology, and the intersecting faultlines of religious extremism, economic upheaval, demographic change, and mass migration have amplified the effects of hidden biases. Our mental errors once affected only ourselves and those in our vicinity. Today, they affect people in distant lands and generations yet unborn. The flapping butterfly that caused a hurricane halfway around the world was a theoretical construct; today, subtle biases in faraway minds produce real storms in our lives. This book grew out of these thoughts. I wanted to place the ideas that I found so exciting, unnerving, and provocative before a larger audience. If science and rigorous studies were to be the backbone of the book, I wanted to show why the research mattered—not just in the ivory tower, but in the public square. I decided to find stories from real life that could illustrate the extraordinary effects of unconscious bias in everyday life. The selection of stories in this book is mine and mine alone. To the extent that they are wrong, misleading, or simplistic, the responsibility lies solely with me. To the extent that they are revealing and insightful—and not merely interesting—the credit mostly belongs to the hundreds of researchers whose work I have cited.

I made a deliberate decision to personify the hidden forces that influence us in everyday life. I coined a term: the hidden brain. It did not refer to a secret agent inside our skulls or some recently unearthed brain module. The "hidden brain" was shorthand for a range of influences that manipulated us without our awareness. Some aspects of the hidden brain had to do with the pervasive problem of mental shortcuts or heuristics, others were related to errors in the way memory and attention worked. Some dealt with social dynamics and relationships. What was common to them all was that we were unaware of their influence. There were dimensions of the hidden brain where, with effort, we could become aware of our biases, but there were many aspects of the hidden brain that were permanently sealed off from introspection. Unconscious bias was not caused by a secret puppeteer who sat inside our heads, but the effects of bias were *as though* such a puppeteer existed. The "hidden brain," in other words, was a writing device, much like the "selfish gene." Just as there were no strands of DNA that shouted "Me first!" no part of the human brain was disguised under sunglasses and fedora. By drawing a simple line between mental activities we were aware of and mental activities we were not aware of, the "hidden brain" subsumed many concepts in wide circulation whose definitions were frequently the subject of dissension: the unconscious, the subconscious, the implicit.

If my debt to the researchers whose work I have cited is immense, my debt to those who shared personal stories with me is incalculable. Many stories in this book describe the effects of unconscious bias on people during moments of great vulnerability. The opening chapter is about a woman who made a serious error identifying the man who raped her. It is a story I would have preferred not to tell—journalistic accounts of rape are troubling for many reasons—but sex crimes offer a powerful window into unconscious bias because they allow us to measure the accuracy of human intuitions against the iron rigor of

DNA tests. I doubt I would have had the courage to share the story that Toni Gustus shared with me. Her honesty and the honesty of many others in this book reminded me of a great truth: Good people are not those who lack flaws, the brave are not those who feel no fear, and the generous are not those who never feel selfish. Extraordinary people are not extraordinary because they are invulnerable to unconscious biases. They are extraordinary because they choose to do something about it.

CHAPTER 1

The Myth of Intention

Five days before her thirtieth birthday, on August 24, 1986, Toni Gustus was out on her patio. It was a Sunday, about four o'clock in the afternoon, and Gustus was in a T-shirt working on some plants. She had just moved to Massachusetts from Iowa; the only contact she had in town was the person who had hired her for a job at the United Way in Framingham. She had found a small two-bedroom basement apartment with a living room that opened onto a sunken patio. When she stood on the patio, the street came up to her chest.

A man strolled by and asked for directions. His eyes seemed glassy and his speech was slurred. Gustus did not know how to direct the man, but her Midwestern upbringing kept her from giving a curt answer and turning away. She told him she was new in town and unsure of the local geography. She pointed him in a direction she thought might be helpful. The man did not turn away. He took another step toward the patio and asked if a different street could take him to the same place. She told him what she knew, but she was starting to feel uncomfortable. It was as if they were suddenly having a conversation. The man took another step to the edge of the patio. Gustus told the man she had to go inside. She turned, and he jumped down onto the patio. He grabbed her arm. She raised her voice immediately and told him to leave. He asked for a glass of water. Gustus could smell alcohol on his breath. She protested, and he started to shove her back into the apartment.

A driver in a passing car saw a man and woman having what seemed to be an altercation on a patio. The driver went to the corner, turned around, and came back for another look. By the time the car got back to the spot, the patio was empty. The driver moved on.

The intruder was not much taller than Gustus. She was about five foot five, and he may have been five foot nine or ten. But he was considerably stronger. The moment he shoved her into the apartment, she started fighting. She screamed, and he clamped a hand over her mouth. He was carrying a portable music player, and Gustus seized the headphones cord and wound it around his neck. He seized her throat. They struggled, trying to subdue each other, until Gustus felt she was going to pass out. Something more primal than fear kicked in. Gustus let go of the headphones cord and went passive. It wasn't just that he was stronger: He was so drunk that she feared he might asphyxiate her and not even know it. No matter what happened, she wanted to get out alive.

The moment he started removing her clothes, another instinct kicked in. Gustus started to memorize details about the man. He was white and in his early twenties. He had a little black cross on one arm that may have been ink or may have been a tattoo. He had dark blond hair that fell over his forehead and his ears. His hair was parted in the middle. His nose was long in proportion to his face. His eyes were blue and relatively narrow. He had a tapered jaw. On and on she went, looking for distinctive features. She swore to herself, *I am not going to forget this face.*

After he raped her, the man allowed her to dress. He put on his clothes. He was not done; it appeared he wanted to have a conversation. Gustus could not believe he wanted small talk. In a sympathetic voice, he told her that "Sometimes it is not good for women when it is like this."

Gustus was stunned: He had no idea what he had just done. He was subdued for now, but who knew how long it would last? Screaming for help was out of the question; she had tried that, and no one had responded. She had to get out of the apartment. Calmly keeping up her end of the small talk, she told the rapist she needed a glass of water from the kitchen. She asked if he wanted a glass, too. He did nothing to stop her from walking out of the living room. The door to the apartment was next to the kitchen, and Gustus simply opened the door and kept walking. A strange calm descended upon her. She knew what she had to do. From a drugstore, she called her boss and told him what had happened. He drove by, picked her up, and took her to the police station.

Police officers administered a rape kit, and immediately asked Gustus to tell them everything distinctive about the rapist. Gustus unloaded every detail she had memorized about the man—the nose, the chin, the eyes, the hair. The man had been wearing a blue and white shirt, a blue windbreaker, and jeans. An artist came up with a composite picture that Gustus thought was fairly accurate. She told the police the man's voice was slurred, but she was good with voices and had memorized how he sounded.

By the time the police arrived at the crime scene, the rapist was gone, but he had left his windbreaker behind. There was a burrito wrapped in plastic and foil inside one pocket. Police officers traced it to a convenience store. There was a black-and-white-film security camera in the store, and the police showed Gustus the grainy video. She recognized the rapist the moment she saw him even though the tape did not show his face. Gustus had memorized the man's body language, the way he carried himself.

The police showed her photos of a number of possible suspects and pictures from local high school yearbooks. None of the photos matched the rapist. About a month after the crime, the police asked Gustus if a drifter they had picked up was the man. Gustus said no. In early December, the police picked up a man who matched the composite picture. Late one evening, police detectives brought Gustus a set of fifteen photos. Gustus pointed to the photo of the man the police had picked up, but she said she needed to see him before she could be sure. Through a one-way mirror at the police station, Gustus thought she saw the rapist. She was cautious by nature, and asked if she could hear the man's voice. The police held a door ajar so Gustus could hear the suspect speak. Gustus told the police she was 95 percent sure that the man in custody was the rapist. His name, she learned, was Eric Sarsfield.

Gustus spent Christmas that year with her family, in a small Illinois town across the Iowa border. She had thought a lot about Sarsfield in the days after she'd identified him. She was quite certain he was the rapist but was worried about the sliver of doubt at the back of her mind. Gustus was the sort of person who took responsibility for everything; no matter the situation, she asked herself what she had done wrong, or what she could have done better. Was her sliver of uncertainty only a manifestation of this trait to doubt herself? There was a Presbyterian church in town that Gustus had long known; it was a place of refuge and comfort. She was a person of faith, and the church always renewed her. She used to sing in the choir, and the choir director had been her voice teacher.

Sitting in the safe space of the church, ensconced by family, Gustus suddenly felt the burden of doubt lift from her shoulders. She was not 95 percent sure that Eric Sarsfield was the rapist; she was 100 percent certain.

She testified against Sarsfield. When asked how certain she was that the man sitting in the defendant's chair was the rapist, Gustus said she was sure. The defense, of course, pointed out that Gustus had initially not been certain. But there were many things about Gustus and the crime that made her testimony compelling. She had seen her assailant for an hour in broad daylight on a sunny day. She was an extraordinarily diligent witness with a keen memory for every distinctive detail about the rapist. Her trustworthiness was unimpeachable, her caution exemplary. She was not the kind of person to say Sarsfield was guilty if she had the slightest doubt. Sarsfield pleaded innocent, but that did not mean much. Gustus told herself that it was possible he had no recollection of the crime because he had been so drunk.

The jury was out for several days. As usual, Gustus took responsibility for the delay. She remonstrated with herself for being so cautious at first. She was now afraid that the doubt she had initially expressed would cause the jury to set free a dangerous man—a rapist who would go on to harm other women. She wanted to see Sarsfield convicted and put behind bars. In the end, when the jury found him guilty, Gustus felt a tremendous relief. The months since the crime had been terribly difficult, and she wanted to move on with her life.

She put the case out of her mind. Over time, she learned that Sarsfield had appealed his conviction, that he'd been turned down, and that he had gone to prison. Gustus got married and settled down.

In 2000, fourteen years after the crime, Gustus received a letter from the district attorney in Middlesex County. It said new evidence had come to light in the case and asked her to come in for a chat. The letter instantly triggered doubts—and dread. Gustus turned to her husband and said, "Oh my God. Something has happened and it is not really him." She learned that a DNA test had been conducted using the rape kit that the police had administered on the day of the crime. The test showed that Sarsfield could not have been the rapist. Gustus did not know much about DNA and was full of questions. She spent half her time blaming herself for not taking her initial sliver of doubt seriously, and the other half wondering about the accuracy of DNA tests. She had a talk with a friend who knew about the science of genetic testing and reassured herself that the test was accurate and had been conducted by a reputable laboratory. But her doubts persisted. She had seen what she had seen. She would never have testified against Sarsfield if she had not been sure he was the rapist. She had gone fourteen years being certain that Sarsfield was guilty.

About a year later, a lawyer got in touch with Gustus to ask if she wanted to meet a client—Eric Sarsfield. The lawyer assured her that Sarsfield bore her no ill will and had forgiven her for misidentifying him. Gustus was not sure about a meeting. For one thing, she was still unconvinced that Sarsfield was innocent. But if the test was right and she was wrong, that was horrible, too. An innocent man had spent years in prison, while the real rapist had gone scot-free. Some thirteen years of Sarsfield's life had been erased. It wasn't just the time he'd spent behind bars—Sarsfield had suffered terribly at the hands of guards and other inmates. He was not just broken physically, he was a mental wreck.

Gustus went into therapy to work out her fears and confusions. Finally, she consented to a meeting with Sarsfield, but insisted it be on her terms. Her husband would accompany her, and the meeting would take place in her therapist's office. When Eric Sarsfield showed up, he brought his fiancée and his lawyer.

The moment they greeted each other, Gustus saw something she had not seen before in Eric Sarsfield—not at the police station when she'd initially identified him through a one-way mirror, not when police had held a door ajar so she could hear his voice, and not in court when he'd sat silently before her as she testified. What she saw convinced her that she had made a terrible mistake.

Gustus had had crooked teeth as a child and had worn braces— teeth were something she noticed. The rapist had had even teeth. Gustus had not mentioned this to the police—and they hadn't asked—because everyone had been trying so hard to focus on things about the rapist that were distinctive. There was nothing distinctive about the rapist's teeth.

The moment Eric Sarsfield opened his mouth to say hello, the first thing Gustus noticed was that he had crooked teeth.

The story of Toni Gustus and Eric Sarsfield is a story about multiple tragedies. Gustus was a blameless victim who mistakenly sent the wrong man to prison. Sarsfield was traumatized for having been wrongly incarcerated. But there was a third victim, too: all of us. The man who raped Gustus was never apprehended. He may have harmed others, and may do so again.

The tragedies illustrate the immense consequences of unconscious bias in our lives. Toni Gustus made a mistake, but it was not an error based in malice or hatred. It was an unintentional error of the mind. Her testimony and her confidence that she had identified the right person were truly powerful. The jury that convicted Sarsfield made a mistake, too, but it was not a mistake caused by recklessness or ill will. In hindsight, we know the jury underweighted the doubt Gustus initially had and ignored problematic aspects of the case—Sarsfield had been drinking the night Gustus identified him, and the slurred voice she heard through the door that the police held ajar may have sounded more like the rapist's than it would have otherwise. The police may have subtly prompted Gustus to finger Sarsfield as they showed her the photo array. But asked to choose between a compelling eyewitness and data that did not quite add up, the jury trusted the emotional testimony of an eyewitness who said she was certain about what she saw.

The case highlights the most distinguishing characteristic of the biases that are the subject of this book: We are not aware of their existence. The endless photos that the police showed Gustus after the crime weakened her memory of her rapist, *even though it did not feel that way to her.* Her relief at being home with family and in her church soothed away her doubts, *even though she felt she was being rigorous.* As Gustus diligently recounted the rapist's features, she ignored a crucial detail, *even though she felt she had reported everything.*

The police and prosecutors believed Sarsfield was guilty and failed to think critically about their conclusions. The jury got swept up. Everyone was wrong, but no one felt anything was wrong. Gustus desperately wanted to get things right. It is particularly instructive that she remembers the precise moment when her doubts vanished. In the safe sanctuary of her church, she exhaled and told herself, *"It is him."*

There is abundant research showing that our mood states—comfort and peace, anger and envy—influence our memory and judgment. Gustus's doubt about Sarsfield was a source of discomfort; the church offered Gustus comfort. The two things had nothing to do with each other—except that it is impossible to feel both comfort and discomfort at the same time. Discomfort, not comfort, was Gustus's real friend in the situation. By soothing it away, she erased the signal she had that something was wrong. Instead of attending to the fire, she unintentionally disabled the fire alarm.

It is also instructive that both Gustus and the police focused on distinctive details about the rapist, while ignoring the routine. Unconscious algorithms in the brain prompt people to pay more attention to the unusual—a tattoo or a voice—than to the everyday. The one physical feature that could have distinguished the rapist from Sarsfield—his teeth—was discarded not because it was hidden from view but because it was too ordinary to mention.

What happened to Toni Gustus is not an aberration. The influence that emotions wield over judgment and countless other cognitive biases surfaces repeatedly in multiple dimensions of our lives. These biases affect everything from how we form personal relationships and make investments, to how we deal with terrorism and war. If it doesn't feel that way, it is because the central feature of unconscious bias is that we are not aware of it.

We think of ourselves as rational, deliberate creatures. We know why we like this movie star rather than that, this president or that television anchor. Just ask, and we can tell you why this political party has all the right answers and that one does not. Our daily actions always seem to have clear reasons behind them—we brush our teeth so we don't get cavities, we hit the brakes to stop our cars, and we get upset when someone cuts in line because that is unfair.

Scientists have long known that there are many brain activities that lie outside the ken of conscious awareness; your brain regulates your heart, keeps you breathing, and makes you turn over in your sleep at night. None of these things feels strange or disturbing. We are perfectly happy to delegate such mundane chores to—to what? To some hidden part of our brain that does all that boring stuff. If we ask ourselves what portion of our mental world is conscious and deliberate and what portion lies outside our awareness, it feels as though most of our mental activity lies within the bright circle of conscious thought.

Even a cursory examination of this theory, however, suggests flaws. You have no awareness, for example, of how your brain is taking visual images from this page, translating symbols into recognizable letters, combining the letters into words and sentences, and producing meaning. All you—meaning your conscious brain—must do is decide to read, and the rest flows seamlessly. You know your brain must be doing all those things, but you have no awareness of it. Similarly, when I ask you your name, you are not aware of how your conscious brain retrieves "Jack" or "Susan" or "Barack." You know the answer, but you don't know *how* you know the answer.

Okay, we tell ourselves. So reading and other everyday activities involve aspects of brain functioning that we aren't fully aware of. But we are still aware of most of what our minds do—certainly all the things that are important. By "important" we mean the activities of higher thought, the conversations we have or the way we reach our opinions. Let's think about some of those things. Take the last conversation you had with that quarrelsome neighbor. As usual, he said something that set you off. It is clear his words upset you, but were you really aware of what was going on in your brain as you lost your temper? One moment you were pruning a hedge, the next you felt blood rushing to your temples and hot words were springing from your mouth. It was almost . . . automatic. But if you didn't consciously decide to get angry, where did the anger come from? Or let's consider something more pleasant. You see someone across a crowded room, and your eyes connect. Your breath catches. Where did the feeling of attraction come from? You didn't make a list of the person's features, compare it against a list of your own preferences, and decide you were attracted. No, it happened in an instant. You locked eyes and, without knowing why, your heart lurched.

All right, we say. So we are not always deliberate when it comes to emotions. But that's because they are emotions. They are supposed to be messy and ill-defined. That still leaves lots of room for conscious thought. There are many situations where we are completely aware of what we do: We decide to invest in a stock after a careful analysis of the market. We hire a job candidate based on a careful analysis of her qualifications.

In recent years, a number of experiments have demonstrated that these intuitions are also flawed. Overweight job applicants, to cite just one example, are widely perceived to be less intelligent and successful—and lazier and more immoral—than identically qualified people of normal weight. In an unusual demonstration of this bias, psychologist Michelle Hebl once sat a job applicant in a waiting room with volunteers who were to later decide whether to "hire" the applicant. In some cases, volunteers saw the applicant sitting alone, in other cases, volunteers saw the applicant sitting next to a person of average weight, and a third group saw him sitting next to someone who was overweight. When the job applicant sat next to someone overweight, he was later perceived to have lower professional and interpersonal skills—and deemed less worthy of hire—compared to when he sat alone in the waiting room or next to a person of average weight. Without their awareness, volunteers were not only penalizing overweight people, but someone who was merely in the *vicinity* of an overweight person.

Intersecting lines of scientific research show that even in higher kinds of thinking, hidden forces often sit beside us and subtly pull us in one direction or another. These biases do not influence only the uneducated and the irresponsible. It is difficult to imagine an eyewitness more thorough, more diligent, and more responsible than Toni Gustus.

The discovery of a world of unconscious cognitive biases has come about much in the manner of an archaeological dig: Researchers scraping beneath the bright circle of conscious thought slowly came to realize that the circle was really a hole that sat atop another structure. The deeper they dug, the more they uncovered, until they eventually found an entire pyramid of unconscious brain activity. Discoveries about a hidden world in our heads have come so fast and have spanned so many aspects of human functioning that it has prompted some very smart people to ask an astonishing question— not "Why do we have a hidden brain?" but "Why do we have a *conscious* brain?"

To understand where this question comes from, imagine you are standing at the base of the newly excavated pyramid. If you crane your neck, you can see the aperture of light at the top—the circle of conscious awareness you once thought encompassed everything. As you draw your gaze back, the aperture grows tiny and you see more and more of the superstructure beneath it. At a certain point, you stop asking why there is a hidden pyramid below the apex of conscious awareness and start asking why the pyramid needs a hole at the top.

There are many explanations for why we have a conscious brain and a hidden brain. One is that we regularly encounter two kinds of experiences, those that are novel and those that are familiar. The conscious mind excels in novel situations because it is rational, careful, analytical. But once a problem has been understood, and the rules to solve it discovered, it makes no sense to think through the problem afresh every time you encounter it. You apply the rules you have learned and move on. This is the dimension in which the hidden brain excels. It is a master of heuristics, the mental shortcuts we use to carry out the mundane chores of life. Learning most skills is really about teaching your hidden brain a set of rules. When you first learn to ride a bicycle, you pay conscious attention to how far you can lean to one side before you topple over. Once you master the rules of how gravity, balance, and momentum interact, your conscious brain relegates bike riding to the hidden brain. You no longer have to think about what you are doing; it becomes automatic. When you first learn a language, you approach it deliberately. But once you master the language, you don't have to consciously think about retrieving the right word, or coming up with the correct syntax. It becomes automatic.

The conscious brain is slow and deliberate. It learns from textbooks and understands how rules have exceptions. The hidden brain is designed to be fast, to make quick approximations and instant adjustments. Right now, your hidden brain is doing many more things than your conscious brain could attend to with the same efficiency. The hidden brain sacrifices sophistcation to achieve speed. If you missed the spelling error in the last sentence, it is because your hidden brain rapidly approximated the correct meaning of "sophistication" and moved on. Telling you it fixed an error would have only slowed you down.

Since your hidden brain values speed over accuracy, it regularly applies heuristics to situations where they do not work. It is as though you master a mental shortcut while riding a bicycle—bunch your fingers into a fist to clench the brakes—and apply the heuristic when you are driving a car. You clutch the steering wheel when you need to stop, instead of jamming your foot on the brake. Now imagine the problem on a grander scale; the hidden brain applying all kinds of rules to complex situations where they do not apply.

When you show people the faces of two political candidates and ask them to judge who looks more competent based only on appearance, people usually have no trouble picking one face over the other. Not only that, but they will tell you, if they are Democrats, that the person who looks more competent is probably a Democrat. If they are Republicans, there is just something about that competent face that looks Republican. Everyone knows it is absurd to leap to conclusions about competence based on appearance, so why do people have a feeling about one face or another? It's because their hidden brain "knows" what competent people look like. The job of the hidden brain *is* to leap to conclusions. This is why people cannot tell you why one politician looks more competent than another, or why one job candidate seems more qualified than another. They just have a feeling, an intuition.

The idea that what seems conscious and intentional might actually be the product of unconscious forces echoes through history from Plato to Freud to Hollywood. In Plato's famous cave, prisoners who see nothing but shadows all their lives come to believe that the shadows are real. It is only when the prisoners emerge from the cave into sunlight that they see the difference between reality and unreality. Plato's liberated prisoners experience an epiphany. Freud aimed to give his patients a similar bolt of insight when they realized how their lives had been circumscribed by some long-ago trauma. In *The Matrix,* Hollywood asked if our actions were subtly controlled by hidden puppeteers, who are robots. When Keanu Reeves's character squinted his eyes, he was able to see streaming three-dimensional structures of ones and zeroes, which is how Hollywood conceptualized the world of robotic control. In all these cases, an "aha!" moment brings the walls crashing down, as people realize they have been manipulated.

I might as well admit something: You will never see the working of your hidden brain this way. The disbelief you may feel when you hear that your everyday actions are routinely influenced by things outside your conscious awareness cannot be erased by any amount of evidence. No matter how much you learn about the hidden brain, you will never *feel* it manipulating you. No Keanu Reeves can help you. You are permanently stuck inside this matrix, because that is the way your brain is designed. To become otherwise does not mean liberation. It is to become something other than fully human.

Like you, I am stuck inside the matrix. I feel I have reasons for the things I do. I am certain about the conclusions I reach. Like you, I am offended if anyone tells me that I do not know my own mind. And like you, I dismiss as absurd the idea that even my perceptions—my basic abilities to see and hear—are regularly swayed by the machinations of my hidden brain. In the course of reporting and of writing this book, I have learned that all those things *are* true. But they still don't *feel* true.

When a magician performs an illusion, people strain to see through the deception. Implicit in this effort is the belief that illusions are always *out there.* You enjoy a magic show because illusions are supposed to be different from the stuff of reality. But what if they aren't? What if we are being constantly fooled, tricked, and hoodwinked—not by some actor dressed in a cape but by our own brain? And which is the more successful illusion, the one that ends with a bow and applause, or the one that feels so real we never stop to think about it?

The shift in understanding about human behavior has been quiet, but its implications are seismic. Nearly all our social, political, and economic institutions are based on an assumption of how human beings behave that is at best incomplete and at worst fundamentally wrong. We see evidence for this all the time in the ways our institutions, governments, and economic systems fail us; in the endlessly recursive conflicts that nations and peoples have with one another; in the most dreadful moral disasters that humans have perpetrated on one another—or that humans have ignored. Our incomplete understanding of human behavior causes us to make errors in our personal lives, in the way we choose partners and the way we behave as consumers, and in the way we respond to politicians and to warnings of disaster. These errors pervade the criminal justice system and they poison the workplace. The mistakes are so fundamental to the way we think about the world that we have enshrined them in international treaties and in constitutions.

Our vulnerability to unconscious manipulation explains how a few schemers can hold entire political systems hostage. It explains failures of national and global resolve in dealing with challenges as serious as climate change. It explains tragedies such as genocide that seem aberrational each time they occur but that repeat themselves with monotonous regularity. Evidence for the hidden brain is really all around us, hidden in plain sight. The clues pervade our lives, the choices we make, our moral judgments. Our blindness to bias seems willful—until you remember that the central feature of unconscious bias is that it is unconscious.

The new understanding of human behavior constitutes a revolution no less intriguing—and perhaps more powerful—than the discovery that Newton's laws of motion collapse at the level of quantum mechanics, or that the sun really does not revolve around the earth, or that human beings appeared on earth as the result of a logical but impersonal force called natural selection. Just as it once seemed inconceivable that an object can be in two places at the same time, or that the movement of the sun across the sky is an illusion caused by the earth rotating in the opposite direction, or that whales and cows are distant cousins, so also it seems inconceivable that much of our lives takes place outside the boundaries of our own awareness. The extraordinary new discoveries about the hidden world in our heads feel personal, moreover, in a way those other fantastic conclusions do not. If you now feel as I once did when I first began learning about these ideas, you might even be a little offended that anyone would say you have a very limited understanding of what is happening in your own head, that the feeling of "common sense" we all experience is an illusion no less fake—and far more spectacular—than the sun's daily journey across the sky.

The ideas in this book are organized into concentric circles, with the early chapters detailing small and sometimes humorous examples of the hidden brain at work, and later chapters tackling bigger issues. Chapter 2 shows the hidden brain at work in four diverse settings—at an office beverage station in England, on the floor of the New York Stock Exchange, at a restaurant in the Netherlands, and in a scientific laboratory in Philadelphia. Chapter 3 demonstrates how the hidden brain influences everything from table manners to the unwritten rules of flirting—and the extraordinary consequences that breakdowns in the hidden brain can have on our lives. Chapter 4 explores how the hidden brain produces stereotypes in the minds of small children, and the continuing effects such stereotypes have on adult behavior and relationships. Chapter 5 explores the world of unconscious sexism. Chapters 6 and 7 explore the unconscious influence that groups wield in highly charged situations. Chapter 6 is about the effects that large groups wield over people during disasters, and Chapter 7 is about the power that small groups have in shaping extreme behavior such as suicide terrorism. Chapter 8 looks at the effects of unconscious prejudice in the criminal justice system, and Chapter 9 examines the role of the hidden brain in politics. Chapter 10 explores how unconscious factors influence our perceptions of risk and our moral judgment, and affect policies that touch the lives of millions.

CHAPTER 2

The Ubiquitous Shadow

The Hidden Brain at Work and Play

Unconscious bias reaches into every corner of your life. At any given time, many dimensions of your hidden brain are at work. Some cooperate with one another; others clash. What is common to all the actions of the hidden brain is the modesty with which it works. Like an attentive assistant that knows you better than you know yourself, the hidden brain anticipates your needs but claims no credit for laying out your shirt, choosing your tie, or making your coffee. That is a wonderful convenience when tasks are mundane and heuristics are applied appropriately. It's when things go wrong, when heuristics are applied in error, or when the hidden brain makes an association that doesn't quite work, that we find ourselves asking, "What was I doing?" or "What was I thinking?" It happens to all of us—there are times when our actions are so at odds with our conscious beliefs and intentions that we don't quite know why we laughed aloud when someone made a mean-spirited joke, or why we lashed out in anger at someone we love. We can't explain why we set the alarm to go off at six P.M. instead of six A.M., or why we hit the gas pedal when we meant to hit the brake. We don't know why we choked during a big test or were tongue-tied when it came to standing up for ourselves in a dispute. *Why didn't I say something?* we wonder afterward. *Why did I do that? How could I have been so foolish?*

This chapter aims to show how widely the effects of unconscious bias touch our everyday lives. The examples that follow are drawn from disparate domains, and show the hidden brain at work in a private setting, a professional setting, a social setting, and an intimate setting.

The Spotlight Effect

The beverage station was located in a nondescript office in Newcastle in northeastern England. It was no different from thousands of other office stations where tea, coffee, and milk were dispensed using an honor system. A sheet of paper was posted on a cupboard door at eye level. Under the banner of a small photograph, the notice specified the cost of tea (thirty pence), coffee (fifty pence), and milk (ten pence). People assembled their beverages and dropped money in an honor box. An office maven sent out emails every six months or so, reminding people to pay for their beverages. But like many other office stations, this one was located in a spot where people could not be observed. If they were honest and paid for their tea and coffee, no one gave them a pat on the back. If they did not pay, no one caught them.

The setup had been in place for several years. Recently, without the knowledge of the several dozen people who used the beverage station, a researcher named Melissa Bateson started tracking how much milk was dispensed each week. She also counted the money in the honor box. She did both things for ten weeks.

You would think the money collected would be roughly the same from week to week, especially if the office workers drank the same amount of tea and coffee. In the first and eighth week, in late January and mid-March, people drank the same amount of milk. But the honor box in the first week held £8.25. In the eighth week, it held £1.17—seven times less. Did people decide to be more honest at the start? No, employees did not know Bateson was studying their honesty. Besides, the money collected in the ninth week, in late March, was more than double the amount collected in the second week of the experiment, in early February. During half the study—weeks one, three, five, seven, and nine—Bateson collected three times as much as she did during weeks two, four, six, eight, and ten. What was different about the odd-numbered weeks?

Each week, Bateson replaced the notice on the cupboard that re-minded people to pay for their drinks. The text detailing the prices of coffee, tea, and milk was identical, but she changed the small dec-orative picture at the top of the notice. For the five odd-numbered weeks, Bateson downloaded photos from the Internet showing dif-ferent pairs of watching eyes. Honesty levels soared. During even-numbered weeks, she printed pictures of different flowers—daisies, marigolds, roses. Honesty plummeted.

Office workers were later quizzed about the notice. People shook their heads, mystified. *No one had noticed the photo was different from week to week.* Yet this subtle change produced a giant effect on honesty. When Bateson subtly communicated that people were being watched—even if the eyes were only a grainy image downloaded from the Internet—people were far more honest than when they poured their coffee in the company of marigolds.

You could draw a small lesson and a large lesson from this exper-iment. The small lesson is that a picture showing a pair of eyes with a penetrating gaze seems to make people more honest in their private actions than a picture showing daisies. The big lesson is that people are powerfully influenced by things that they never consciously regis-ter. The workers did not notice the photographs, yet they were influ-enced by them. (See Figure 1.)

Why did people fail to notice that marigolds had been replaced by a photo showing a pair of eyes? Think about it this way: Your atten-tion is like a spotlight that can illuminate anything you choose to focus on. But the spotlight can't illuminate everything at the same time. If you are thinking about work or an office conversation, you might not notice that the photograph on the wall shows a pair of eyes or a flower. If you remember to pay attention to the decor, you don't notice it is bright outside—and people have been shown to give larger tips, make more aggressive investments, and generally report more optimism about their lives and romantic relationships when it is bright and sunny, compared to when it is overcast.

In fact, if you were to make a detailed inventory of everything you could possibly focus on at any given moment, the list would run to dozens of pages. There are smells and tastes; ideas, moods, and tones

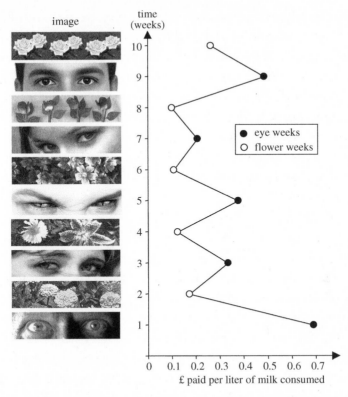

Figure 1. Pounds paid per liter of milk consumed as a function of week and image type.

of voice. Focusing on any one thing is trivial; focusing on everything at the same time is impossible. If you really did sit down to make that inventory, you would see that at any given moment, you are not aware of most of the cues around you. Right now, for example, you are reading and thinking about the words on this page. But until I remind you about it, you are not paying attention to the texture of the book jacket, or whether the temperature is right. You can, of course, refocus the beam of your attention on anything, but doing so means something else will disappear from the spotlight.

What happens to things that are outside the spotlight of our conscious attention? They don't vanish altogether, because this would be dangerous. It would be irritating to be reminded about your peripheral vision all the time, because much of the time nothing important is happening there, but you want to be notified about important things.

So as the spotlight of your conscious attention moves to other things, your hidden brain remains vigilant to your peripheral vision. In situations that do not require conscious intervention, the hidden brain simply responds to what it sees without informing you about what it has done. When it comes to a notice posted on a cupboard, the hidden brain notices the small picture on the notice has changed from week to week. Since the hidden brain specializes in rapid analyses and lacks the sophistication to distinguish between a photograph and an actual pair of eyes, it subtly prompts you to behave as if you were really being watched.

The Irresistible Heuristic

A few thousand miles from Newcastle, another experiment was under way at the same time Melissa Bateson was tracking her beverage station. Economists have long puzzled over how investors deal with new entrants to the stock market. There is no mystery when it comes to a well-known company such as Google going public; investors know a lot about such companies. But in many cases, new stocks are volatile because investors are still learning about companies. Rumors about internal company developments and earnings can send prices spiraling upward or can trigger a rush for the exit. Mathematicians have come up with complicated formulas to track changes, and have developed algorithms to predict minute decimal shifts in share prices. When billions of dollars of stock are traded each day, small differences mean enormous profits and losses.

Psychologists Adam Alter and Daniel Oppenheimer recently decided to try their hand at this game. Did they study the complexities of the stock exchange, the underlying strength of companies, and oil futures? No, no, and no. Did they have vast encyclopedic knowledge of where the economy was headed? Nope. Did they have insider information? Decidedly not. The psychologists looked at whether companies had names that were pronounceable or names that were unpronounceable. They presented a group of volunteers with a series of made-up company names that would wrap your tongue in knots—Aegeadux and Xagibdan, Mextskry and Beaulieaux—as well as a set of company names that were easy to pronounce, such as Jillman and Clearman, Barnings and Tanley. If the companies Queown and Ulymnius were like complex paintings from Vincent van Gogh's dark period, full of dark skies and menacing colors, the companies Adderley and Deerbond were like paintings brought home from school by happy five-year-olds, a yellow sun with a smiley face peering down on a house with a puff of smoke coming out the chimney. Alter and Oppenheimer found that without their awareness, volunteers were influenced by the names of companies they studied. They tended to overvalue companies with easy names and undervalue companies with difficult names.

But surely names would not affect how companies fared on the real stock market? What sane investor would base investment decisions on names? Alter and Oppenheimer tracked ten stocks with easy-to-pronounce names and ten stocks with hard-to-pronounce names on the New York Stock Exchange. They found that companies with easy-to-pronounce names outperformed companies with hard-to-pronounce names by 11.2 percent on their very first day of trading. After six months, the difference was more than 27 percent. After a year, it was more than 33 percent. If you'd put a million dollars into the stocks with easy names and a million dollars into the stocks with hard names, the group with easy names would have outperformed the group with difficult names by $330,000.

It got better (or worse, depending on your point of view). Instead of looking at names, Alter and Oppenheimer looked at companies' ticker symbols. A review of share prices on the New York Stock Exchange and the American Stock Exchange showed that companies with easy-to-pronounce stock ticker codes (such as KAR) outperformed companies with hard-to-pronounce ticker codes (such as RDO) by 8.5 percent on their first day of trading and by more than 2 percent after one year of trading. Remember the mathematicians who track the market? They get excited by differences in decimal points. Two percentage points is big money.

Alter and Oppenheimer found the pronounceability effect went away with time. Once investors learn about the companies, they start basing decisions on more important things than names. Pronounceability matters only until investors develop proficiency in the skills that really matter. But why would investors base their initial decisions on something as trivial as a name? Unlike with the office workers in Newcastle, you don't have to ask whether investors were aware that they were being influenced by the names of companies. They were not. If they'd known about the bias, they would have compensated for it, and the difference in stock performance would have vanished.

Like the beverage drinkers in Newcastle, the investors that Alter and Oppenheimer studied felt they were making deliberate choices. Without their awareness, however, their decisions were swayed. Their hidden brains associated the names of companies that were easy to pronounce with a sense of comfort, and the names of companies that were difficult to pronounce with a sense of discomfort. Comfort is linked to familiarity and safety, which is why investors chose some stocks and drove up the prices. Discomfort is associated with risk and unfamiliarity, which is why investors avoided those stocks and under-valued them. Applying heuristics—shortcuts linking comfort with safety and discomfort with risk—to situations for which they have not been designed is a recipe for trouble.

The Three-Legged Race

I recently typed "In de Cramer 142 Heerlen, 6412PM" into Google Earth. I saw the planet on my screen slowly spin. The Atlantic Ocean passed by in half a second, England was a blip, the English Channel a droplet of water on the side of my glass. Cities and local landmarks emerged, and I zoomed in on trees, roads, and cars in the town of Heerlen in the Netherlands.

Google Earth didn't tell me this, but the rooftop on my computer screen was an IKEA store. Across from the IKEA was an Applebee's restaurant with about thirty tables inside. The restaurant was family-friendly, casual, and moderately priced.

Inside the restaurant, a waitress took orders. She was about seventeen or eighteen years old. When customers asked for beer and fries, the waitress wrote down the order and repeated it verbatim. "*Bier*," she echoed, or "*friet*." When other customers asked for "*bier*," the waitress said "*pils,*" a Dutch synonym for beer. For "*friet,*" she said "*patat,*" another synonym. She wrote down every order.

For one group of customers, the waitress mimicked the customers verbatim. For another group, she acknowledged their orders by using a synonym and saying "yes." Tips given by the customers were counted. When the waitress mimicked customers, her tip went up. The difference was not trivial. On average, customers who were mimicked gave the waitress tips that were *140 percent larger.*

The waitress did not know the aim of the experiment, so it was not as though she treated one set of customers better than the other. I called Dutch psychologist Rick van Baaren, who conducted the study. He told me mimicry works best when it follows the natural rhythms of conversation. If you instantly repeat what someone tells you, it will be obvious and irritating, like a five-year-old repeating back to you everything you say. But when you repeat what you hear after a short delay, you communicate something important: *I am listening to you. I have understood you. I agree with you.*

What is fascinating is that the waitress communicated exactly those things to the other customers, too. By using synonyms and saying yes, she told these customers that she had heard them and understood their instructions. By writing down every order, she emphasized that she would accurately communicate the orders to kitchen staff. But language is more than just verbal information. Much of what we say goes beyond the literal meaning of the words we use. Using tone, inflection, and various patterns of speech, we communicate affection, anger, and gratitude, loneliness and longing. I am not drawing your attention to the well-known difference between verbal and nonverbal communication. I am drawing your attention to the difference between conscious and unconscious communication. Without their awareness, customers who were mimicked felt they received better service.

The next time you are in a park, a restaurant, or an office, watch any two people talking. The more in sync they are, the more likely they will be to subtly mimic each other. If you get close enough to hear what they are saying, you might hear them repeating each other's phrases. They might even have the same rhythms of speech, the same body language—their hidden brains are prompting them to reflect concordance. When people hear something they agree with, they respond enthusiastically and quickly. When they hear something they disagree with, they are microseconds slower to respond, because the hidden brain knows that an impasse lies ahead and is girding for conflict.

The psychologists Tanya Chartrand and John Bargh once videotaped people in conversation with a lab assistant. The assistant was instructed to rub her face or shake her foot throughout the conversation. The videotape revealed the subjects of the study rubbing their faces and shaking their feet in response. When quizzed later on, none of the people remembered adopting these tics. Nor did they report noticing the assistant's face rubbing and foot shaking. Unlike psychologists who deliberately manipulate behavior to see what effect it has on others, most of our modulations in speech and action happen unconsciously and unintentionally in the course of everyday communication. I unconsciously respond to your unconscious signals, and you to mine. The fact that neither of us is aware of this dance does not mean it is irrelevant. Remember, even as the Applebee's customers and the waitress were exchanging information at a deliberate and explicit level—orders and acknowledgments for beer and fries—they were also exchanging information at an unconscious and unintentional level. If you looked only at the explicit information exchanged, you would not understand why some customers gave extra generous tips.

When we hear about the Newcastle beverage station or the volunteers who rub their faces and shake their feet in response to a lab assistant's actions—or an eyewitness who makes an "obvious" error—we can't help but feel we would never be susceptible to such manipulation. Of course we would notice that the person sitting before us was shaking her foot or rubbing her face. The photo obviously shows a pair of eyes one week and marigolds the next. The rapist's teeth are straight; the suspect's are crooked. The cues are not hidden. When Dutch psychologist Rick van Baaren came up with his Applebee's experiment, the waitress was initially reluctant to participate because she felt the mimicry would be obvious. Customers would ask her what the hell she thought she was doing. Of course, no one did.

What the restaurant experiment reveals is that your hidden brain does not work in isolation. It forms networks with other hidden brains. I unconsciously pick up the unconscious cues you send me, and I unconsciously respond to them. Without being aware of it, we are constantly adapting to different contexts and people, modulating not just our rhythms of speech, but the very content of our ideas. This effect is especially powerful in situations where people are trying to form emotional connections: When you want to create a bond with another person, your hidden brain subtly whispers, "Say this" or "Don't say that."

The Selfish Brain

Two friends of mine are prominent Alzheimer's disease researchers. John Trojanowski and Virginia Lee co-direct the University of Pennsylvania's research on neurodegenerative disorders. But what I want to tell you about these scientists does not have to do with neurofibrillary tangles and beta-amyloid plaques. It has to do with John and Virginia themselves.

John speaks in full sentences. He is attentive to detail in everyday conversation. When I interviewed him some years ago for an investigative article, the picture he painted was like a John le Carré spy story—intricate, detailed, subtle. Listening to John was like watching a painter develop a canvas, only instead of brush and paint John employed a series of perfectly-thought-out sentences. He included so much detail that I found myself having to concentrate really hard to pick out the important points. Like any good le Carré novel, John's account was not about bombs and car chases and hijacked airplanes but about the passing detail of an unlatched gate.

At first glance, John and Virginia seem like an odd couple. He is six foot three inches tall, looks a little like Mick Jagger, and is expansively genial. She is of Asian ancestry, petite, and has the coiled restraint of a cat. At second glance, they look even more like an odd couple.

Where John is verbose, Virginia is staccato. When they get angry, he exudes icy dignity and she flashes fire. John follows a simple rule in everyday conversation—why say something in one sentence when you can say it in two? Virginia strips language to its tensile outlines, eliminating subjects and objects in most sentences, and waging an unrelenting war of annihilation against all modifiers. When she says "Yes!" or "No!" her eyes bristling with impatience, you have the sense that what she really means to say would take ten minutes but she can't spare that kind of time.

"When Virginia's angry with you," one friend of theirs told me, "it's like she's going to take a knife and slit your throat. When John's angry with you, he'll make you feel so guilty that you will take a knife and slit your own throat."

"A friend calls us fire and ice," John said. "You can guess which is which."

I once visited John and Virginia's lab. As I was talking with an office administrator, Virginia rushed up.

"Here," she said, and dropped a folder before the administrator, whose name was Karen Engel. "We'll talk about it tomorrow." She whirled and was gone.

"John would have talked about it for ten minutes," Engel said, nodding at the folder. "He is not one to make rash decisions. He wants consensus."

Perhaps you know people like John and Virginia; their clashing personalities are a cliché of television sitcoms. Experts in human relationships will tell you that while such clashing personalities are good for comedy, they are definitely not good in real life. People like John and Virginia who clash, disagree, and get on each other's nerves because they have different personalities are exactly the kind of people who should never be left alone in a room together. As colleagues, experts will say, people like John and Virginia are doomed to conflict. And if a professional relationship between people like them is likely to be doomed, a personal relationship between them would be a catastrophe. Don't think rancor and bitterness, think mushroom clouds.

What I haven't told you about John and Virginia is that they have been married to each other for more than thirty years. And more than most couples I know who have been married half as long, it is obviously they are very much in love. Opposites attract, you say. Research studies contradict you on that—at least in that studies show that similar people tend to get along better in the long run—but never mind. Let's assume opposites do attract. What I find astonishing about John and Virginia is that they not only live together and love each other, but they have formed a potent professional partnership that has placed them among the ranks of the most prolific and widely respected scientists in the world. At Penn, John and Virginia collaborate to produce dozens of research papers in prestigious scientific journals. They haul in millions of dollars in grants. Everything they do is in concert, collaboration, and consultation with each other. Someday, admirers whisper, they might win the Nobel Prize in medicine—together.

Bear in mind that this is a couple that argues about minutiae. Neither will give ground on such all-important questions as whether the forks should go in the dishwasher with their pointy ends up or their pointy ends down. When John and Virginia clash, they revert to personality. John becomes more and more precise, attending to tinier and tinier details, his emotions hidden behind layers of ice. Virginia grows more and more didactic, interrupting John and showing considerable exasperation at his verbal pyrotechnics. When they spar, I can see her mentally pick up projectiles and fling them at him while he sits, steely-faced and impassive, green peas whizzing by his nose.

When they went on vacation recently, they argued about the right way to make breakfast cereal. When he tried to recall what the fight was about some days later, John came up short. It was so trivial he could barely remember the details—except that the fight was not only heated, but a recurring conflict every day of their vacation. If you had seen them during these breakfast cereal duels, you would not have guessed that together in their professional life John and Virginia have bucked the neuroscience community on the causes of Alzheimer's disease. They have often been willing to stake out ground that is at odds with the conventional wisdom, the kind of position that requires them to depend on each other for intellectual and emotional support. Taking such gambles in science is not easy. It is a little like being lost at sea, menacing gray-green water from horizon to horizon, and striking off in one direction on your own, while all the other boats head off together in the opposite direction. It needs confidence and it needs each member of the couple to have complete trust in the other.

In everyday life, however, friends and co-workers do not wonder how John and Virginia work so well together. They wonder how John and Virginia can coexist.

I imagine a marital counselor giving advice to John and Virginia. After hearing about the breakfast cereal fights, I see him wondering about whether the two of them are really suited for each other.

John, for example, will start to describe how his day goes: "We get up at seven o'clock—"

"We get up at seven-thirty," Virginia sharply interrupts. "John, you *think* that you wake up at seven."

The marital counselor raises his eyebrows imperceptibly. *They argue about small things,* he says to himself. *Do they give each other lots of space?* No. He learns that they share their professional lives, going from the same house to adjacent cubicles in the same office. Do they gingerly avoid each other in their professional life? No. They are often at each other's throats in public.

"I've never encountered the volatility I see between them," a lab manager named Jennifer Bruce once told me. "If it happens often enough, people just say, 'Oh, they're at it again.' "

Bob Dome, another colleague, told me that he was taken aback when he first met the couple. "Virginia is hyperkinetic. And John always speaks very slowly, so Virginia is always telling him to shut up or get on with it. I was shocked when I first met them. I didn't know they were married."

Even their jokes have an edge. At a lab meeting with two dozen people in attendance, John once talked about the role that brain injuries might play in the development of Alzheimer's disease. He explained that the insidious thing about these injuries is that their effects might not be visible, even to highly sophisticated brain scanners.

"I fell off a horse when I was sixteen and I had a brief amnesia," he said. "It went away, but that's the kind of thing that predisposes somebody to Alzheimer's disease. I haven't taken an MRI [brain scan], but even if I did, I wouldn't find anything."

"How do you know?" Virginia asked, deadpan. The room erupted in laughter, and John looked displeased.

I see the marital counselor shaking his head as he learns from John that their heated criticisms of each other at work regularly bring them both "to the brink of tears."

"When we don't agree, it is not really clashing," Virginia interrupts, disagreeing with her husband about whether they disagree with each other. "If I don't agree with him, I tell him."

I see our imaginary therapist leaning back in his chair with a heavy sigh when he realizes the only thing that keeps them from each other's throats is traffic safety. "We have one very important rule—we still bicycle to work," John told me. "Whatever we discuss, we cannot fight on our bicycles, because that is dangerous."

But John and Virginia also have a secret, perhaps the most important secret that extraordinarily talented type A couples can have. To understand what it is, I want to introduce you to the work of a social psychologist named Abraham Tesser.

Some years ago, a young woman approached Tesser and told him that she had done well in a recent class but was feeling awful because a close friend of hers had done even better. Social psychologists are always on the lookout for behaviors that are not idiosyncratic to individuals but that say something about human nature in general. Tesser sympathized with the woman who confided in him, but her remark got him thinking. Would the woman have felt as bad if the person who had outperformed her had not been a close friend? Alternatively, if the friend had done well at something that the woman did not care about herself, would she have experienced jealousy? Tesser intuitively guessed the answer to both questions was no. When a stranger does well at something, we can enjoy their accomplishments. In fact, when we know something about basketball or poetry, we are better able to understand the skill involved in dunking a ball or turning a rhyme. Most of us take great pleasure in watching gifted athletes and performers do things we could never dream of doing ourselves.

When close friends or lovers do well in activities that do not interest us, the same thing happens. The wife who would never be caught dead in a garden can take pride in her green-thumbed husband who has turned the backyard into a horticultural exhibit; the aspiring high school football star feels his chest puff with pride when his younger sister is chosen for the lead role in the school play. In fact, Tesser sensed that in these situations, people feel happy partly because they get to bask in reflected glory. *There is my cousin, who is the first violinist in the symphony!* a person might think. Or, *There is my son, the doctor!*

But something interesting—and potentially unpleasant—happens when someone whom we are close to excels in a domain where we would like to be seen as excellent ourselves. The writer who is outshone by his writer girlfriend feels a conflict. He feels pleasure at the success of someone he loves and gets some reflected glory, but he also feels taken down a peg. He doesn't want reflected literary glory; he wants his own literary glory! This is why the twelve-year-old who gets bumped from the lead role in the school play is likely to come home bemused if she loses the starring role to a stranger, but is likely to come home in tears if she loses the part to her twin sister.

"If the relationship is close, the jealousy gets even worse," Tesser told me. "You have these two reactions to the other person—'Your success pulls me up,' but on the other hand, 'Your success makes me feel like crapola.'"

Tesser conducted a series of experiments that confirmed his hunches. At its core, the conflict between pride and jealousy in other people's accomplishments hinges on a mechanism in the hidden brain designed to watch out for our narrow selfish interests. We show ourselves in a positive light when we excel at something, but we are also seen positively when we are associated with someone who excels—the brother of the beauty pageant winner is not just another guy. Some of his sister's glory rubs off on him. Usually these two mechanisms in the hidden brain are not in conflict. Tesser's insight was that when someone who is close to us excels at something that we want to excel at ourselves, these two drives are unconsciously put into conflict with each other. The glory of our successful friends and siblings rubs off on us. But because we hunger for their kind of glory ourselves, their success makes us feel mediocre. This is why the woman who confided in Tesser was upset at being outperformed by a close friend.

Tesser found that people feel very powerful resentment when their partners are successful in domains that are integral to their own identity. This resentment is so powerful that volunteers in experiments sabotage their friends and lovers to keep them from doing well at things the volunteers see as their own core strengths. Wordsmiths presented with a test of verbal ability, for example, will help strangers and undermine their lovers, in order to keep partners from outperforming them. Although husbands and wives say they are unrestrainedly happy about the successes of their partners, videotaped interviews show that people's expressions of pleasure are leavened with dismay when they find their spouses have outdone them in domains they want to claim as their own. The people Tesser studied were not bad people; they had no awareness of what they were doing. Like the woman who approached Tesser to ask why it was she felt dismayed her friend had outperformed her, these husbands and wives were not consciously aware of why they felt the way they did. Not only would they not be able to explain their behavior to others, they would not be able to explain their behavior to themselves, which is how it always is with the hidden brain.

In one especially interesting analysis, Tesser examined the relationships between famous male scientists and their fathers. He found that when the father and son were scientists in the same field, the success of the son predicted an emotionally distant parent-child relationship. When father and son were in different fields, the success of the son predicted emotional closeness with the father. Even when it comes to our own children, in other words, having a child outperform us in a domain where we have long sought excellence ourselves can be threatening to our self-esteem. All fathers bask in the reflected glory of their sons' successes, but when a father and son share similar interests, a persistent voice at the back of the father's head asks why such success was denied to *him*.

All this, as you might guess, spells trouble for two people like John Trojanowski and Virginia Lee. They are married to each other, which means they are close, and their professional lives and feelings of achievement are tied up in the same things. They are both smart, ambitious, and competitive. It's not just that both of them are academics. One of them is not doing social science while the other does clinical science. No, they are both in exactly the same field, working in the same university, out of the same office. They even have the same job title. Given the differences in their personalities, Tesser's research would predict that John and Virginia would quickly become envious of each other, and that jealousy and competitiveness would poison their relationship.

But as I said, John and Virginia have a secret. It can be summed up in a single word: complementarity.

Although they appear to be doing identical things and have identical interests, John and Virginia have figured out how to do slightly different things—to divide up their everyday tasks so that they work in complementary ways rather than competitive ways. They have unconsciously harnessed the selfishness of the hidden brain to their mutual advantage. They have agreed, for example, that she is the expert when it comes to biochemistry and cell biology—the basic tools of bench science. They have also agreed that he is the expert on clinical issues—and a lot of scientific work involves working with patients. They have also divided up the human resources needs of running a large laboratory, which is like a small business. Virginia thinks of herself as being a "lab rat," and there is nothing she likes as much as discussing science with postdoctoral fellows. John is much more social and enjoys talking to collaborators, the press, and the outside world.

"The strategy to make sure our partnership did not undermine each other was not do the same thing," John said. "We have different skill sets and different management skill sets. Even though we say we work with each other all the time, we have to get appointments to see each other."

"It never started out as, 'This is what I do and this is what you do.' It started out as 'This is what we do together,'" Virginia added. "It naturally sorted out. If, at the end of the day, I am not in town, John can substitute for me. We don't really stake out an area but go with whoever is better at it."

Given how similar their interests are and the extremely competitive structure of modern science, it is astonishing that John and Virginia have perfectly complementary strengths. But Tesser's research suggests blind luck probably played a modest role in their division of responsibilities. When couples are emotionally close, Tesser found they automatically and unconsciously stake out complementary domains. It is almost as though, recognizing the potential threat that competitiveness poses to an intimate relationship, the hidden brain nudges people toward complementarity. Tesser found that if one partner has a strong preference to do task A over task B, but the other partner has an even stronger preference for task A, the first person unconsciously switches preferences and says he actually prefers task B. On his own, John might well have been a lab rat and Virginia an outgoing communicator, but in the context of their relationship they have unconsciously adopted roles that allow them to see each other as collaborators instead of competitors.

John and Virginia have also—consciously and deliberately—set up rules to reduce the risk of competitiveness. By specializing in different tasks, all of which are essential to the functioning of their laboratory, they have increased their dependence on each other. John knows he needs the engine of bench science that Virginia provides; Virginia knows she needs the engine of research grants and collaborations that John generates. Every publication that goes out from their lab has both their names on it.

They both insist all recognition be shared equally, and are prepared to make sacrifices to see that this happens. John once applied for a prestigious million-dollar grant that neither he nor Virginia thought was within their reach. To their surprise, John won the grant. But before he accepted, he told the organizers the grant would have to have both their names on it. The private organization giving out the grant balked; after all, John had applied for the grant on his own. John told the group that unless the grant was given to them both, he was going to turn down the million dollars.

"Initially they did not want to do it, and I said, 'Sorry. We don't want the money,' " John told me. The organization relented and gave the grant to both of them.

"Neither of us would do as well on our own," Virginia agreed. "But together we work very well."

"People tell me, 'You don't do anything unless Virginia gives you permission,' " John added. "What it is, is there is no single boss in our operation at work or home, and to some men that seems weak. I don't mind acknowledging that nothing I have accomplished would have been possible without Virginia."

I am skeptical about the accuracy of this claim. John and Virginia are immensely talented people and would very likely have been successful if they had never become partners. But I am certain that their belief in this claim is essential to the success of their personal and professional partnership. With all their personality differences, John and Virginia have to see their individual success as intertwined with the success of the other person. Absent that belief—that bias—they would lose a very important pillar of their love. The unconscious bias of the hidden brain to look out for itself can be an immensely destructive force in personal relationships, but it can also be harnessed to create dense networks of interdependence. Unlike most couples who have been married for more than three decades, John and Virginia hate spending a single night away from each other. When either is invited to give a talk in another city, each invariably arranges for the other to come along, too, like opposite poles of two magnets that cannot get enough of each other.

CHAPTER 3

Tracking the Hidden Brain

How Mental Disorders Reveal Our Unconscious Lives

The reason people have no awareness of the hidden brain is that it is usually not accessible through introspection. Turning the spotlight of our attention inward does not reveal a subterranean world. But there are times in the course of everyday life when we are suddenly made aware of the hidden brain—not by its presence but by its absence.

Scientists, researchers, and clinicians regularly encounter patients with hidden-brain impairments. As Abraham Tesser and others have shown through experiments, and as Freud intuited through experience, the hidden brain regularly causes people to make the same errors over and over in their lives. Couples that sabotage each other in order not to be outshone have no idea they are sabotaging each other, let alone why they are doing so. One of the most powerful forms of psychotherapy developed in recent years is called cognitive behavior therapy. Simply put, the technique teaches patients to become mindful of unconscious thought patterns. The alcoholic may feel his addiction is completely beyond his control, but it turns out there are patterns to his behavior: He tends to drink after he gets a paycheck, or when he walks by a favorite bar, or after a fight with his wife. Fighting alcoholism is partly about becoming aware of these triggers and consciously setting up mechanisms to guard against them—to have a paycheck direct-deposited into a bank account, for example, or to walk a different route home that does not go by the bar.

It's the same with depression and other mood disorders. People feel their emotional problems are largely caused by external events. There is little doubt that losing a job or a spouse can be devastating, but a core insight of all talk therapy is that a large portion of how we feel about our lives rests within ourselves, in unconscious patterns of thought and habit. Treating psychiatric ailments with medications achieves the same thing. Neurochemical changes make patients feel better about themselves. No one intuits the presence of a neurotransmitter, but depression and the effective treatments for it show that we need neurotransmitters to function properly. In recent years, high-tech brain scans have allowed us for the first time to observe the physical brain in action—to directly glimpse dimensions of the hidden brain at work.

While these insights are increasingly well established in clinical science, the role of the hidden brain is disregarded in most other realms. We may concede that schizophrenia and depression have something to do with the hidden brain, but commonplace things such as table manners, politeness, and honesty seem driven by conscious intent: People are polite because they choose to be polite, and they are honest because they want to be honest. It takes an unusual disorder to reveal that the basic elements of everyday life—morality, kindness, and love—rely on the unconscious mind.

Brian and Wendy McNamara live in Oakville, Ontario, just outside Toronto. In keeping with their friendly personalities, both Brian and Wendy chose sociable professions. Brian became national sales manager for the computer maker Hewlett-Packard. Wendy sold casual clothing for Weekenders. She called people on the phone and arranged to come over to their homes to make presentations of the latest fashions. Both Brian and Wendy were very good at what they did. In 2002, Brian accepted an early retirement package and settled into a life of semi-retirement. He was happy to kick back, even if it meant giving up the perks and bonuses that had come with his high-profile job.

Brian and Wendy were close and enjoyed each other's company. For Brian, retirement meant they could focus on things they loved to do together—travel, antiques hunting, and exploring different wineries. Life seemed full.

In 2004, thirty years into their marriage, Wendy had a partial hysterectomy to remove a fibroid growth. She took a long time to recover. Around the same time, Brian sensed Wendy's drive was slowing down—where she once had demonstrated a lot of get-up-and-go in making sales calls, she now just sat around. Brian thought it might be time for her to kick back, too. He sounded her out about retiring from the clothing business and doing something else, such as volunteer work. Wendy was not enthusiastic about the idea, but she made no move to pick up the pace on her business responsibilities.

Over the following weeks and months, Brian felt something else was amiss: The woman who had been his high school sweetheart seemed to be growing increasingly distant. He would propose things to do together, fun things, and she wouldn't say yes and she wouldn't say no. When he cuddled up to her, she seemed uninterested in affection—not angry but indifferent. In late 2005, Brian took Wendy's sister into his confidence. Evelyn Sommers is a clinical psychologist, and Brian told her about Wendy's lack of emotional connection to work, to life, and to him. They discussed the possibility that Wendy was suffering from depression, an outgrowth of her lengthy recovery from surgery, or the scale-back in lifestyle that had come with Brian's retirement. Brian felt that the time he now had to enjoy life as a result of retirement was well worth the lost perks and bonuses, but was it possible Wendy secretly did not feel the same? Brian asked Wendy if she wanted to talk to a psychologist. She was neither enthusiastic nor averse. As usual, she was indifferent. She met a psychologist half a dozen times in late 2005 and early 2006. When Brian asked her how the sessions went, she gave monosyllabic answers. Brian hoped she was unburdening herself to the therapist.

The couple had always been intimate, but that was falling away, too. Brian kept asking Wendy what was happening to them. "Are we falling out of love?" he would urgently ask. "Are we parting?" Wendy would turn his plea for connection into an argument: "Do you want to leave me?" "No," he would say. "I just want to understand what is going on."

There was little by way of overt fighting; if their marriage was dissolving, it seemed to have gone from warmth and love to distance and indifference without making the traditional pit stops at anger, resentment, and conflict.

If there was any anger, it mostly came from Brian. He would go out of town on trips for a couple of days to do some consulting, and come home to find newspapers strewn around the house. There would be unwashed plates and cups on the dining table. Wendy used to be the kind of person who pushed her chair back into place after getting up from a table, and who put her cup in the dishwasher after drinking her coffee. What was going on? Brian felt lonely. It was difficult to communicate to other people what was wrong because once he started talking about it, it felt like small stuff. He and Wendy had always enjoyed shopping for groceries on weekends and then cooking a meal together. Now when he asked her what she wanted to eat, she would shrug. When they did bring groceries home, Wendy would sometimes put her shoes right back on and say she was going out for a walk. It wasn't possible to communicate the gravity of things like this to another person. But to Brian, who craved emotional connection with his wife, the incessant accumulation of minor events felt like the stuff of divorce. Maybe they were just falling out of love, he thought. Maybe it was his fault, too, in ways he did not fully understand. Brian felt terribly sad but knew it was hardly earthshaking. They were going through what millions of couples had gone through before them.

But there were some things that were just strange. When they went for walks, Wendy closely examined the bark on trees. She studied whorls in the wood, and pointed out patterns that resembled human faces. She ran her fingers across the bark, over and over, as though trying to divine some secret message. She was an amateur painter and had an arts background, and Brian marveled at her ability to find incredibly subtle patterns in bark and on rocks.

When they were in the car together, Wendy counted the wheels of passing transport trucks. That one has eighteen wheels. This one has twenty-four. On a drive to Brian's sister's house, he once saw her intently studying the passing forest. He could hear her quietly counting to herself. When she got to two hundred, he finally asked her what she was counting. "Dead trees," she said.

One summer day, when Brian made a quick pit stop at a store to pick up some beer, Wendy jumped out of the car and followed him inside. A young couple had caught her eye; the man had a series of elaborate tattoos down one arm. Wendy approached the stranger fearlessly. "You have wonderful tattoos," she said. "Can I see them?" The young man was taken aback, but Wendy disarmed him. Her charming personality and winning smile made behavior that might have seemed weird coming from another person just seem unusually friendly. Before Brian managed to hustle her away, Wendy told the stranger about patterns in his tattoos that he had not seen himself.

Brian felt the strange events were like shadows. They were here one moment, gone the next. If Wendy did something odd one day, she did not repeat it the next day. To Brian's precise mind, there was no connection between counting dead trees and Wendy's growing propensity to send off checks to buy books she did not want to read.

But the odd events kept occurring—with increasing frequency. Wendy went up to men she didn't know, admired their hair, and asked if she could touch their beards. Sometimes she didn't ask. Brian feared for her safety. The people she stopped were shocked but guarded. What would happen if she accosted a stranger who was dangerous?

At home, Wendy walked around at night looking at shadows, searching for patterns. She owned a lot of antique glass, and these nocturnal trips often involved visits to her china and dishware collection. She wasn't a Midas reveling in her possessions; she just had an insatiable urge to run her fingers over ridges of all kinds and was drawn to intricate patterns in glassware. The couple had stopped sleeping in the same bedroom because Wendy was so restless. Brian sometimes woke up in the middle of the night to see his wife standing silently by his bed, watching him. "You need to go back to sleep," he would say, and she would obediently comply.

The couple had a grown son living in the house, and the young man had closely cropped hair. Wendy loved to run her hands over her son's scalp, feeling the texture. But it got to a point where it became weird and annoying. Both Brian and his son asked Wendy to stop. She started sneaking up and ambushing her son. It was silly, but when she didn't stop after repeated pleas, Brian felt such behavior constituted abuse.

Wendy had been a great animal lover, but she now grabbed hold of the cat, set her electronic keyboard to play "The Charge of the Light Brigade," and vigorously rocked the poor animal back and forth until it was terrified. When she dropped the cat, she was mindless about the height of the fall. If the cat was left in her care, she did not feed it.

In May 2007, Wendy agreed to accompany her sister and mother on a trip to France. Wendy's sister, the psychologist, had planned the trip—she was going to exchange vows with her partner, Larry. It was to be a two-week trip with lots of fun events planned, and Evelyn Sommers told Brian that the change of scenery might do Wendy good. Brian sat Wendy down for a heart-to-heart chat before she left. "You need to think carefully about what you want when you come home," he told her. "You need to ask yourself if you want to live here, if you want to be with me."

Things unraveled as soon as the flight got under way. Wendy drank copiously. It was out of character; she had always been the one to stop herself and others after the first glass or two of wine. When they arrived at their destination, Wendy continued to drink, but there was something different about the way she consumed alcohol. Wendy had always been a social drinker; the alcohol had been incidental to social connection. The social connection now seemed incidental to the alcohol. Wendy's sister had rented a house from friends, who themselves lived a couple of doors away. Without anyone knowing, Wendy would slip out and go over to the home of her sister's friends—people she knew only slightly. "Hi," she would say brightly, "can I have something to drink?" The dazzling smile would appear, and her new-found hosts would comply, even as they eyed each other questioningly.

For the first time since Wendy had begun to change, she was not with Brian but with other family members. In the close proximity that comes with travel, Wendy's sister started to understand what Brian was going through. The trip was to have been a respite, but Wendy had instead become an unwelcome distraction. Evelyn confronted her sister. But as usual, Wendy was indifferent to criticism. When the family returned to Canada, Evelyn was distraught. She told Brian she was certain something serious was wrong. This was not depression.

Brian felt an enormous relief. It wasn't just him. Other people who knew and loved Wendy were able to tell something was amiss. But what could it be? He took Wendy to see their family doctor. "Why are you here?" the doctor asked. "Yes," Wendy agreed, turning to Brian with an air of curiosity, "why are we here?" Brian told the doctor about the drinking, the apathy, the indifference. The doctor raised the possibility of depression, and Brian said that Wendy had already seen a psychologist and that it had gone nowhere.

Brian told the doctor about Wendy's insatiable urge to rub her fingers over her son's scalp—and the heads of strangers with kinky hair. Wendy also seemed constantly fatigued; inasmuch as she was restless at night, she also spent a lot of the day just lying around. The doctor told Wendy she was going to order some tests. She wanted blood work and tests to measure brain functioning. The doctor then changed the topic. After a few minutes, she abruptly asked Wendy about the tests. "Do you recall I suggested doing a blood test and other measurements?" Wendy looked at her blankly. "No," she said. Brian felt another surge of relief. Someone in the medical community had picked up on something.

After the tests were completed, the doctor referred Wendy to a neurologist at the Sam and Ida Ross Memory Clinic at the Baycrest Geriatric Health Care System in Toronto. There were more tests. Finally, the neurologist Tiffany Chow produced a diagnosis: Wendy had a disorder known as frontotemporal dementia. Although Wendy's symptoms for this disorder began around the time she had her partial hysterectomy, in all likelihood the two issues were not related. The McNamaras had simply had two pieces of bad luck arrive at the same time.

The frontal and temporal lobes are craggy outgrowths of the brain handed down to us by our evolutionary ancestors. The Taj Mahal and the Eiffel Tower, spaceships and classical art, laws and governments—civilization itself—are products of these brain areas. We do much of our important thinking here. We analyze and forecast things, make choices, and form judgments. As with the rest of the brain, much of what the frontal and temporal lobes do is unconscious. They shape our ability to judge social situations and make aesthetic judgments. And they provide us with the prick of conscience when we do something wrong.

There are many neurological disorders that affect the brain, but none may be as curious as frontotemporal dementia. Unlike Alzheimer's disease, which begins by robbing the memory while leaving other aspects of brain functioning intact, frontotemporal dementia affects a part of the brain that subtly and secretly regulates our social behavior. The frontal and temporal lobes tell us whether it is polite to reach across a crowded dinner table for a dish, and how to greet someone we know only slightly. They tell us whether the person who catches our eye across a crowded bar is just scanning the room or looking meaningfully at us. They allow us to experience the pleasures of comradeship and teamwork. People with frontotemporal dementia often have extremely acute powers of observation and analysis—meaning that the analytical parts of their brain are working fine—but they don't have table manners. In Wendy's case, the gradual disintegration of her ability to judge socially appropriate behavior from inappropriate behavior took nothing away from her ability to rapidly count the wheels of transport trucks and to identify subtle patterns on the bark of a tree.

The vast majority of rules of human interaction are not written down or even articulated. There is no rule book that tells you when it is appropriate to knock on someone's door and suggest a drink. When you do it, whom you do it with, and how often you do it all matter. In India, where I grew up, it was perfectly appropriate to knock on a friend's door without calling ahead. Phoning a close friend or relative to say you were going to come over could be taken as a sign you did not consider the person close enough to show up unannounced. In North America, barging into someone's house without warning is rude. It doesn't take long when you transplant someone from India to the United States, or from the United States to India, to quickly grasp that the social rules have changed. People adjust to new rules swiftly and automatically, because the hidden brain is highly skilled at orienting itself in new cultural contexts. Healthy people grasp and follow social rules without conscious effort. We do not realize how important these rules are, because we don't do the work of acquiring and following the rules—our hidden brain does it for us.

If you ask a person why she does not reach across a crowded dinner table for a dish, or why she leaves the last potato for someone else, or how she knows one glance in a bar is meaningful but another is not, she will tell you that she has thought about each question and figured out the answer. It isn't true. She may consciously claim responsibility for her answers, but it is really her hidden brain that conducts those analyses, and we know this is true because patients with frontotemporal dementia who do socially inappropriate things have their powers of analysis intact. They can reason their way through life, but it turns out that reason is an inadequate guide in many social situations. It is only when the machinery of the hidden brain breaks down that we suddenly recognize its importance.

Much of this book is about errors and biases caused by the hidden brain. The automatic conclusion is that bias is bad and we should do everything we can to rid the brain of unconscious thinking. If we could only think consciously all the time, we would avoid all the mistakes of the hidden brain. That is partially true, but it is also true that the hidden brain can be our friend. It tells us how to navigate the world, it creates the foundation for our lives as social creatures, it enmeshes us in the web of relationships that make life meaningful. Without the hidden brain, we would not be supercomputing machines that everyone envies. We would be sad creatures, locked out from the very things that make life precious. We would lose the ability to work collegially with others, to form lasting friendships, and to fall in love. Our hidden brain is like the wetness of water that the fish never notices—but can't live without.

Morris Freedman, a frontotemporal dementia expert at the Baycrest Center where Wendy McNamara was diagnosed, told me that patients with this disorder often end up in trouble with police and other authorities. It turns out that the most important aspect of being a law-abiding citizen is the ability to understand social rules. We don't avoid shoplifting merely because we consciously know it is wrong, or because it is against the law. Most of us don't shoplift because our hidden brain tells us it is a violation of rules of social interaction. It is the fear of social opprobrium—the contempt of store clerks and security officials and fellow customers if we should get caught, or the shame that would befall us if our friends and colleagues learned about our actions—that keeps people honest, not all the laws in the world.

It doesn't feel that way, of course. Most people will tell you they don't shoplift because they are honest folks who can consciously tell right from wrong. It is only when we see patients with a disorder such as frontotemporal dementia that we realize that most of us can claim very little credit for our conscious notions of morality. Patients with frontotemporal dementia don't become bad people, and they don't stop being able to tell right from wrong; they simply stop caring about shame and social opprobrium. These patients will tell you their actions are wrong—but it doesn't bother them. This is why patients with frontotemporal dementia don't just lose their marriages and their friends on account of apathy and indifference; they regularly get into trouble with the law. They also lose their jobs, because it turns out that much of our professional lives is not about the excellence of our work but about the creation and maintenance of social bonds.

One study of sixteen patients with frontotemporal dementia found that among them, the group was guilty of "unsolicited sexual approach or touching," hit-and-run accidents, physical assaults, shoplifting, public urination, breaking into other people's homes, and even one case of pedophilia. The patients readily acknowledged their actions were wrong—but showed no remorse. They knew they were breaking the law, but it didn't matter to them.

Many of our social institutions—and laws in particular—implicitly assume that human actions are largely the product of conscious knowledge and intention. We believe that all we need for a law-abiding society is to let people know what is right and what is wrong, and everything will follow from there. Sure, we make exceptions for people with grave mental disorders, but we assume most human behavior is conscious and intentional. Even when we acknowledge the power of unconscious influence, we believe it can be overcome by willpower or education. When confronted by people who say they understand the law but break it anyway, we lock them up and throw away the key, because in our schema, these have to be bad people. The law does not realize that most law-abiding behavior has little to do with conscious knowledge and motivation. Wendy McNamara, for example, regularly walks into the homes of her neighbors without knocking. Brian McNamara told me that he has explained the situation to everyone who lives nearby so people don't feel their houses are being broken into. The McNamaras have the good fortune of being surrounded by understanding and compassionate neighbors—and Wendy McNamara is blessed to be married to a man with endless patience and understanding.

"These patients go to a store and see something they want and pick it up and walk out without thinking of the consequences," Freedman told me. "They call their boss fat. Normal people may think their boss is fat, but they are not going to say it. These patients lose the inhibition.

"These patients get arrested for going up to children and asking for a dollar," he added. "If someone sees a person going to a playground and asking kids for a dime and patting kids on the head, they call the cops."

Brian McNamara told me that about nine months after Wendy returned from France with her mother, sister, and her sister's partner, Larry, the family received terrible news—Larry had passed away. "It was a nonevent for Wendy," Brian McNamara told me. "She had known this man for four to five years. There was no sadness. There wasn't even a silence or a shock when I told her. I told her Larry had passed away and there would be a memorial for him, and she had no reaction."

A few years ago, researchers posed a series of dilemmas to patients with damage to a brain area that is implicated in frontotemporal dementia. Some of the dilemmas were trivial, others difficult.

The simpler dilemmas included situations such as this: "You are driving along a country road when you hear a plea for help coming from some roadside bushes. You pull over and encounter a man whose legs are covered with blood. The man explains that he has had an accident while hiking and asks you to take him to a nearby hospital. Your initial inclination is to help this man, who will probably lose his leg if he does not get to the hospital soon. However, if you give this man a lift, his blood will ruin the leather upholstery of your car. Would you leave this man by the side of the road in order to preserve your leather upholstery?"

There were dilemmas with higher stakes: "You are a fifteen-year-old girl who has become pregnant. By wearing loose clothing and deliberately putting on weight you have managed to keep your pregnancy a secret. One day, while at school, your water breaks. You run to the girls locker room and hide for several hours while you deliver the baby. You are sure that you are not prepared to care for this baby. You think to yourself that it would be such a relief to simply clean up the mess you've made in the locker room, wrap the baby in some towels, throw the baby in the dumpster behind the school, and act as if nothing had ever happened. Would you throw your baby in the dumpster in order to move on with your life?"

And finally, there were dilemmas where you had to choose between two bad options, both of which involved serious harm to other human beings: "Enemy soldiers have taken over your village. They have orders to kill all remaining civilians. You and some of your townspeople have sought refuge in the cellar of a large house. Outside you hear the voices of soldiers who have come to search the house for valuables. Your baby begins to cry loudly. You cover his mouth to block the sound. If you remove your hand from his mouth his crying will summon the attention of the soldiers who will kill you, your child, and the others hiding out in the cellar. To save yourself and the others you must smother your child to death. Would you smother your child in order to save yourself and the other townspeople?"

The researchers found something curious. Patients with damage to parts of the brain that regulate social behavior did not reach different conclusions from the others. Rather, when it came to the highly charged problems, where people had to choose between two actions that both had terrible consequences, these patients did not experience the *distress* that normal people felt. They reacted rationally, without emotion. In the scenario involving enemy soldiers combing through a village, the crying child would die anyway if the party hiding in the cellar were discovered, so it is irrational not to smother the child and save the lives of all the other people. Most normal people, however, find the idea of smothering their own child—or any child—unbearable. Patients with damage to a brain area known as the ventromedial prefrontal cortex had no trouble stripping away the emotional component of the problem. From a purely mathematical perspective, it is always better to save many lives instead of one.

Research studies into brain disorders that affect social behavior suggest that our basic notions of right and wrong do not spring from what we learn in textbooks and Sunday school, or from laws handed down by messiahs and legislators, but from parts of the brain we hardly understand. Joshua Greene, a Harvard neuroscientist and philosopher, told me that much of what we call ethics and morality, in fact, might not be handed *down* to us by holy books and human laws, but handed *up* to us by algorithms in the hidden brain, ancient rules developed in the course of evolution. People with normal brain functioning do not need to be taught to care about social relationships, and social relationships lie at the heart of all morality.

Does this mean people have no responsibility for immoral actions? Of course not. *We have responsibility for not only our conscious minds, but our unconscious minds as well.* Not everyone who shoplifts has frontotemporal dementia. But what the extreme examples of these patients provide is the insight that it is the hidden brain, rather than the conscious brain, that creates a society that is law-abiding and just. If we want a moral society, we must actively recruit the help of the hidden brain. We must devise laws that take advantage of our awareness of social rules, and don't just take advantage of our knowledge of the rules that get written down.

In the example of the Newcastle beverage station, people did not notice that the photograph on the cupboard was changing from week to week, but the reason a pair of watching eyes made a difference at all is that the hidden brain cares about other people's opinions. It is much easier to be honest in situations that encourage and broadcast transparency than in situations where our actions are secret.

Frontotemporal dementia is not the only disorder that affects the hidden brain. From schizophrenia and autism to anxiety and depression, patients with a wide range of mental disorders experience damage or dysfunction to parts of the brain that are responsible for unconsciously regulating our behavior. Addictions to heroin, cocaine, or nicotine hijack pathways in the unconscious brain. Once rewired, the hidden brain powerfully manipulates the conscious mind to act against its own will and to justify behavior that is obviously self-destructive. In the case of autism and schizophrenia, a variety of unconscious brain mechanisms go awry. Decreases in gray matter in a part of the brain known as the superior temporal gyrus, for example, appear to be correlated with the delusions and hallucinations that many patients with schizophrenia experience. Changes in brain regions known as the amygdala and the prefrontal cortex appear to be the reason patients with schizophrenia often have trouble reading other people's facial expressions. The ability to read expressions feels like a conscious skill, but turns out to be a largely unconscious process—and an essential component of social judgment.

A close friend of mine developed schizophrenia some years ago. When we got together for a meal at a restaurant, we happened to get a waiter who was surly. To my friend, the waiter's manner felt threatening—his hidden brain could not distinguish between rudeness and hostility. My friend grew increasingly suspicious, and when I tried to reassure him about the waiter, I became part of the problem. When the waiter placed our food before us, my friend handed me his plate and loudly demanded I give him my plate. He wanted to eat my food and he wanted me to eat his food. The waiter and I exchanged glances. I got the feeling my friend felt the waiter and I were somehow in cahoots—and that we had conspired to have his food poisoned.

It was an unlikely scenario, to be sure, but not categorically impossible. How do most of us tell the difference between a surly waiter and a homicidal maniac? We don't conduct investigations, we don't march into restaurant kitchens to see what's being sprinkled on our food. Everyday life depends on our ability to make a series of unconscious assumptions, and one of them is to trust that the food served to us at a clean restaurant is good food.

Our hidden brain makes rapid judgments about the likelihood of various scenarios, and dismisses the unlikely ones before they can even appear over the horizon of conscious thinking. This is why most of us do not suspect the careless driver who rear-ends our car of trying to kill us, or believe that the medical secretary who asks for our Social Security number is part of an identity-theft crime syndicate. In a world where we have nothing to go on but our rational minds, the simplest things can paralyze us because it can take huge amounts of time for our conscious brain to think about every scenario deliberately. If we didn't have our hidden brain to weed through thousands of scenarios and to guide our attention to the most pertinent questions, we would quickly become overwhelmed, because bad things can potentially happen to us in every conceivable situation. Everyday life requires us to *suspend* rationality, to be mindless about countless risks.

There is no cure as yet for disorders such as schizophrenia, autism, or frontotemporal dementia. Patients with Wendy's disorder who are in otherwise excellent health can easily outlive their caregivers, which worries Brian McNamara endlessly. He has started to work again, and has enrolled Wendy in a day program to practice her social and physical skills.

On a recent visit I paid to the McNamaras, Wendy greeted me at the door with a beaming smile and the single word "Cute!" Brian and Wendy and Evelyn Sommers, who was visiting, took me back to a kitchen table overlooking a yard, where Wendy used to grow plants. I asked Wendy if she had green thumbs, and she said, "Maybe so." A moment later, she added, "Cute!" I realized the word was not a judgment but a tic.

Brian showed me a couple of watercolors Wendy had painted many years ago; one showed a cottage snuggled among trees, bathed in dappled sunlight. It was the work of a sure hand and a keen eye. When Brian sets Wendy before paint and brushes now, all she manages are broad strokes one above the other, like a child's rainbow. Inasmuch as Wendy is more sensitive than ever to form and line and color, she no longer has access to the unconscious skills that all artists must possess—the ability to grasp the *feeling* of a picture and the drive to express that feeling.

Wendy abruptly interrupted our conversation about painting to inform me that I had a hole in my right earlobe. I told her this came as news. (I later found a deep declivity in my earlobes that I had not noticed before.) She asked me to turn my head so she could inspect my other ear. When I obliged, she told me my ears were kinky, and small for my head. I had expected Wendy to say and do socially inappropriate things. Her pleasant smile and cheerful demeanor robbed her comments of any sting; I found myself drawn to her authenticity. I told her that narcissistic people might be willing to pay good money to sit before her and have her observe things about them that no one had noticed before. "Maybe so," she said.

There were some pinecones on the table, and Wendy played with them, passing one hand and then the other over the ridges. She showed me how the ridges were open at the top and bottom of the pinecone, but closed at the middle. Brian asked her how the pinecone felt to her, and she said, again, that the ridges were open at the top and bottom, and pressed in at the middle—she had no access to how the pinecone *felt*. Wendy rose and wandered over to a bowl of potpourri and symmetrically ran her hands over a number of objects.

Although she is in the thrall of compulsions, Wendy does not have the feelings typically associated with satisfying or denying compulsions. If there is an open bottle of wine available, Wendy can drain it like water, but if she asks for wine and Brian tells her no bottle is open, she feels nothing.

As Brian and Evelyn and I talked, Wendy wandered in and out, sometimes hanging on the periphery of our conversation, and other times walking out of the room. At one point, with Wendy back at the kitchen table, we talked about the visit to France. Evelyn reminded Wendy about her late partner, Larry.

"You remember Larry, my Larry, don't you?" Evelyn asked.

"Maybe so," Wendy replied with a bright smile.

"You know he died?"

"Cute!"

Wendy loaded dishes into the dishwasher, slowly exploring the ridges and contours of every plate and cup. She washed her hands with soap and water several times, and lingered over a towel, her fingers moving over the texture of the cloth like a blind person.

She returned to make a comment about my shoes. She asked if she could see the underside of my left sole. I lifted my shoe, and she smiled happily. She then inspected the sole of her sister's shoe.

Wendy did not seem offended as Brian and Evelyn talked about frontotemporal dementia. She acknowledged that doctors had given her a diagnosis, but she spoke as one given a doubtful tip about a racehorse. When I asked her if she disagreed with the diagnosis, she smiled pleasantly and said, "Maybe so." One reason frontotemporal dementia is much harder on caregivers than on patients is that victims lack awareness of what they have lost.

Wendy never gets angry. It has been years since she shed a tear. She can watch suspenseful shows on television with detachment, observing sound and light and color while remaining untouched by the story. Day-to-day life around her can be lighthearted, even funny. Wendy's comments about my ears made everyone laugh in the same way intensely honest observations from a child can make grown-ups laugh. Being around Wendy was like watching a comedian relate a tragedy— all laughs, cracks, and quips. The sadness lay in what was never said.

CHAPTER 4

The Infant's Stare, *Macaca,* and Racist Seniors

The Life Cycle of Bias

When my daughter was a few days old, I prowled back and forth in front of her as she lay swaddled in her bassinet. She watched. As I circled the room, she kept her eyes fixed on mine until the rim of the bassinet obscured her vision. The moment I reappeared, she homed in again. I wasn't being a proud father; I was conducting an experiment. If you know anything about infants, the fact that my daughter tracked my eyes as I walked around her room will not strike you as surprising. Indeed, her behavior will seem so commonplace that you might wonder why I mention it—or put it down to the usual vanity of parents who insist that ordinary things about their children are somehow extraordinary.

The fact that infants are so adept at tracking their parents as they move about *is* actually quite extraordinary. It is also one of the earliest visible examples of the hidden brain at work. Without thought or effort, my daughter was doing something that has stumped supercomputers for years. Consider the problem from an engineering perspective. Let's say you want to design an intelligent camera to spot a pair of eyes. If the face is in front of you, you would teach the camera to locate two blobs that are symmetrically positioned on either side of the nose (once you teach the camera to recognize a nose). But faces are usually not in front of us. Most of the time, they are off to one side or another, displaced in any one of a thousand possible angles. Sometimes all we can see is a single eye. If a face should vanish and reappear, our camera would have to not only recognize that a face (and not a pumpkin) had come into view, but calculate at what angle the face was being presented. If the camera worked through trial and error, it might produce thousands of errors before it found the right answer. The reason my daughter tracked my eyes effortlessly is that she arrived in this world with the innate ability to distinguish faces and eyes from other objects. Brightly colored toys could capture her attention, but they were only interesting things in a world that awaited exploration. My face and eyes, on the other hand, were already meaningful.

In the long journey of learning and survival that lay before her, my daughter's ability to lock eyes with me was a crucial step. The faces of her parents, after all, were not just objects in an object-cluttered world; they were her link to food and water, to comfort, protection, and security. Babies the world over face radically different challenges for survival, but all the problems have the same solution—the loving attention of parents.

The hidden brain is designed to preferentially recognize faces over other objects. Across generations, infants who formed a bond by locking on to the eyes of their parents were more likely to survive than infants who found trees or dogs or rocks more interesting. Italian researchers once showed that newborns who were just a day old preferred geometric shapes that resembled a human face over shapes that did not. It takes barely five hours of face-to-face time for an infant to develop a preferential attachment to her mother's face over that of a stranger. This is extraordinary when you consider how similar faces are to one another, and how limited and helpless newborn infants are in virtually every other domain of physical and mental performance.

Our preferential ability to recognize faces—and certain faces, in particular—makes the human brain very different from a computer. My daughter's brain was *designed to be biased,* to pay attention to faces at the expense of other objects, and to some faces at the expense of others. You can see why such a bias is useful. As infants, it allows us to latch on to our parents. As children, it helps us recognize a friend across a crowded playground. As young adults searching for mates, it gives us the ability to make exquisitely sensitive distinctions in matters of beauty and attractiveness. Throughout life, faces are our guides to the feelings and predispositions of those around us; facial expressions let us know when our neighbor is upset; they tell us whether the cute sophomore is interested in going out on a date; they warn us about people who intend to do us harm. If you were designing a brain from scratch, you would want to bias it to pay attention to faces over other objects.

In recent years, scientists have found an area in the brain—called the fusiform face area—that specializes in recognizing human faces. It is activated when we see a face, and also when we remember a face. Brain imaging studies show the fusiform face area is activated only by human faces (and not by other objects or by faces of other animals) and is sensitive to faces presented in full view, in profile, and as cartoons. This part of the hidden brain even lights up in response to two-tone pictures that provide minuscule amounts of information— and that require us to mentally "fill in" a picture in order to recognize a face.

The unconscious influence of the fusiform face area explains why people regularly see human faces in random patterns of nature. Shortly after Iraqi dictator Saddam Hussein was executed in 2006, for example, many people in Iraq swore they saw the dictator's face imprinted on the moon. When I looked at a photograph of that moon over Iraq, it took me a few seconds to spot Saddam Hussein's visage, but there it was, all right—his eyes, nose, even his mustache. The coincidence said less about the supernatural than about the way the hidden brain has a systematic bias to recognize anything that looks like a face. There is a good reason people in Iraq, rather than people in Kazakhstan, noticed the Saddam-like image. The Iraqis had seen the dictator's face thousands of times. Their hidden brains had learned to preferentially recognize that face—even in the craters of the moon.

Researchers once found that people shown a Lexus whose front grille was turned up in the form of a human smile (with the headlights serving as eyes) liked the car better than when the ends of the grille were turned down in the shape of a frown. As usual, volunteers in the study were not aware that a subtle face recognition bias had influenced their judgment. Many people also show strong, automatic, and unthinking preferences for animals that have humanlike features. Beluga whales and dolphins, with their smooth heads, cherubic eyes, and mouths shaped in humanlike smiles, are more appealing to us than sea lampreys and octopi. Two dark splotches of fur cause giant pandas to look like they have large eyes, and the hidden brain associates large eyes with babies. It is not surprising that the panda has become a global symbol for conservation. (Zoos have to take great care to keep pandas, which can be dangerous, away from people—because the hidden brains of zoo visitors tell them that pandas are cute and cuddly.)

Cartoons routinely show animals whose faces have been anthropomorphized—bears and tigers in children's cartoons not only talk a human language, but have their features altered to look humanlike. When we see a mouse that looks like a real mouse and a mouse whose features have been altered to look like a human, our hidden brain places a finger on our internal scale and causes us to find the anthropomorphized mouse more pleasing. We may consciously know that mice are vermin, carriers of deadly diseases, and opportunistic scavengers. But when you widen and move a mouse's eyes from the sides of its head to the front, give it a high-wattage smile, and conceal its grubby paws in yellow boots and white gloves, the hidden brain fools us into thinking this mouse is an endearing creature. You don't need a scientific experiment to prove this. Just run to the nearest encyclopedia and look up "Disney, Walt."

I have spent a fair amount of time on the brain's affinity for faces to show how pervasive the effects of this simple bias can be. But this seemingly innocuous bias can also have not-so-benign consequences. Experiments show that our unthinking tendency to find baby features adorable biases us to trust adults who happen to have large eyes and cherubic features over adults who do not look childlike—even when the adults with childlike features are liars.

The brain's bias for familiar faces also makes it easier for us to recognize those from our own ethnic group than members of less familiar ethnic groups. Our hidden brains arrive in this world with the instant ability to orient themselves in any culture. A Chinese infant born in China will form a preferential attachment to Chinese faces.

Through countless encounters with cooing relatives, doting parents, and smiling strangers, most of whom are Chinese, the baby learns to make extremely fine distinctions between Chinese faces. People who have little or no contact with Chinese people, by contrast, have a harder time making fine distinctions between Chinese faces, especially in situations that call for rapid judgment.

When a Chinese person is asked to spot the difference between two Chinese faces, the mental work is automatic—such challenges have been encountered so many times that the hidden brain has mastered rules to solve the problem without input from the conscious brain. When someone is asked to make distinctions between two people from an unfamiliar ethnic group, the challenge is met by the conscious brain, because it is novel. With effort, the conscious brain of a novice can arrive at the same conclusion as the hidden brain of an expert, but it takes a second longer. Someone who grows up in rural China and is transported to predominantly white Iowa will think most Iowans look alike. But the playing field isn't level. Patterns of global cultural consumption—Hollywood movies and the spread of American popular culture—mean that people in Ethiopia, Korea, and China are far more likely to have repeated exposure to Caucasian faces than the other way around.

I occasionally get mistaken for other Indian Americans at work. It upsets me, of course, and the moment my colleagues recognize the error, they are mortified. I feel that my Indian American colleagues and I look very different, but that is because over a matter of decades I have come into close contact with tens of thousands of Indians and Indian Americans. My exposure to so many South Asian faces has taught my hidden brain to make rapid and fine distinctions among such faces. Mixing up faces of people belonging to unfamiliar ethnic groups does not make us bad people, but it does say a lot about whom we are familiar and unfamiliar with. We are most likely to mix up people when we are stressed or distracted: The conscious mind has its hands full, and the hidden brain leaps to the wrong conclusion.

If you believe human behavior is mostly driven by conscious thinking, such errors can produce grave misunderstandings. In 2006, African American Congresswoman Cynthia McKinney of Georgia got furious when a Capitol Hill police officer failed to recognize her. She walked around a metal detector, as members of Congress are allowed to do, and when a white police officer pursued and challenged her, she struck him in the chest. The story line developed predictably from there: McKinney and several African American leaders said the incident was emblematic of racism in American society and of the extra vigilance that people of color endure at the hands of police. An NAACP leader said the officer had treated McKinney with "disrespect." Conservative groups, meanwhile, lambasted McKinney for striking an officer. The following year, McKinney was defeated in her attempt to retain her seat in Congress.

If you think about the incident with the hidden brain in mind, you can see how the police officer who failed to recognize McKinney might have been guilty of an unconscious race *bias,* in that he might have been less likely to make a similar error with a white congressman. Most congressional representatives are white men, and it's a safe bet that most of the people authorized to walk around metal detectors on Capitol Hill are white men. Through sheer repetition, the hidden brains of Capitol Hill police officers will have learned to recognize the faces of white congressmen more or less automatically. Identifying congressional representatives who belong to a less familiar group— African American women—can take a second longer because the mental processing has to be carried out by the conscious brain. The officer most likely intended McKinney no disrespect, and she was wrong to strike him.

·From the point of view of the congresswoman, I can understand why she got angry. If you are a person of color, the sad truth is that you are much more likely to be the victim of these errors in the United States, even if you are a member of Congress. It feels unfair and is hurtful—and if the incidents happen often enough, *your* hidden brain comes to assume that the wounds are being inflicted intentionally. McKinney was not responding calmly, rationally, or deliberately. Her hidden brain responded automatically to an insult, just as the police officer reacted automatically to an unfamiliar person walking around a metal detector. Like Iagos manipulating unwitting Othellos, the hidden brains in both cop and congresswoman were the real villains of this story. The national commentariat missed the subconscious forces because the commentariat always assumes that words and actions reflect conscious intent—the default position in our society is that the hidden brain does not exist. To McKinney's supporters, the cop had to be a racist. To her detractors, she was a crazy woman who shouted "Racism!" without provocation.

A harmless—indeed, necessary—bias in early infancy thus creates problems in later life that are maddeningly difficult to control. In criminal justice settings, interracial eyewitness identifications are far more prone to error than situations where witnesses and suspects belong to the same race. Courts dismiss the idea that some eyewitnesses should be taken more seriously than others, because the scales of justice—like Capitol Hill police officers—are supposed to be color-blind. Many of the institutions in our society, as I have said, are premised on the notion that deliberate and conscious thinking are all that matter. We assume eyewitnesses who mean to be accurate are accurate. The data, however, prove that unintentional and unconscious bias regularly plays a role in eyewitness errors. Ignoring the role of race, rather than taking it into account, is what produces outcomes that are racist.

When do automatic and "mundane" biases in the hidden brain start to influence our relationships with others? Remarkable research by a Canadian psychologist shows that these biases start to shape our social perceptions and judgment from the time we are toddlers.

The Whiteside Taylor Daycare in Montréal is no different from hundreds of other facilities in North America that care for the very young. Infants and preschoolers play, fidget, eat, and cry. A few years ago, a psychologist named Frances Aboud visited Whiteside Taylor with an interesting proposition. She wanted to recruit some of the children at the day care for a psychological experiment.

The day care agreed, and Aboud went about getting permission from parents of the children. When all the paperwork was squared away, Aboud gathered eighty white children from the day care and from a few local elementary schools. The youngest child she studied was three years old. Aboud, who has sharp, striking features and is of

Lebanese descent, gave her young volunteers half a dozen positive adjectives such as "good," "kind," and "clean" and half a dozen negative adjectives such as "mean," "cruel," and "bad." Aboud asked the children to match each adjective with one of two pictures. The drawings always showed a white person and a black person. She provided a short explanation of each adjective. She would say, "Some men are selfish. They don't care about anyone but themselves. Who is selfish?" and ask the children to point to the drawing of either a black man or a white man. Or she would say, "Some women are sad. They are left alone with no one to talk to. Who is sad?" and ask them to point to the drawing of either a black woman or a white woman. Aboud also showed the children drawings of a black boy and a white boy and told them, "Some boys are cruel. When their dog comes to meet them, they kick their dog. Who is cruel?" She showed the kids drawings of a white girl and a black girl and said, "Some girls are ugly and people don't like to look at them. Who is ugly?"

Seventy percent of the children Aboud studied assigned *nearly every* positive adjective to the white faces and *nearly every* negative adjective to the black faces.

As disturbing as it may seem, there is nothing unusual about the Whiteside Taylor Daycare or the biases of the young children in its care; similar studies going back many years have found identical results among a range of preschoolers and elementary school children across North America. It doesn't make much difference, by the way, if you allow the children to assign positive adjectives to both the white and the black faces and allow them to not assign negative adjectives to either face. Young children, on average, still assign more negative adjectives exclusively to the drawings of black faces and more positive adjectives exclusively to the drawings of white faces.

Research into the biases of young children provides us with a useful window into the hidden brain, because children are rapidly forming associations—and associations are the way the hidden brain learns many of its rules. The doings of the hidden brain, moreover, stand out more clearly among young children than among adults because small kids have not learned to consciously fight the hidden brain's automatic conclusions.

But Aboud's work also forces us to think about bias and prejudice through a new lens. It is absurd to think of the toddlers at Whiteside Taylor as hostile bigots. These children were still learning to blow their noses. If we cannot blame the children, whom should we blame? Well, perhaps the fault lies with the parents or teachers of these children? Where else could they have learned such hateful stuff?

To answer that, Aboud assessed the racial views of children at the Harold Napper Elementary School just outside Montréal. She also assessed the views of their parents and teachers. Aboud found no correlation between the views of the children and the views of their parents. Nor was there a correlation between the views of the children and the views of their teachers. The children were simply not being exposed to a regular diet of hate speech that told them that blacks were cruel and ugly and that whites were clean and good. So where did those ideas come from?

Aboud decided to start by understanding what these children thought was going on in the minds of the adults around them. So she recruited yet another group of young white children from kindergarten and the first grade. She administered the version of the racial bias test that allowed children to assign positive and negative adjectives to the black or the white face, to both faces, or to neither.

Unsurprisingly, Aboud found the same pattern of results as in the earlier studies—children assigned many of the negative words exclusively to black faces and many of the positive words exclusively to white faces. Aboud then showed the children photos of two research assistants. One was white and the other black. Aboud asked the children to guess how the research assistants might assign the positive and negative adjectives to the white and black faces: She challenged the kids to guess the racial views of the research assistants. The children believed that the research assistants would reach exactly the same conclusions they did. They believed that the white and black assistants would mostly assign the positive adjectives to white faces and the negative adjectives to black faces.

Aboud had the two research assistants visit the children. She had them read stories to the kids with positive interracial themes. She wanted to test the intuitively appealing idea that stories with positive themes would reverse the children's attitudes. The stories were about pairs of black and white friends. One was about two boys named Billy and Carl. Both loved to ride around on their bikes, and both hoped their parents would buy them new bikes for their birthdays. The boys spent time at each other's homes, and were warmly welcomed by each other's families. They confided their hopes about the new bikes to each other. When one of them received a new bike, they celebrated together. When the second boy was not given a new bike for his birthday, he confided his disappointment to his friend. The friends supported each other—right up to the point when the second boy's parents got him a surprise present—a go-cart. In the final scene of the picture book, the two friends entered a race together and came in first with the go-cart. The story, as you can tell, had unambiguously positive racial themes. Both the friends were warm, caring, and attractive children. They liked each other, and their families liked each other, too.

Did it make a difference to the kindergartners? The children loved the stories, but to Aboud's dismay, the stories made virtually no difference in their racial attitudes toward black people. Not only did they continue to assign negative adjectives to the black faces, they continued to believe that the research assistants, including the woman who was black, would hold identical views.

Another story the research assistants read revealed a surprising twist in the nature of the children's bias. The tale was a fantastic account of three young boys, Alex, Joel, and Zachariah, who were playing on a river in a rubber raft. Alex and Joel were white. Zachariah was black, a serious child who liked books and reading. As they daydreamed, their raft took them out to sea—where they encountered a crocodile. The beast attacked them and flipped Alex and Joel into the sea. It then came after Zachariah, who alertly used a bandanna to tie its snout shut. Zachariah then pulled his friends out of the water and, crocodile in tow, headed back to land. Once on the dock, Zachariah untied the crocodile's snout, even though one of his friends thought the beast should be left to its own devices. But Zachariah knew the crocodile was endangered. As Alex and Joel slept over at Zachariah's home that night, the little black boy stayed up until eleven P.M. writing letters to the president to urge more animal conservation efforts.

As you can tell, the little black boy was an unusual hero. Zachariah fought off the crocodile, saved the lives of his friends, was kind to the crocodile because he knew about conservation issues, and sacrificed his own sleep in order to write to the president. But when the researchers asked the kindergartners to describe what they had learned from this and other stories, the children tended to misremember the positive actions of black characters as positive actions of the white characters in the stories. Without being aware that they were doing so, the children stripped Zachariah of his heroism and assigned the credit for his brave and clever actions to his white friends. In other words, every piece of information that Aboud was giving the kindergartners was being filtered through a lens that systematically advantaged whites and systematically disadvantaged blacks.

"That was so distressing because it was clear the black kid had saved his friends," Aboud said. *Where were the children getting their obnoxious views?*

Some of Aboud's colleagues suggested that the parents of these children were lying to the psychologist, that they were secretly communicating racist messages to children while pretending to be tolerant. Aboud thought this was extremely unlikely; if anything, the parents she'd encountered had been worried about discussing racial matters at all out of fear that it might prompt their children to believe that race mattered and eventually lead them to intolerant attitudes. Furthermore, even if the parents had secretly taught their children to be bigots, why would the children believe the research assistants were similarly biased? The research assistants were clearly trying their best to communicate positive things about blacks and interracial friendships. Why were the children hearing something completely different?

Aboud decided there were two separate puzzles to solve. The first question was, Why did the kids believe that the adults in their lives shared their views—when they clearly did not? The second question was more basic: How did kids form their racial attitudes in the first place?

Hidden in Aboud's data was a clue to the first answer. There were differences between younger and older children when it came to how accurately they guessed the views of the research assistants before and after the children heard the positive stories. When the oldest kids heard the white research assistant read stories with extremely explicit and positive interracial themes, they later concluded the research assistant felt positively toward blacks. Their own views about blacks continued to be negative, but for the first time, these kids were able to tell that an adult did not share their views.

Frances Aboud was an admirer of the Swiss psychologist Jean Piaget, and she thought a Piagetian concept might explain why the youngest kids assumed adults shared their views. Very young children assume that *everyone* shares their views of the world. It requires a certain level of maturity for a child to realize that people can have entirely different perspectives.

This would explain why the youngest children not only believed that the research assistants shared their biases, but why they felt that their parents and teachers had the same attitudes, when in reality all the adults were trying to teach the kids to have positive views about people from other ethnic groups. The children were projecting their own views onto the adults in an immature and egocentric manner. When the research assistants read positive stories to the kids, Aboud had assumed—erroneously—that the children would accurately figure out what the adults thought about interracial friendships. But young children find it difficult to infer what is happening in other people's minds.

Aboud sent the research assistants back into the classroom, but this time, instead of just reading the stories and assuming the kids would draw the right message, the research assistants were told to go out of their way to be explicit about what they took away from the stories. The assistants praised the heroics of the black characters, and explicitly pointed out the warmth of the interracial friendships. When the racial attitude of the kids toward blacks was tested again, the kindergartners now looked a lot like the older kids. They still assigned positive adjectives to whites and negative adjectives to blacks, but they were able to see how the research assistants did not share their views.

"Parents are afraid of saying anything about race to their kids because they are afraid it will make their children prejudiced," Aboud said. "I say, 'Heap on the positive stuff.' "

But this still raises the basic question: Where did the attitudes of the kids come from? We can confidently say the biased views were *not* coming from parents and teachers, but we still don't know where they *were* coming from. Remember, the children did not hold random views on racial matters—large numbers of them, especially the youngest kids, had nearly identical views. They believed whites were good and nice and clean, and that blacks were cruel and ugly and dirty.

The answer lay in the different ways the hidden brain and the conscious brain learn about the world. Aboud asked me to imagine that I was a young white child who suddenly found himself in an ordinary suburban neighborhood in North America. For the purposes of this thought experiment, imagine that I am friendless and parentless—no one tells me what to think, or what conclusions to draw. I am a child, so I lack the maturity to draw very sophisticated conclusions. What would my hidden brain learn as it tried to make sense of the world? It would conclude, for one thing, that most people who live in nice houses are white. Most people on television are white, especially the people who are shown in positions of authority, dignity, and power. Most of the storybook characters I see are white, and it is white children who mostly do heroic, clever, and generous things. My hidden brain—fluent in the language of associations—would conclude that there must be an unspoken rule in society that forces whites to marry other whites, because everywhere I look, most of the white husbands seem to be married to white wives. There also must be unspoken rules about who can visit whose homes, because most of the time when friends visit each other, they belong to the same race.

In my three-year-old brain, I don't think of black people as bad, but I think of them as *different*. I might even think they have *chosen* to be different, that they have chosen to have different skin color, that they have chosen to marry other black people, and that they have chosen to live in black neighborhoods and visit with black friends. Now imagine that I pick up this message not once or twice but thousands of times. I run into exceptions regularly, the black family that lives in the palatial mansion down the street, the interracial couple on the next block, the gay or Latino friends who drop by now and then. But to my hidden brain, which is interested only in generalities, the overall force of the cultural message is overwhelming. My beliefs are inaccurate inferences, but they don't feel like inferences. To my hidden brain, they feel like solid conclusions. Everywhere I look, I see evidence to back them up.

Small children who are trying to rapidly orient themselves in the world can draw conclusions that superficially match the facts but are completely wrong. If my three-year-old brain had the verbal and conceptual ability to communicate my conclusions to grown-ups, they would quickly explain to me why I was wrong. But I don't, and in any event, it's no use telling the hidden brain that patterns are superficial, that there really isn't a rule that whites can marry only whites, or that men can fall in love only with women. Remember, the hidden brain has one simple, blunt-edged priority: to quickly acculturate us to our world and give us a set of simple tools to enable us to make quick decisions.

Many experiments in recent decades have found that black children hold views on racial matters that are more or less identical to those of white children. Black children are likely to associate positive things with white characters rather than black characters. Little black girls may feel white dolls are prettier than black dolls. Educators and parents have tried to expose kids to counter-stereotypical books, movies, and images. That is exactly the way to keep the hidden brain from forming the wrong associations, but Frances Aboud's work shows us just how strong, persistent, and explicit the counter-stereotypical messages need to be to have any effect.

When my own daughter turned three, to cite a personal example, her favorite game was "doctor." Whenever she asked me to play with her, she told me to be the doctor, and she would take on the role of nurse. She was occasionally willing to assume the role of doctor, too, but she would insist we *both* be doctors. She was absolutely unwilling to let me play nurse. I told her there were no rules about who could be a nurse and who could be a doctor, but it was like pushing a boulder uphill. I finally asked her why nurses had to be female, and she explained, with the calm logic of a child, that she had never seen a storybook where a man was a nurse.

If I were to show you a photo of a white man and ask you to imagine what the man's spouse looks like, your conscious brain would tell you the man could be married to a white woman or a black woman, a Latina or an Asian. He might be married to another man; he might be single. Your hidden brain, on the other hand, doesn't care about the full range of possibilities. When you ask the question, the answer pops right out: The white man is going to be married to a white woman. It doesn't matter to the hidden brain that the rule of thumb is sometimes wrong. The point is that it is *usually* right, and the answer can be produced at lightning speed. This is why interracial couples in the United States—even in this late day and age—attract second glances.

When we see a man kissing another man, the preconceived associations in the hidden brain tell most Americans that this is not what men do. Of course, we can quickly shush our hidden brain and act blasé. But when we are juggling many things, when we are under pressure, or when we are simply busy doing something else, it becomes difficult to suppress the automatic associations of the hidden brain. At such times, the hidden brain's rapid conclusions about the world become especially powerful. If we are asked to make a judgment about these men in some other context—their job performance, for example—we may get the feeling they are not quite right for the job without knowing how we leaped to that conclusion.

When I say "we" have automatic biases about gay people, I really do mean everyone—straight people *and* gay people. Just as black children tend to have positive associations with white faces rather than with black faces, gay people can unconsciously harbor the same associations as straight people. This should not be cause for surprise: Gays usually see many more straight families than gay families in real life, on TV, and in books. If the hidden brain learns through repetition, why would the unconscious associations of gay people be much different from the unconscious associations of straight people?

The picture painted by this work stands in sharp contrast to the conventional way many people think about prejudice. Bias among toddlers is not triggered by a steady diet of hostile messages, or indoctrination by bigoted parents and teachers. It reflects instead that we really have two systems of learning within our heads, that these two systems develop more or less independently, and that we pay almost no attention to one of them. Our society resolutely believes the conscious mind is all that matters, and so all our educational and legal efforts focus on it. We have schools with multicultural messages and rainbow flags. We have organizational experts who preach the importance of sensitivity and understanding. We have laws to punish hate crimes. Many of our interventions are based on the belief that prejudice involves conscious intention or hostility, that it is largely the result of ignorance, and that education is the best way to overcome it. As you can see from Frances Aboud's work, each of these beliefs is wrong in a fundamental way. The children at Harold Napper Elementary were not being taught by their teachers that whites were superior to blacks; all the efforts at the school were trying to communicate tolerance, not prejudice. Separate from what the children were learning consciously, however, they were unconsciously learning something else altogether.

What is disturbing to me about Aboud's work among the very young is not that children are biased. It is that pervasive bias can occur without anyone—parents, teachers, or the children themselves—wanting it to happen. Everyone involved, in fact, can desperately want the children to reach the opposite beliefs, and the children will still associate positive adjectives with white faces and negative adjectives with black faces. They will misremember the heroics of a little black boy called Zachariah as the heroics of his white friends. And in time, as I will show, children carry these hidden beliefs into adulthood.

Some sixty-five million years ago a giant asteroid hurtled into Mexico's Yucatán Peninsula. The geological record suggests that the impact triggered dust storms and tsunamis that wiped out many species, including the dinosaurs. The rate of extinction was so dramatic that scientists today call the asteroid impact an extinction event.

Interracial friendships between schoolchildren in America suffer an extinction event sometime in middle school. Studies show that by the time kids are in the seventh grade, they have far fewer interracial friendships than they did in the fourth grade. Declines in interracial friendships have also been found in many other countries. This isn't just something that happens to white and black children in the United States—the same phenomenon has been documented among Dutch, South Asian, and Turkish children in countries as varied as Britain, the Netherlands, and Canada. Like the asteroid that wiped out the dinosaurs, something seems to happen in middle school that causes children to form in-groups and become less likely to form close friendships with children from other backgrounds. This sets the stage for friendships that teenagers develop in high school and beyond.

The research findings about childhood friendships is especially depressing because friendship is a magic key to understanding people from other backgrounds. Frances Aboud has found that children who have a close friend from another race—where the children offer each other emotional security, trust, and loyalty—have more positive attitudes toward the other race in general. And children who lack such close friendships have more negative attitudes toward the other race.

One of the puzzling things about the extinction event in interracial friendships is that it occurs at precisely the time when children are getting beyond simplistic biases. Aboud and others have found that by the time children are seven or eight or nine, they are able to assign both positive and negative adjectives to people of all races. When the hidden brains of these children come up with simplistic and stereotypical conclusions, their conscious brains are now mature enough to overrule those conclusions. In fact, when Aboud had children who were at different stages of emotional maturity discuss racial issues with each other, she found that more mature children invariably debunked the views of children who were still thinking at a preschool level. When a prejudiced child was placed in conversation with someone more mature, the more mature child, with the more tolerant views, invariably changed the views of his partner—because mindless heuristics invariably yield to conscious reasoning. Here is one illustrative exchange between two children that Aboud studied:

GA: Lots of black people, you can't trust them. Like, I had a black friend and he was nice to me, but he's not really nice because he—
MP: Does that mean, though, that black people are always gonna be bad?
GA: No, not always.
MP: Right.
GA: But some—
MP: Only some. Same for whites, same for Chinese.

If racism among very small children is largely the result of the conscious brain not being mature enough to overrule the broad generalizations of the hidden brain, why would interracial friendships suffer an extinction event at precisely the point when most children develop the maturity to see that people from all groups have positive and negative qualities? Aboud decided to study the question among two hundred forty black and white students at Montréal's Westmount Park elementary school, a multiracial school featuring large numbers of white, Caribbean black, Southeast Asian, and South Asian students. Her plan was simple: She interviewed students in the fall and again in the spring of a single academic school year and asked the children about their friends. If John reported Dick was his best friend, Aboud checked with Dick to make sure he said John was his best friend, too. Aboud and her colleagues also asked other students to describe whether John and Dick spent time together, and by comparing these responses, she definitively established which pairs of students were mutual friends and mutual best friends. In the spring, Aboud and her colleagues repeated the process. By comparing the results, Aboud minutely documented the evolution of same-race and interracial friendships over a six-month period.

The changing nature of these friendships was revealing. Nine- and ten-year-old children, as you might imagine, add, drop, and change friends quite often. If you were to look at one set of twenty fifth graders, for example, Aboud found about half had a friend belonging to another race. By the second set of interviews, only two of these friendships were still intact. But the same thing was happening with friends belonging to the same race. Perhaps eighteen of twenty students had a best friend belonging to the same race during the first set of interviews, and only ten of these friendships endured over the six-month period. Children were adding new friends at a furious clip, too. But there was a subtle difference in the way they added and dropped friends—different-race friends were slightly more likely than same-race friends to get dropped, and new interracial friendships were slightly less likely to be formed. The difference would not have been obvious to a casual observer. It might not have been obvious even to parents, because the underlying pattern was hidden in a lot of "noise"—a cycle of rapidly changing friendships. But the results were hardly subtle. Whereas the youngest children in Aboud's group had roughly the same number of same-race and different-race friends, the oldest children in her group had one and a half times as many same-race friends as different-race friends. A parent who saw an encouraging racial variety at their child's seventh-, eighth-, and ninth-year birthday party might notice a monochromatic racial makeup at their twelfth or thirteenth birthday party and wonder how that happened.

When the asteroid hit the Yucatán Peninsula sixty-five million years ago, it would have instantly killed most terrestrial creatures in the immediate area. But much of the damage to life would have come in the weeks and months that followed. As plant life was choked off by hovering dust clouds, the devastation would have traveled rapidly up the food chain. If you were a dinosaur in what is now Montana, life around you might have declined over several years, not in a Hollywood-style explosion.

But slow, steady declines in habitat and ecosystems can be just as deadly as sudden cataclysms. Many of the hidden brain's most powerful effects similarly involve subtle changes that assume gigantic proportions because they influence us steadily over time.

If you were to intercede in a child's life, for example, in order to encourage the child to form more interracial friendships, you would hardly know where to begin. Clearly no individual friendship tells you anything very meaningful; if the vast majority of interracial friendships are lost within a short period of time, so also are the vast majority of same-race friendships. The apartheid model simply does not apply—it is not as if children are being forced apart and taught to hate one another. The hidden brain is insidious not because it whacks us on the back of the head but because it places the tiniest of fingers on our inner scales. By the time children are in the seventh grade, those tiny differences leave them with far fewer different-race friends than they had in grade four.

This phenomenon tells me that the way we usually think about prejudice is deeply problematic. In 2007, for example, the international news media was drawn like honeybees to the story of the Jena Six—a racial conflict in a Louisiana town that inflamed national passions when white students hung nooses from trees to send a threatening message to black kids. Commentators saw this as a disturbing sign of toxic racial polarization among kids in small-town Jena. The events in Jena were troubling, but they pale in comparison with the tectonic shifts that happen every day in America's middle schools—earthquakes that go unnoticed. By the time American children are in high school, most are firmly entrenched within their own racial groups; many have forever lost the magic keys of friendship that might have allowed them to understand what it is like to be a person from another race. Nooses hung from trees make for sensational coverage, but they are merely the end product of a process more subtle and more sinister.

Our fascination with cases such as the Jena Six reflects our bias for stories with easy villains and heroes. When we look for villains in the larger story of prejudice among children, we come up short. What is disturbing to me about the extinction event in interracial friendships among children is that, as with the preschoolers Aboud studied, it can occur without anyone explicitly wanting it to happen.

The extinction event in childhood friendships turns out to be a natural outgrowth of children's development. Around the time kids are seven or eight, they start to seek out memberships in groups as a way to cement a sense of their own identity. Developing these identities is both normal and important. Racial identity is only one of the many dimensions children gravitate toward. They also start to identify with sports teams, with cultures, and with nations. Researchers in England once had a group of six- to seven-year-old children and a group of ten- to eleven-year-old children think about English people who said nice things about the German soccer team ahead of the 2002 World Cup soccer championship. It will not surprise you to learn that the English children generally disliked people who said nice things about the German team. What is interesting and instructive, however, is that the older children were far more likely than the younger children to say that they would exclude "traitors" from their groups. For the youngest kids, people with contrarian ideas were not defined by their views; for the oldest kids, views about soccer defined who could be in the in-group and who had to be excluded. The extinction event that Aboud has studied among middle school children was not triggered by hostility and animosity but by the simple fact that race is one of many categories that define people, and ten- or eleven-year-olds are eager to start defining themselves.

It might be easier to understand this phenomenon if we remove the element of race from the equation. If the work by Aboud and others is correct, the same biases that children demonstrate on racial issues should show up for other dimensions of identity.

Aboud conducted another study on friendships at Montréal's Courtland Park International School. Unlike the school with a large number of students from different races, this school had mostly white children. But it was unique in that it had a large number of children from English-speaking households and a large number of children from French-speaking households. Instruction at the school was in both English and French—at lunchtime on Wednesdays, the school switched all conversation and classroom instruction from one language to the other. The idea was to offer the children an immersive experience in two languages and two cultures.

Aboud found the same decline in friendships among English- and French-speaking children as she had with black and white children at the other school. Cross-cultural friends were more likely to get dropped and less likely to be added, leaving children from the two cultures gradually segregated, in psychological terms, even as their school did its best to physically integrate them. When Aboud asked some of the children why they dropped friends who belonged to the other culture, the children said that while they had no personal problem with cross-language friends, it made group activities difficult because there were usually other children from their own linguistic group who had a problem with an interloper. Sometimes no one would actually say anything. But conversation would come to a halt when a child from the other culture joined the group. Children would stop telling secrets midsentence. It did not take long for "interlopers" to get the message.

The fact that racial biases occur "naturally" does not mean they are inevitable. What is inevitable is that children will gravitate toward in-groups, but there is nothing to suggest that race has to be one of the dimensions children use to define themselves. If children can be encouraged to form loyalties to groups that transcend race—to a nation or a school or even a sports team—parents and educators can harness the automatic biases of the mind to drive children from different races together, rather than apart. It is fruitless to try to fight bias by telling kids that unconscious attitudes are wrong. What works is to co-opt the hidden brain in the service of tolerance.

Prejudices among children are disturbing, but it is easy to think that cognitive errors in early childhood have nothing to do with our judgments, decisions, and attitudes in later life. Thinking about bias in terms of the hidden brain, however, can provide us with what scientists call a "parsimonious" explanation—a single explanatory framework that describes the nature of prejudice across the life span, from the very young to the very old. Most of us agree it would be absurd to punish five-year-old children for their biases, particularly when, as we've just discovered, they arrive at those biases innocently, but most of us have no problem blaming adults who display racial prejudice. Small children may not know better, but adults should. Or at least that's what we tell ourselves.

So when former senator George Allen of Virginia called an Indian American "*macaca*" and offered him a "welcome to America" before the 2006 U.S. midterm elections, those gaffes cost Allen his seat and cost the Republicans control of the Senate—the first pebble in an avalanche that ended in the 2008 elections, where the GOP lost both houses of Congress and the White House. And when Michael Richards—the much-beloved Kramer from the television show *Seinfeld*—reminded a black heckler at a comedy club that uppity blacks used to be strung up with nooses, he was quickly and publicly censured for his egregious violation of social norms. The subtext of all the ritualistic breast-beating and finger-pointing on talk shows and in op-ed pages boiled down to one simple question: *Shouldn't these people have known better?*

The answer to that question is yes—and no. When it comes to prejudice, there are some surprising similarities between the preschoolers that Aboud studied and the likes of George Allen. What mostly changes between the ages of five and fifty-four are not the associations of the hidden brain but the ability of the conscious mind to restrain those associations.

Researchers once conducted tests that measured the conscious and unconscious racial attitudes of six-year-olds, ten-year-olds, and adults. They found all three groups had similar unconscious attitudes—they were pro-white. But when the six-year-olds, ten-year-olds, and adults were asked to explicitly state their views, the ten-year-olds reported feeling less prejudiced than the six-year-olds, and the adults denied being prejudiced altogether.

Were the adults lying when they said they were not prejudiced? Of course not. The reason people consciously reject stereotypes is that they know that generalizations about entire groups are dumb. When we ask people about their views, they tell us what they consciously know. But that doesn't tell us about their *unconscious* attitudes and associations. Why should adults, who live in the same world as preschoolers, form different unconscious associations? It's not as if adults live in a world where interracial marriages are the norm and there are just as many gay families in the neighborhood as straight families. Why would their hidden brains, which learn through blind repetition and association, arrive at different conclusions?

I want to be very clear: I am not saying most adults consciously believe racial or sexist stereotypes. When we are explicitly asked to state our views, our conscious brain and hidden brain sit down for a chat, and our conscious brain wins the debate every time, because reasoned analysis is always superior to dumb heuristics. If the conscious mind is the pilot and the hidden brain is the autopilot function on a plane, the pilot can always overrule the autopilot, *except when the pilot is not paying attention.*

Let's go back to George Allen and Michael Richards. Does the hidden brain explain their outbursts? Let's turn the question around. Let us assume that Allen and Richards did not have a hidden brain, that their comments were the product of conscious intent. George Allen's crack now seems even more peculiar than it already did. (Who calls someone a "*macaca*," anyway?) If Allen had been consciously trying to slur the Indian American at his rally, he was engaging in intentional political suicide. The young man Allen addressed was taping him on a video camera—and he was working for Allen's opponent in the Senate race. Sure enough, Allen denied being suicidal. In his flustered attempt to explain his comments, he said, "It's contrary to what I believe and who I am." Likewise, after Michael Richards was excoriated on national television for his comments at the comedy club, he confessed he had no idea where his words had come from. He swore they were at odds with how he really felt.

Now let's put the hidden brain back into the equation, and take the conscious brain out entirely. You can actually do this in experimental settings—not through brain surgery but through techniques that distract people's conscious attention and keep them from consciously restraining the automatic associations of the hidden brain. When social psychologists devise such situations, the automatic biases of the hidden brain show up loudly and clearly. Under pressure, the conscious brain can get overwhelmed. Its ability to mask the hidden brain declines, and we observe the beliefs and attitudes we normally conceal. This is why, under the glare of spotlights and cameras, people often say dumb things. It astonishes us when we see small children assign nearly every positive word to white faces and nearly every negative word to black faces, just as it outrages us when a politician or a prominent entertainer—people who really "ought to know better"—voice hateful ideas. But what is really happening in all these cases is that people are deprived of conscious control over their unconscious attitudes. In the case of toddlers, the conscious mind has simply not developed to the point where it can exert much control over the hidden brain. In the cases of the George Allens and Michael Richardses of the world, stress and pressure can overwhelm the conscious mind and temporarily unmask the hidden associations that lie beneath the surface. People under pressure are more likely to voice hateful ideas and associations—or mix up one Chinese face with another—simply because the conscious mind has its hands full and cannot override an "autopilot" error.

Since our entire political discourse is premised on the assumption that the hidden brain does not exist, however, our ability to talk about race in the United States is severely hampered. Take a look at this conversation that Allen had with *Meet the Press* host Tim Russert about the "*macaca*" comment. I have italicized two sentences.

RUSSERT: Critics say that "*macaca*" is a racist slur, and that you used it because he was dark-skinned. What did you specifically mean when you said, "Welcome to America and the real Virginia?" Why did you use those words toward a dark-skinned American?

ALLEN: Tim, I made a mistake. I said things thoughtlessly. I've apologized for it, as well I should. *But there was no racial or ethnic intent to slur anyone.* If I had any idea that, that that word, and to some people in some parts of the world, was an insult, I would never do it, because it's contrary to what I believe and who I am.

RUSSERT: Well, where'd the word come from? *It must've been in your consciousness.*

ALLEN: Oh, it's just made up.

RUSSERT: Made up?

ALLEN: Just made up. Made-up word.

RUSSERT: You'd never heard it before?

ALLEN: Never heard it before.

If Allen really did make up the word "*macaca*," he invented a word that happened to have a long and racist history. It's patently unbelievable, of course, but this response was prompted by Russert's argument that Allen must have *meant* what he said. Russert was saying, *If I can show George Allen meant to demean a person of color, that will prove he is a racist.* The politician was saying, *If I can show I did not intend a slur, that will prove I am not a racist.* Both men were focused on Allen's conscious *intentions.* But what if the word *"macaca"* came out of Allen's hidden brain? Contrary to what Allen was trying to imply to Russert, he is still responsible for the slur—because we are responsible for the doings of our hidden brain. But contrary to what Russert was trying to imply to Allen, the Republican may not have been consciously motivated by the slightest racial animosity.

Most Americans think of Allen's comments and Richards's views as abhorrent—and they are. But unpleasant and inaccurate associations lie within all of us, which is why when we see someone slip, our reaction should not be "We finally caught that racist bastard!" but, "There, but for the grace of God, go I." When we focus mountains of newsprint and television time on these incidents, we implicitly set ourselves off as different from the George Allens and the Michael Richardses. We convince ourselves that biased attitudes are the exception, when dozens of research studies have shown that they are really the norm—among blacks and whites. I am not saying everyone associates brown people with *"macaca"*—I had to run to a dictionary myself to find out what the word meant. What I am saying is that we all have mindless associations in our hidden brain that surface when we are not on guard.

I promised to show you how the hidden brain can offer a unifying explanation for prejudice across the life span. Many studies have found that older people have higher levels of prejudice than younger adults, and the conventional explanation for this phenomenon is that elderly people grew up in an age when prejudiced attitudes could be expressed freely—or were even the norm. In other words, racist attitudes stem from consciously racist beliefs.

There can be little doubt that people consciously do have different attitudes and beliefs. This is true of kids, adults, and the elderly. There are people who explicitly feel African and Asian nations ought to be re-colonized, that black people in the United States ought to be slaves, and that Jews should be sent to concentration camps. But I believe these consciously biased people are in a very small minority. The disproportionate attention we pay to them distracts us from the far greater challenge—the unconscious biases of the majority, including people in positions of visibility, influence, and authority.

One scientist recently showed how the hidden brain is responsible for prejudice among the elderly. William von Hippel at the University of Queensland in Australia found that elderly people were more likely to express prejudice when they had diminished ability to control their minds—in exactly the same way Wendy McNamara became careless about social norms and niceties as her ability to exert "executive control" was stolen from her by frontotemporal dementia. Prejudice among the elderly, von Hippel found, was closely related to the extent of conscious control elderly people could exert over their hidden brain. Elderly people who were more easily confused by distractions in laboratory experiments were also the most likely to express prejudiced views. Many displays of prejudice among elderly folk, von Hippel argued, were no different from the propensity of elderly volunteers to get into quarrelsome arguments when they were tired. Elderly patients were three times more likely to engage in "gratuitous arguments" in the afternoon than in the morning.

In another experiment that I could hardly believe when I first read about it, researchers reduced prejudice among adults by giving them some sugar. Some volunteers were given lemonade sweetened with sugar while another group was given lemonade sweetened with the sugar substitute Splenda. Sugar, of course, rapidly boosts energy levels in the body and the brain, while Splenda does not. The researchers then evaluated the attitudes of the volunteers toward homosexuality. They found that volunteers who got the drink with sugar displayed less overt prejudice than the Splenda volunteers. The brain is one of the body's biggest energy gluttons. If people need executive control to restrain hidden stereotypes, volunteers who got the nonsugar drink had less mental fuel to shackle their hidden brains.

The work by von Hippel meshes perfectly with Frances Aboud's work among the very young and with a growing body of research into prejudice among adults. Elderly people who have lost executive function behave in exactly the same way as thirty-year-olds deprived in experimental settings of conscious control over the hidden brain. The politician in the heat of an election campaign or the entertainer confronted by a heckler in a darkened theater, meanwhile, can be momentarily reduced to thinking like Frances Aboud's preschoolers.

"More and more, I have gotten to think that some part of our brain is still stuck where we were at four and five and eight, and it is always there," Aboud told me. "Under stress, people do regress to an early mode."

When people cannot control their hidden brains—because they are young and immature, or because they are adults whose minds are temporarily distracted, or because they are elderly and literally losing brain matter—they are more vulnerable to the associations that are always present in the hidden brain.

This is why when you ask adults who "ought to know better" why they said and did certain things, they will tell you they have no idea. We often feel such protestations are disingenuous, but I believe that people are mostly telling the truth when they say they do not hold consciously bigoted views. They are sincere when they report they do not consciously harbor hostility, hate, or malice toward people from other groups. But that does not mean their hidden brain shares their egalitarian views. Thomas Jefferson was a great man, but it is not remotely self-evident to the hidden brain that all men are created equal.

CHAPTER 5

The Invisible Current

Gender, Privilege, and the Hidden Brain

illy Ledbetter's life followed a clockwork routine. When she worked the night shift at the Goodyear Tire & Rubber Company plant in Gadsden, Alabama, she came home from work around nine-thirty in the morning. She took a hot bath, laid out her work clothes for her next shift, and slept until the afternoon. At around five, she set off again for the plant. Her shift did not start until seven, but the route from her home in Jacksonville involved a stretch of about ten miles on a country road, where she sometimes got stuck behind a slow vehicle.

The rubber plant was solid, stolid work. During each shift, managers such as Lilly were given instructions that told them what they needed to get done. If the instructions—which were called a "schedule"—required Lilly's team to make tread belts one night, she had to make sure she had all the components and labor in place before the shift started. The shift ran for twelve hours, but Lilly usually got to the plant early and stayed late. Lilly had once worked for a group of gynecologists, but she felt she was not cut out for medical work. She joined Goodyear when she was forty, straight out of a position with H&R Block. The tire company was a man's world, and Lilly was the only female manager on the night shift. It didn't bother her. If she kept her head down and worked hard, she knew she would be treated the same as everyone else.

One evening in 1998, Lilly reached work around six o'clock. She went to an upper floor where the managers had their mailboxes. There were a number of documents in her mailbox, and inserted among them was a torn sheet of paper. On the fragment were four names—first names. One was hers. The others were area managers who worked with her, doing identical work. The four managers supervised identical crews, worked the same hours, handled the same responsibilities, and had the same level of experience. Lilly was the only woman in the quartet.

Next to the names were numbers. Lilly instantly recognized the number next to her name. It was her salary: $3,727 a month. She looked at the other numbers and instantly felt sick. The other managers' salaries ranged between $4,286 and $5,236 a month. Lilly made $44,724 a year. Her co-workers made $51,432 to $62,832 a year.

Lilly's cheeks flushed. She looked up to see if anyone was watching her. No one seemed to be taking any notice. Lilly rushed to the women's room and collapsed on a sofa. She stared at the paper. She did not feel angry; she felt ashamed, small, and humiliated. "What am I going to do?" she asked herself. "How do I do anything?"

She slipped the paper into her pocket, determined not to show her feelings, but all through her shift the realization that her company valued her so much less than her co-workers gnawed at her. She crossed paths with another manager, a man who was being paid much more to do the same work. Lilly said nothing, but she ached inside.

Lilly did not want to think of herself as a victim of discrimination. Over the years at the Gadsden plant, there had been people who'd been nasty to her, but there had also been plenty of people who'd been friendly. There had been times, for example, when her supervisors had failed to tell her what her team needed to get done during a shift, even as her colleagues received their schedules. She would fall back on personal relationships to get out of the jam—friends in the scheduling department would pass along the instructions. When she had run-ins with supervisors, she put it down to individual chemistry. When a department foreman told her, "God damnit, Lilly, your department looks like a whorehouse!" Lilly coolly told her supervisor, "I don't know. I have never been in one."

Another time, when corporate bigwigs from Akron came down to Gadsden for a visit, Lilly learned that two of her colleagues had been invited to meet the bosses at a social event after work. She asked a manager what time she needed to be at the gathering, and was told she didn't need to attend. She stayed home and fretted, but there was not much else to do—it wasn't like she could barge into a social event uninvited.

After some poor performance reviews, a supervisor told her that if she would only go "down to a local hotel with him," the reviews would start saying Lilly was a good worker. When Lilly complained about sexual harassment, the company changed her supervisor, but she felt she was thereafter branded a troublemaker. She got left out of meetings, which made it harder for her to do her job. Setbacks usually made Lilly more determined. She had grown up on old Westerns, where the cowboy gets spat on and cursed at but keeps his cool, and the world comes around in the end. Whenever she felt dispirited, Lilly told herself, "I'm not a quitter."

Despite her determinedly sanguine attitude, Lilly did sometimes suspect she was being paid less than her co-workers. She heard rumors, for example, that some of her colleagues were making twenty thousand dollars a year in overtime. Lilly worked overtime hours that were as long as anyone else's, but she did not make nearly that much money. The fragment of paper she received—nineteen years after she started working at Goodyear—was the first piece of tangible evidence to support her suspicions. Lilly was working a shift with a complicated two-week cycle; the next time she got a day off that fell on a weekday, she drove an hour west to Birmingham, to the Equal Employment Opportunity Commission, and filed a complaint. The EEOC was backlogged but told her that she had a strong case and encouraged her to work with a private lawyer.

In the lawsuit that followed, Lilly learned she was earning seventy-nine cents to the dollar of her male counterparts. The numbers on the piece of paper were only base salaries; they had other consequences. Her salary determined how much she got paid for overtime. It determined how much she could set aside in her personal retirement account, and how much she contributed to Social Security. Eventually it affected how much pension she received, and all the other sources of her retirement income. Lilly figured if she had been compensated fairly, her income in retirement would have been twice as large as it actually was.

Goodyear countered in court by producing a number of Lilly's performance reviews, which were below par. Lilly's salary had lagged behind her counterparts', the company argued, because she was an underperformer. Lilly argued that she had been evaluated unfairly because she was a woman. She pointed out that in 1996, Goodyear itself had given her a top performance award. The company put a manager on the stand who said the company had given Lilly the high rating because her salary had been lagging behind her peers and the company had been trying to justify giving her more money. Far from discriminating against Lilly, Goodyear suggested, the company had been biased in her *favor*, and had given her merit raises she did not deserve.

The case eventually made its way to the Supreme Court, which dismissed Lilly's complaint on the grounds that the discrimination she alleged had taken place a long time before. A central tenet in the law, the Supreme Court ruled, is that people need to file complaints promptly. Chief Justice John Roberts openly worried that if the Supreme Court were to consider Lilly's allegations, the courts might be flooded by cases from people alleging discrimination in earlier eras. Goodyear had denied Lilly only two raises in the 180 days before she first reached out to the EEOC, and the court ruled there was insufficient evidence to show that those two decisions constituted discrimination. Lilly pointed out the obvious: She could not have filed a complaint earlier in her career because until she found that scrap of paper in her mailbox, she did not have evidence she was being paid less than her co-workers.

Gender issues were an undercurrent in the decision. Justice Samuel Alito, who had recently replaced Justice Sandra Day O'Connor, the first woman to serve on the Supreme Court, wrote the majority opinion. Justice Ruth Bader Ginsburg, who was then the only woman on the court, dissented along with Justices Stephen Breyer, John Paul Stevens, and David Souter. In an unusual move, Ginsburg read her dissent aloud from the bench. "In our view," she said, "this court does not comprehend, or is indifferent to, the insidious way in which women can be victims of pay discrimination."

Ginsburg personally sympathized with Lilly's long silence at Goodyear. Like Lilly, the Supreme Court justice had herself gone years being silent about the effects of sexism in her career. It was the norm for women of Ginsburg's age not to go to law school; the norm that if they did go to law school, they would have a difficult time getting good clerkships; the norm that they would be paid less than their male counterparts. The fact that Lilly had not complained for nearly twenty years about her treatment at Goodyear was unremarkable to Ginsburg. When the Supreme Court justice went to law school at Columbia in the 1950s, there were no women's bathrooms in the building. "If nature called, you had to make a mad dash to another building that had a women's bathroom," she recalled as she discussed her feelings about the Lilly Ledbetter case. It was "even worse if you were in the middle of an exam. We never complained; it never occurred to us to complain."

Lilly Ledbetter never found out who left the scrap of paper in her mailbox. Her case—decided on the timing of her complaint rather than on its substance—became a signature example of the capriciousness of discrimination laws, and the failure of such laws to account for real-world circumstances. One of the first bills signed into law by President Barack Obama was the *Lilly Ledbetter Fair Pay Act of 2009*. It was designed to give many victims of pay discrimination a fair hearing. The new law would have allowed Lilly's complaint to be judged on its merits, rather than on a technicality.

Lilly Ledbetter was widely hailed as a crusader for justice. She danced with President Obama at an inauguration ball. She got no financial recompense for her troubles, but she did get one of the pens Obama used to sign the Fair Pay Act into law.

As Lilly Ledbetter's case was being dismissed by the Supreme Court on the grounds that it was not timely, America was engrossed in the 2008 Democratic presidential primary race between Hillary Clinton and Barack Obama, the first female and African American presidential contenders in history to each have a serious shot at winning the presidency. Clinton, the early front-runner, faltered in the late winter. As she raced to catch up with Obama, her campaign and supporters repeatedly argued that she was the victim of sexism.

A few months before the primary race began, I wrote a column in *The Washington Post* about the role that sexism plays in the way people perceive female leaders. I talked about how a pattern emerged in the way the online encyclopedia Wikipedia, which is the open-source creation of its users, described women leaders. Margaret Thatcher was "Attila the Hen." Golda Meir, the first female prime minister of Israel, was "the only man in the Cabinet." Indira Gandhi, India's first female prime minister, was called the "Old Witch." And Angela Merkel, the first female chancellor of Germany, was the "Iron Frau." The conventional explanation for why women leaders are widely perceived to be ruthless and conniving—and to have lost their caring, feminine side—is that politics is a tough sport and women who climb to the top must have rough elbows. But before these women became leaders of their countries, I found that they had been described in very different ways. Merkel had been nicknamed *das Mädchen*—"the girl." Indira Gandhi had been called *gungi gudiya,* or "dumb doll." How did "the girl" become the "Iron Frau"? How did the "dumb doll" become the "Old Witch"?

If these women leaders had wills of iron and attitudes like Attila, why had dumb blonde stereotypes been attached to them *before* they'd assumed power? I argued in my column that people have unconscious stereotypes about men and women, and also about the nature of leadership—which is linked in our minds with strength, decisiveness, and manliness. When a woman assumes a leadership role, our unconscious stereotypes about leadership come into conflict with our unconscious stereotypes about women. The hidden brain reconciles the conflict by stripping women of their feminine, caring side. Our hidden brain makes women leaders appear ruthless and dislikeable for no better reason than that they happen to be women leaders.

There is fascinating experimental research to back this up. Madeline Heilman at New York University once conducted an experiment in which she told volunteers about a manager. Some were told,

"Subordinates have often described Andrea as someone who is tough, yet outgoing and personable. She is known to reward individual contributions and has worked hard to maximize employees' creativity." Other volunteers were told, "Subordinates have often described James as someone who is tough, yet outgoing and personable. He is known to reward individual contributions and has worked hard to maximize employees' creativity." The only difference between what the groups were told was that some people thought they were hearing about a leader named Andrea while others thought they were hearing about a leader named James. Heilman asked her volunteers to guesstimate how likeable Andrea and James were as people. *Three-quarters* of the volunteers thought James was more likeable than Andrea. Using a clever experimental design, Heilman determined which manager each volunteer preferred: Four in five volunteers preferred to have James be their boss. Andrea seemed less likeable merely because she was a woman who happened to be a leader.

Hillary Clinton's supporters had ample evidence that their candidate was treated in a sexist fashion. Cable news was chock-full of overt sexism. Conservative talk show host Rush Limbaugh, for example, said, "Will this country want to actually watch a woman get older before their eyes on a daily basis?" Hillary Clinton was compared to Lorena Bobbitt (of penis-chopping fame) and likened to "everyone's first wife standing outside a probate court." Tucker Carlson said on MSNBC, "When she comes on television, I involuntarily cross my legs." Clinton was widely described as unlikeable and untrustworthy. She endured numerous sexist taunts—"Iron my shirt," for example, and the ever popular "bitch."

But did Clinton lose the primary race to Barack Obama because of sexism? Millions of her supporters, men included, were convinced that was the case. But opinions tended to fall along lines of political allegiance. Obama supporters, women included, were much less likely to attribute the outcome of the primary race to sexism. (Many Obama supporters noted that Clinton *benefited* from a different bias—some of her supporters explicitly said they would never vote for a black man.) Many political consultants also argued that Clinton made critical political errors in the race. And Clinton did win eighteen million votes, more than any successful Democratic presidential primary candidate before 2008. Candy Crowley of CNN said it was not clear if the "attacks were being made because she was a woman or because she was this woman or because, for a long time, she was the front-runner."

The existence of unconscious sexism can be scientifically proven in laboratory experiments. We know that unconscious sexism caused the laboratory volunteers in Heilman's experiment to find Andrea the manager less likeable than James the manager, because two groups of volunteers, divided at random, reached different conclusions about the likeability of the managers. Since the only thing that varied between the groups was whether they were told the manager was named Andrea or James, we can confidently say the outcome was produced by that single difference.

Bias is much harder to demonstrate scientifically in real life, which may be why large numbers of people do not believe that sexism and other forms of prejudice still exist. Many people think we live in a "post-racial" and "post-sexist" world where egalitarian notions are the norm. Indeed, if you go by what people report, we do live in a bias-free world, because most people report feeling no prejudice whatsoever.

I am personally convinced that Lilly Ledbetter was the victim of discrimination and wasn't just a mediocre employee who got her just deserts, but if you pressed me to prove my case scientifically, I would have to say I do not have conclusive proof. The jury that first heard Lilly's case concluded that she was the victim of discrimination. But a legal conclusion is very different from scientific certainty. We do not know what really happened inside the Gadsden plant, year in and year out. We cannot tell whether the manager who spoke insultingly to Lilly, or the manager who excluded her from a meeting with the big bosses from Akron, did so because she was a woman or because of some other factor. Even if sexism is endemic, it is conceivable that the insulting manager regularly insulted both men and women. That doesn't make him less of a jerk, but it does raise the question of whether he insulted Lilly *because* she was a woman. Similarly, it is not as if Lilly never got a merit raise. For any year in which she was denied a raise, we do not know whether Lilly was passed over because she was not up to par or because of sexism. Sexual harassment is obviously disturbing and illegal, but the connections between harassment and the wage gap Lilly suffered are far from clear. It is possible that the supervisor who propositioned Lilly was an isolated bad apple who in no way reflected how the company evaluated Lilly's performance and determined whether she deserved raises.

It may sound like I am going out of my way to give Goodyear the benefit of the doubt, but what I am trying to explain is how so many people can plausibly argue that bias is merely in the eye of the beholder. I am intuitively sure that Lilly suffered discrimination, but I cannot prove this scientifically because, for every outcome I see, there is always more than one possible explanation. Discrimination would certainly explain the pay disparity, but I have to concede it is also possible that Lilly was not as skilled as her colleagues.

This is true even though there is very clear evidence that women on average are paid less than men for doing the same work. Women working full-time earn about seventy-seven cents to the dollar as compared with men working full-time. Many people argue that this disparity arises because men and women choose different kinds of professions, work different hours, and are likely to take different amounts of time off to raise families. But even if you take all the confounding variables into account, women who work full-time and have never taken time off to raise a family earn about eighty-nine cents to the dollar as men in identical professions. While it is possible that *some* of those women are paid less than men because they are not as good, it is implausible that women *on average* are less competent than men.

The problem, however, is that every time we are asked to think about a situation that might involve discrimination, we have to deal with a single case, not averages. Judges might feel that sexism is real and that women on average are more likely than men to face an uphill climb, but that is not helpful in any individual situation.

If we wanted to settle the question scientifically, what we would really like to know is how Lilly Ledbetter would have been treated if she'd been a man. Would the supervisor have compared her work area to a whorehouse? Would she have received mediocre performance reviews and been passed over for raises? Would her colleagues and co-workers have been more helpful? If we could turn Lilly Ledbetter into a man and have her go back to the Gadsden plant in 1979, we would instantly have incontrovertible proof about the absence or presence of sexism. If (she) received all kinds of privileges, if (she) were given access to networks and mentoring, we would know—scientifically—that the reason she'd been excluded from those things in her real life was because she was a woman. And even the most skeptical among us would want to take Goodyear and nail its ass to a tree.

The same goes for Hillary Clinton. I can confidently say that women leaders on average are perceived to be tougher and more ruthless than they really are, and less warm and caring. But while we have intuitions about the role of such biases in any individual situation, the data cannot conclusively tell us whether a *particular* woman candidate failed because of sexism or because she was an inferior candidate. In any individual case, it is impossible to tell apart accurate perceptions of ruthlessness from unconscious beliefs that link female leaders with ruthlessness, because they both produce exactly the same perception in our minds. A woman leader can appear ruthless because of our own unconscious bias or because she actually is ruthless. As we will see in a chapter devoted to the issue of unconscious bias in politics, the fact that conscious and accurate assessments, and unconscious bias, can both produce the same perceptions in our mind is a major reason unconscious biases flourish and can be actively fanned by those who profit from them. Those who encourage our unconscious biases can plausibly tell us our views are the product of careful analysis, not bias.

The reason unconscious bias is so insidious and so powerful is that it can influence voters without their being aware of it. Explicit bias—Limbaugh and the other openly sexist commentators—got the headlines during the Democratic primary, but implicit bias may have determined the outcome. Overt sexism may have ultimately had very little effect. Millions of Democrats were repulsed by Limbaugh and the other misogynists, and the overtly sexist comments may have even driven *up* support for Clinton. Unconscious bias, on the other hand, may have prompted millions of voters to reject Clinton for reasons that ostensibly had nothing to do with her gender. How can we tell, with scientific certainty, that unconscious bias caused Hillary Clinton to lose? Real life does not provide us with control groups. If Hillary Clinton were a man, (s)he might still have lost.

Hillary Clinton and Lilly Ledbetter are examples of a pervasive challenge in applying the scientific research into bias to the context where it matters most—the lives of individuals. When a woman is passed over for a job or a raise or a plum assignment, when a presidential candidate loses or an employee gets fired, fair-minded people cannot say for certain whether the outcome was because of bias or because of other factors. Neither can bosses, voters, or the victims themselves. The experimental and observational data are very good at telling us that sexism exists, and that it *may* play a role in an individual case, but we have to acknowledge that other factors are invariably involved in any individual situation. There are certainly weak women political candidates and inferior women employees, and it would be a serious error to attribute every defeat and demotion of women to sexism.

It may seem quite obvious to you that the outcomes Lilly Ledbetter and Hillary Clinton experienced were the product of sexism. But the fact that that argument cannot be made with scientific certainty is, I believe, why many people dismiss bias as being merely a matter of opinion. The distinction between personal opinion and scientific fact is important: It doesn't matter whether anyone personally agrees with Heilman's data about volunteers finding a female manager less likeable than a man with identical qualifications. The powerful thing about scientific proof is that it renders personal opinions irrelevant. A scientific fact does not depend on our belief in it to exist, and it does not vanish because we disbelieve it.

What would be remarkably instructive in real life is if women in various professions could experience life as men, and vice versa. If the same person got treated differently, we would be sure sexism was at work, because the only thing that changed was the sex of the individual and not his or her skills, talent, knowledge, experience, or interests. Individual human beings could become their own control groups.

As it turns out, there are men who were once women, and women who were once men. Transgendered people allow us to scientifically apply the research on sexism to the lives of individuals because when a man becomes a woman or vice versa, the person's educational background, professional expertise, and life experience remain the same. If a woman who becomes a man suddenly finds himself privileged in all kinds of subtle ways, or a man who becomes a woman suddenly finds herself shackled, we can unhesitatingly—and scientifically—say sexism is to blame.

There is compelling empirical evidence to show that when men transition to becoming women, they experience all kinds of disadvantages that they did not experience when they were men. Their incomes, on average, fall. When women transition to becoming men, they find they have all kinds of new privileges. Their incomes, on average, rise. Transmen—people who transition from female to male—often report aspects of their professional lives getting easier. Transwomen—people who transition from male to female—often report the reverse.

The sociologist Kristen Schilt has tracked this phenomenon. Between 2003 and 2005, she followed the lives of twenty-nine transmen in Southern California. The transmen were white-collar and blue-collar workers, professionals, and retail salesmen. They ranged in age from twenty to forty-eight. They included people who were white, black, Latino, Asian, and biracial. Eighteen of the twenty-nine were open, meaning their co-workers knew they had once been women. Eleven of them were "stealth" transmen.

Overwhelmingly, the men told Schilt that they were being treated better than they'd been treated as women. Some enjoyed their new-found privileges, others felt uncomfortable.

One thirty-nine-year-old white man who worked in a blue-collar job told Schilt: "I swear they let the guys get away with so much stuff! Lazy-ass bastards get away with so much stuff, and the women who are working hard, they just get ignored. . . . I am really aware of it.

And that is one of the reasons that I feel like I have become much more of a feminist since transition. I am just so aware of the difference that my experience has shown me."

Carl, a thirty-four-year-old "stealth" transman, told Schilt about the hardware store where he worked after he made the transition: "Girls couldn't get their forklift license, or it would take them forever. They wouldn't make as much money. It was so pathetic. I would have never seen it if I was a regular guy. I would have just not seen it."

A Latino attorney told Schilt that an attorney at another law firm had complimented his boss for firing an incompetent woman and hiring a new lawyer who was "just delightful." The attorney at the other firm did not know that the incompetent woman and the delightful new lawyer were the same person.

One transman told Schilt that he was not asked to do different work after the transition, but doing his work suddenly became much easier. He recalled that before the transition, he would often be told that crews and trucks were not available when he needed some help. "I swear it was like from one day to the next of me transitioning. [I would say,] 'I need this, this is what I want,' and—" The man snapped his fingers. "I have not had to fight about anything."

Another study that Schilt conducted with Matthew Wiswall analyzed the salaries of forty-three transgendered people after the volunteers made transitions from male to female or female to male. Schilt and Wiswall found that men who became women reported a decline of 12 percent in their earnings. Women who became men reported an increase of 7.5 percent in their earnings.

"While transgender people have the same human capital after their transitions, their workplace experiences often change radically," Schilt and Wiswall wrote in a paper they published in *The B. E. Journal of Economic Analysis & Policy.* "We estimate that average earnings for female-to-male transgender workers increase slightly following their gender transitions, while earnings for male-to-female transgender workers fall by nearly ⅓. This finding is consistent with qualitative evidence that for many male-to-female workers, becoming a woman often brings a loss of authority, harassment, and termination, but that for female-to-male workers, becoming a man often brings an increase in respect and authority. These findings . . . illustrate the often hidden and subtle processes that produce gender inequality."

I am going to show how such changes manifested themselves in two lives, but I want to make a couple of things clear first. Transgendered people do reveal something powerful about sexism, but they are also victimized in other ways. Many encounter scrutiny, suspicion, and hostility, with homophobia mixed in. Two transgendered people agreed to speak with me on the record about their experiences, because both care deeply about the wounds that sexism has inflicted on American society. Before I tell you their stories, I want to acknowledge their courage—and my debt.

Joan Roughgarden and Ben Barres are biologists at Stanford University. Both are researchers at one of the premier academic institutions in the country; both are tenured professors. Both are transgendered people. Stanford has been a welcoming home for these scientists; if you are going to be a transgendered person anywhere in the United States, it would be difficult to imagine a place more tolerant than Palo Alto and the San Francisco Bay Area. In the interest of full disclosure, I should mention that I am a graduate of Stanford's MA program in journalism—and I have warm memories of and high regard for my alma mater.

Ben Barres did not transition to being a man until he was fifty. For much of her early life, Barbara Barres was oblivious to questions of sexism. She would hear Gloria Steinem and other feminists talk about discrimination and wonder, "What's their problem?" She was no activist; all she wanted was to be a scientist. She was an excellent student. She was captain of her high school's math team. When a school guidance counselor advised her to set her sights lower than MIT, Barbara ignored him, applied to MIT, and got admitted in 1972.

During a particularly difficult math seminar at MIT, a professor handed out a quiz with five math problems. He gave out the test at nine A.M., and students had to hand in their answers by midnight. The first four problems were easy, and Barbara knocked them off in short order. But the fifth one was a beauty; it involved writing a computer program where the solution required the program to generate a partial answer, and then loop around to the start in a recursive fashion.

"I remember when the professor handed back the exams, he made this announcement that there were five problems but no one had solved the fifth problem and therefore he only scored the class on the four problems," Ben recalled. "I got an A. I went to the professor and I said, 'I solved it.' He looked at me and he had a look of disdain in his eyes, and he said, 'You must have had your boyfriend solve it.' To me, the most amazing thing is that I was indignant. I walked away. I didn't know what to say. He was in essence accusing me of cheating. I was incensed by that. It did not occur to me for years and years that that was sexism."

In her sophomore year, Barbara found herself stymied as she looked for a lab where she could in effect become an apprentice to an expert professor. She had an excellent record, but none of the top labs wanted her. A female professor said yes, but Barbara felt this lab was second-best. In academia, as in many other professions, finding a good mentor is a powerful first step that affects the rest of a person's career.

By the time she was done with MIT, Barbara had more or less decided she wanted to be a neuroscientist. She decided to go to medical school at Dartmouth. Gender issues at med school were like the issues at MIT on steroids; one professor referred Barbara to his wife when she wanted to talk about her professional interests. An anatomy professor showed a slide of a nude female pinup during a lecture. During the first year of Barbara's residency, when she was an intern, she found herself clashing with the chief resident. "When you have to learn to do a spinal tap or do a line, at some point only one person can do the procedure. What I noticed is that every time a male resident would do the picking, he would pick a guy to do the procedure. I had to often say, 'He did it last time. It is my turn this time.' "

But things changed in large and subtle ways after Barbara became Ben.

Ben once gave a presentation at the prestigious Whitehead Institute in Cambridge, Massachusetts. A friend relayed a comment made by someone in the audience who didn't know Ben Barres and Barbara Barres were the same person: "Ben Barres gave a great seminar today, but, then, his work is much better than his sister's."

Ben also noticed he was treated differently in the everyday world. "When I go into stores, I notice I am much more likely to be attended to. They come up to me and say, 'Yes, sir? Can I help you, sir?' I have had the thought a million times, *I am taken more seriously*."

When Harvard's former president Larry Summers (who went on to become a senior economic adviser to President Obama) set off a firestorm a few years ago after musing about whether there were fewer women professors in the top ranks of science because of innate differences between men and women, Ben wrote an anguished essay in the journal *Nature*. He asked whether innate differences or subtle biases—from grade school to graduate school—explained the large disparities between men and women in the highest reaches of science. "When it comes to bias, it seems that the desire to believe in a meritocracy is so powerful that until a person has experienced sufficient career-harming bias themselves they simply do not believe it exists. . . . By far, the main difference that I have noticed is that people who don't know I am transgendered treat me with much more respect: I can even complete a whole sentence without being interrupted by a man."

Joan Roughgarden came to Stanford in 1972, more than a quarter century before she made her male-to-female transition in 1998. When the young biologist arrived at Stanford, it felt as though tracks had been laid down; all Roughgarden had to do was stick to the tracks, and the high expectations that others had of the young biologist would do the rest.

"It was clear when I got the job at Stanford that it was like being on a conveyer belt," Roughgarden told me in an interview. "The career track is set up for young men. You are assumed to be competent unless revealed otherwise. You can speak, and people will pause and people will listen. You can enunciate in definitive terms and get away with it. You are taken as a player. You can use male diction, male tones of voice. You can speak definitionally. You can assert. You have the authority to frame issues."

At the Hopkins Marine Station in Pacific Grove, an outpost of the university about ninety miles from campus, Roughgarden ruffled feathers in the scientific establishment by arguing that a prominent theory that described the life cycle of marine animals was wrong. Where previous research had suggested that tide pools were involved in the transportation of certain larvae, Roughgarden reframed the issue and showed that the larger ocean played a significant role. The new theory got harsh reviews, but Roughgarden's ideas were taken seriously. In short order, Roughgarden became a tenured professor, and a widely respected scientist and author.

Like Ben Barres, Roughgarden made her transition to Joan relatively late in life. Stanford proved tolerant, but very soon Joan started to feel that people were taking her ideas less seriously. In 2006, for example, Joan suggested another famous scientific theory was wrong—Charles Darwin's theory of sexual selection. Among other things, the theory suggests that men and women are perpetually locked in a reproductive conflict. Men are supposed to be sexually promiscuous because they stand to gain from spreading their genes as widely as possible, whereas women are supposed to value monogamy because they can have relatively few biological children. Even when women and men escape from this "battle of the sexes," it is only because a temporary truce has been declared. A monogamous husband, for example, "forgoes" his natural inclination to infidelity because his partner offers him something of exceptional value—such as beauty or youth. The theory essentially suggests that conflicting goals are basic to all male-female human relationships—and even purports to "explain" why men rape women. Using ideas from game theory, Joan published a review article in the prestigious journal *Science,* where she explained why she thought the theory was wrong. She drew partly on her 2004 book, *Evolution's Rainbow,* where she detailed the extraordinary range of sexual practices that flourished in the animal kingdom. Thinking about sex purely in terms of reproduction was flawed, Joan argued. Sex was also about building alliances, trading, cooperation, social regulation, and play.

Joan used the example of the Eurasian oystercatcher, a wading bird, in her 2006 paper. In particular, she looked at nests involving three birds, a male and two females. In some of these families, the females fought viciously with each other, whereas in others, the females mated with each other almost as often as they mated with the male. Nests where females bonded sexually were much more likely to have offspring that survived, compared to nests where the females fought each other, since the cooperative nest could call on the resources of three birds to defend offspring against predators. Sex between the females may not have produced offspring, but it had a powerful effect on the survival rate of offspring.

Where Darwin's theory of sexual selection would argue that the competing interests of males and females are what produce a range of sexual behaviors, Joan's theory of "social selection" offered a different viewpoint: Conflict between Eurasian oystercatchers, as perhaps with conflict between human mates, was not the starting point of relationships but an unfortunate outcome. Cooperation, not conflict, Joan argued, was basic to nature. "Reproductive social behavior and sexual reproduction are cooperative. Sexual conflict derives from negotiation breakdown. In Darwinian sexual selection, sexual conflict is primitive and cooperation derived, whereas in social selection, sexual cooperation is primitive and conflict derived."

The scientific establishment, Joan told me, was livid. But in contrast to the response to her earlier theory about tide pools and marine animals, few scientists engaged with her. At a workshop at Loyola University, a scientist "lost it" and started screaming at her for being irresponsible. "I had never had experiences of anyone trying to coerce me in this physically intimidating and coercive way," she told me, as she compared the reactions to her work before and after she became a woman. "You really think this guy is really going to come over and hit you."

At a meeting of the Ecological Society of America in Minneapolis, Joan told me, a prominent expert jumped up on the stage after her talk and started shouting at her at the top of his voice. "If he had hit me, I would have hit him back, but if you have a big man shouting at you, you can feel your tongue getting dry. . . . Once every month or two, I will have some man shout at me, try to physically coerce me into stopping.

"When I was doing the marine ecology work, they did not try to physically intimidate me and say, 'You have not read all the literature,' " she told me. "They would not assume they were smarter. The current crop of objectors assumes they are smarter."

Joan is willing to acknowledge her theory might be wrong; that, after all, is the nature of science. But what she wants is to be *proven* wrong, rather than dismissed. Making bold and counterintuitive assertions is precisely the way science progresses. Many bold ideas are wrong, but if there isn't a regular supply of them and if they are not debated seriously, there is no progress. After her transition, Joan said she no longer feels she has "the right to be wrong."

"It is like we are in a forest and the men are the trees, and what we can do is to water the roots and make the trees flourish, but we can't move the trees," she said. "We can live in the canopy of the forest and be bathed by the light filtered through the canopy. It does not occur to men that a woman can frame the issue and that we are entitled to frame it differently."

Where she used to be a member of Stanford University's senate, Joan told me she is no longer on any university or departmental committee. Where she was once able to access internal university funds for research, she said she finds it all but impossible to do so now. Before her transition, she enjoyed an above-average salary at Stanford. But since her transition, she wrote in an email, "My own salary has drifted down to the bottom 10 percent of full professors in the School of Humanities and Sciences, even though my research and students are among the best of my career and are having international impact, albeit often controversial."

I asked her about interpersonal dynamics before and after her transition. "You get interrupted when you are talking, you can't command attention, but above all you can't frame the issues," she told me. With a touch of wistfulness, she compared herself to Ben Barres. "Ben has migrated into the center, whereas I have had to migrate into the periphery."

I want to tell you another story, a personal story. On its surface, it has nothing to do with the hidden brain, bias, or sexism. But stay with me a second. The story has an unexpected insight into the strange canvasses that Ben Barres, Joan Roughgarden, and Schilt's volunteers have painted for us.

Shortly after I started work on this chapter, I took a vacation with my family. For me, the highlight of our destination—the tiny island of Isla Mujeres in Mexico—was a wonderful snorkeling opportunity off the southwestern coast. When I arrived at the snorkeling spot, it was noon. The water was calm and warm, the December sun glorious. The coral reef that lay a short distance away had been damaged in a recent storm, but it was growing back. At the southern lip of a small bay, officials had cordoned off the reef from swimmers with lines attached to buoys in order to allow the reef to grow. The cordoned-off area was about two hundred and fifty feet from my deck chair. The lines and buoys continued out of sight around a solid wall of rocks.

I have a complicated love affair with the water. I didn't learn to swim until I was an adult. Well into my twenties, I carried the kind of unreasonable fear of water that you do not have if you learn to swim as a child. A considerable part of my enjoyment of the water lies in demonstrating to myself, over and over, that I have conquered my mortal fear. I am a decent swimmer, but I also know my fear has not completely disappeared. When things go wrong in the water, I easily panic.

After several dips, I decided to take one final excursion—this time around the edge of the bay. I felt happy and wonderful and fit; the water was calm. I suspected some of the best snorkeling lay around the edge of the rocks, two hundred fifty feet away. There were no signs posted that warned of any danger. With a good lunch in my stomach, I felt I could easily swim around the edge of the bay and back. I briefly thought about donning a life jacket and flippers, but decided against it. The life jacket would slow me down, and flippers don't allow for the kind of maneuverability I like when I am snorkeling over a shallow reef.

The moment I got into the water and headed for the edge of the bay, I knew I had made the right decision to swim without a life jacket or flippers. I felt strong and good. I had done a lot of swimming that day already and was surprised at how smoothly I was kicking through the water. The trip would be child's play; the way I was feeling, I knew I could easily swim well past the edge of the bay. I struck out purposefully to the lip of rocks. I imagined seeing myself from the deck chairs back on land, disappearing from view around the rocks.

The water felt suddenly cooler as I rounded the lip of the bay. It felt pleasant. I kept within ten or fifteen feet of the line attached to the buoys. From my side of the line, the ocean side, I could see the coral reef growing back within the protective arc. The water was now twenty or thirty feet deep. The reef and the fish were lovelier and more plentiful than anything close to the main snorkeling area. All the other swimmers were staying in the main area. I was alone in the water and hidden from view. It felt delicious, as though I had the whole reef to myself.

My legs and arms felt stronger than ever. Each kick took me several feet; my technique was better than I remembered. I lengthened my stroke, feeling the pull of cool water against my torso. I felt graceful. Without realizing it, through steady practice, I had become a very good swimmer. I felt proud of myself.

I knew from a previous visit that there was a recreational park area to the south with some excellent snorkeling, and I wanted to reach it before turning around. But after swimming ten minutes or so past the lip of rocks, all I could see when I lifted my head from the water was gray sea. *Enough*, I told myself. *Time to turn around.*

I pivoted and started to kick my way back. A particularly lovely piece of coral lay just beneath me. But as I watched for it to go by as I swam past, the coral did not budge. I kicked again and again. It was as though I were swimming in place, stuck with invisible glue to a single spot. My fear of the water, long dormant, opened one monstrous eye.

I instantly realized my grace and skill on the way out had not been grace and skill at all. I had been riding an undercurrent. I would now have to fight it on the way back. The reef did not look beautiful anymore. The water looked too deep. No one on land could see me. Why had I not worn a life jacket? How insane not to have donned flippers. I kicked and pulled and kicked and pulled. I was working much harder than before, but I was not traveling several feet with each stroke; each effort bought me mere inches. My breathing in my own ears sounded labored, a huge pair of bellows shouting over the din of the sea.

I debated whether to turn around and go with the current, in the hope of reaching the recreation area I had seen during my previous visit, and then hauling myself onto land. But I was no longer sure if there even was a recreation area anymore. Perhaps it had been closed—because of dangerous undercurrents. If the recreation area did not exist, I knew I would quickly find myself in water well beyond my swimming ability. Currents from the east and west met in a ferocious battle near the southernmost edge of the island. Experts often say that the best way to fight an undercurrent is to swim out and around it. In this case, that would have meant swimming out to sea, but the thought filled me with terror. I had to go back the way I'd come.

I was gripped by an absolute sense of the lunacy of what I had done. There were no lifeguards in the snorkeling area, no boats. No one could see me. I lived the usual sedentary life of many urban professionals; my athletic exploits were mainly weekend heroics. What had made me think I was really fit enough to swim out so far when I had already exerted myself so much that day?

I had not traveled more than halfway back to the edge of the bay when I decided I could go no farther. I was exhausted by the current. It was all I could do to hold the panic down, to keep pulling and kicking and breathing. I feared the onset of cramps. And over and over, I asked myself how I could have missed the existence of the current until the moment I turned around and had to fight it.

I don't know where the strength came from to make it back. Perhaps it was the image of my daughter, who had just turned two, waiting for me on the shore. When I finally stepped back onto land, I was on the verge of collapse. I had had a narrow escape.

Perhaps it is clear to you why I told you this story. Unconscious bias influences our lives in exactly the same manner as that undercurrent that took me out so far that day. When undercurrents aid us, as they did when Joan Roughgarden first arrived at Stanford, we are invariably unconscious of them. We never credit the undercurrent for carrying us so swiftly; we credit ourselves, our talents, our skills. I was completely sure that it was my swimming ability that was carrying me out so swiftly that day. It did not matter that I knew in my heart that I was a very average swimmer, it did not matter that I knew that I should have worn a life jacket and flippers. On the way out, the idea of humility never occurred to me. It was only at the moment I turned back, when I had to go against the current, that I even realized the current existed.

Our brains are expert at providing explanations for the outcomes we see. People who swim with the current never credit it for their success, because it genuinely feels as though their achievements are produced through sheer merit. These explanations are always partially true—people who do well in life usually are gifted and talented. If we achieve success through corrupt means, we know we got where we are because we cheated. This is what explicit bias feels like. But when we achieve success because of unconscious privileges, it doesn't feel like cheating. And it isn't just the people who flow with the current who are unconscious about its existence. People who fight the current all their lives also regularly arrive at false explanations for outcomes. When they fall behind, they blame themselves, their lack of talent. Just as there are always plausible explanations for why some people succeed, there are always plausible explanations for why others do not. You can always attribute failure to some lack of perseverance, foresight, or skill. It's like a Zen riddle: If you never change directions, how can you tell there is a current?

Most of us—men *and* women—will never consciously experience the undercurrent of sexism that runs through our world. Those who travel with the current will always feel they are good swimmers; those who swim against the current may never realize they are better swimmers than they imagine. We may have our suspicions, but we cannot know for sure, because most men will never experience life as a woman and most women will never know what it is like to be a man. It is only the transgendered who have the moment of epiphany, when they suddenly face a current they were never really sure existed, or suddenly experience the relief of being carried by a force larger than themselves. The men and women who make this transition viscerally experience something that the rest of us do not. They experience the *unfairness* of the current.

"I am no different than I was, so I should, on its face, be able to command just as much authority to reframe issues or have my considered opinion placed on the table as I used to," Joan Roughgarden told me. "In my opinion, because of what I have been through, I don't think my work has ever been better."

CHAPTER 6

The Siren's Call

Disasters and the Lure of Conformity

We have seen how unconscious bias plays a role in simple decisions such as whether to give a waitress an extra-large tip, or to buy a stock with a complicated ticker code. We have seen the effects of the hidden brain in professional settings and in the minds of young children. The remaining chapters of this book each focus on an important issue and examine the effects of unconscious bias in that domain. Subsequent chapters will examine the automatic biases of suicide terrorists, the role of unconscious racism in death penalty sentencing and in presidential elections, and the effects of bias on moral decision-making. This chapter focuses on the role of the hidden brain during disasters.

The Belle Isle bridge in Detroit was not designed with a psychology experiment in mind. But on an August night some years ago, it became a laboratory for the study of human nature. Being on a bridge is in some respects like being in an elevator or on a passenger plane. It's an experience so familiar that we barely register it as an experience at all. But when things go wrong, a bridge can quickly turn into something very different: a confined space where large numbers of people are surrounded by total strangers.

The nineteen cantilevered arches of the Belle Isle bridge span 2,356 feet. Two lanes of traffic run in each direction between Detroit and its favorite public park, the island of Belle Isle. Thirty feet below the cars, the currents of the Detroit River run swiftly toward Lake Erie. On a clear day with no traffic, a car going thirty-five miles an hour can cross the bridge in forty-five seconds. But such speed is inconceivable on summer nights, when traffic clogs the bridge in both directions. Hundreds of cars can be jammed together, inches separating one bumper from the next. Although most people don't think about it, the fact is from the moment they drive onto the bridge until the moment they get off, they are trapped.

The third Friday night in August 1995 was a typical summer night. Countless young people from Detroit came over the bridge to Belle Isle. Cars cruised around a portion of the island known as the strip. People rolled down their windows and drove slowly; the idea was to watch and be watched. Loud music blared from the cars. It was late. Midnight came and went. Somewhere in the crowd, a thirty-three-year-old woman took a drag on a marijuana joint. Deletha Word was four feet eleven inches tall and weighed one hundred fifteen pounds. She had a dog by her side. Deletha was chatting with someone she had met at Belle Isle that evening. What were they talking about? Perhaps just the minutiae of everyday life. Deletha, who was known to her family as Lisa, worked at a grocery store. She was finishing a marketing degree, after which she hoped to pursue a career in fashion. She had a thirteen-year-old daughter.

A young man materialized from the darkness. A suitor. Martell Welch was six foot one and weighed nearly three hundred pounds, a former high school football player. As Deletha's acquaintance would later recount, the petite woman wasn't interested. But the nineteen-year-old was insistent. He reached out and touched Deletha. She pulled back. Martell pressed forward. Words rang out. As he made himself more unpleasant—and more intimidating—Deletha could think of only one way to extricate herself. She jumped into her station wagon and drove off—her hurry so great that she forgot to take her dog. She headed for the bridge. By now, she was thoroughly rattled. When she looked into her rearview mirror, she saw that the hulk had jumped into his car and was coming after her. Deletha stepped on the gas, desperate to get some distance from her pursuer before they reached the bottleneck of the bridge.

Twenty-three-year-old Tiffany Alexander had been at a small gathering at a friend's place that evening. Detroit in August can be hot and sticky, and someone suggested a drive. Tiffany grabbed her cellphone and climbed into the back of a GMC Jimmy. There were two men and another woman in the car. The friends drove to Belle Isle and started a leisurely cruise around the island. They were about three-quarters of the way around when Tiffany, who was sitting behind the driver, saw something out of the corner of her eye. A Plymouth Reliant station wagon shot by. It was going fast, maybe twice the twenty-five-miles-per-hour speed limit. A moment later, another car whizzed past. It was a Chevy Monte Carlo.

By the time Tiffany and her friends reached the bridge, the car chase was over. Deletha and Martell had been brought to a stop by the traffic on the bridge; Martell had caught up with Deletha and had pulled up to her rear bumper. In her panic, Deletha threw the station wagon into reverse, and backed right into the Monte Carlo. There was a jarring bump. Before Deletha could move, Martell jumped out and raced over to the station wagon. There were three other young men in the car with Martell, and they got out, too. As the SUV Tiffany was in pulled alongside the two stationary cars, she saw a large man reach through the window of the Plymouth station wagon and grab hold of a small woman. Martell hauled Deletha up and out. Yanking her partially through the window, he flexed his fingers into a fist and hit her. Martell pinned her against the window frame, and pounded on her like a jackhammer. At the sight of the violence, Tiffany involuntarily slouched down in her seat. She couldn't see Deletha's face, but she could see Martell clearly. Deletha's body hung halfway out the window. Punch! . . . Punch! . . . Punch! . . . The young woman's body shuddered with the blows—Tiffany could not believe it was happening in plain view. Slowly Tiffany's car pulled away from the scene. All the way across the jammed bridge and for a good half mile afterward, Tiffany and her friends talked about the altercation. What could have prompted such violence? What would happen to the woman? Tiffany felt shaken up. She worried about the woman. But it never occurred to her to call the police on her cellphone. Dozens of people, after all, were at the scene—surely someone else would intervene.

Behind Tiffany, other cars stopped around the station wagon and the Monte Carlo. Bystanders formed concentric circles of shock and horror. Martell's assault continued. His three friends—and a gaping crowd—looked on, and did nothing to stop him. Twenty-one-year-old Lehjuan Jones saw the football player drag the woman out of her car, strip off her pants, and swear that he was going to kill her. Three car lengths behind the Monte Carlo, a forty-year-old Detroit bus driver named Harvey Mayberry saw a young woman being dragged along the bridge by a young man. Another bystander, twenty-three-year-old Michael Sandford, saw Martell seize Deletha's hair in his fist. The woman struggled, her arms and legs flailing as Martell spun her around like a rag doll. Deletha was trying to find something to hold on to. Harvey Mayberry, the bus driver, saw Martell slam Deletha's head down onto the hood of his car while screaming about the damage the fender bender had inflicted on his vehicle. Blood covered Deletha's face. People watched, openmouthed. Harvey Mayberry felt paralyzed—it wasn't just Martell he was afraid of; he was afraid of the three young men who were with Martell. Raymont McGore, a dockworker who had come upon the scene, also felt paralyzed. If just one other person had stepped forward to help Deletha, the dockworker felt he might have jumped in, too. But no one in the growing circle of bystanders did anything. Martell hoisted Deletha into the air and proffered the naked woman to the crowd.

"Does anybody want some of this bitch?" he screamed. "Because she has to pay for my car."

Martell flung Deletha down onto the bridge and kicked her. She lay there, helpless, and the crowd gaped. Martell retrieved a tire iron and began to smash Deletha's station wagon; his friends helped him damage her car. All Deletha wanted was to get away. She woozily crossed over to the other side of the bridge, stumbling past stopped cars and wide-eyed occupants. Dozens of people watched her go, a disoriented woman who had obviously just suffered a grievous assault. No one intervened.

Meanwhile, Tiffany Alexander and her three friends came by a police squad car about half a mile after the bridge. They pulled over to see if someone had reported the incident. The cop told them a report had just come in and that police would respond. The friends decided to turn around and see for themselves. Bridge traffic on the way back was clogged. Tiffany's car inched along. Then, up ahead and on the right, beyond a concrete barrier that separated traffic from the sidewalk, Tiffany saw a lone figure walking along the edge of the bridge. Some estimates suggest that from the time the assault began, nearly half an hour had elapsed. Tiffany was close enough to see that Deletha Word was a brown-skinned woman and that her hair was askew. Tiffany and her friends did not get out of their car. The woman stumbled along. Investigators later concluded, from the trail of blood Deletha left behind, that she walked one hundred seventy feet from the scene of the fender bender. When Deletha drew level with Tiffany's SUV, she looked over her shoulder. It was like a scene from a horror movie: Martell was coming after her again. He was now carrying the tire iron. Deprived of escape and surrounded by dozens of gawking witnesses who seemed frozen in their cars, Deletha did the only thing possible. She climbed the outer rail of the bridge. Between forty and a hundred people saw what was happening: a lone woman, helpless and terrified, clinging to a rail, perilously hanging thirty feet above the surging currents of the Detroit River. Tiffany's heart was in her mouth. But none of the bystanders lifted a finger.

"You can't go out that way," Martell taunted. He took another step toward Deletha. He raised the tire iron. He was only six feet away.

Deletha looked at Martell and the gaping crowd. The dark water beneath her was terrifying; she did not know how to swim. But between the swirling river and the indifferent strangers on the bridge, she preferred her chances with drowning. She let go of the railing and plummeted from sight. The crowd gasped. It would have taken less than one and a half seconds for her to hit the water. Within a moment, the current had her in its grip. How long did she thrash in terror? It could have been minutes, or much longer. When her drowned body was finally recovered the following day, it had been in the water for nine hours. The corpse was missing a leg. Somewhere along a ten-mile journey downriver, a boat propeller had severed Deletha's right leg at the hip.

In the days that followed, outrage grew over the incident. It turned out that Tiffany Alexander was not alone in failing to use her cellphone to immediately call for help. For an incident that lasted as long as thirty minutes and had dozens of eyewitnesses, hardly anyone alerted police. Officers were nowhere close to the scene when Deletha jumped off the bridge. Martell even made it home safely that night. He was arrested only the next day after detectives spotted a Chevy Monte Carlo on his street with a hockey mask hanging from the rearview mirror—a description that matched eyewitness reports. Prosecutors matched bloodstains on the hood of the Monte Carlo to Deletha Word. Because people were unable to comprehend how so many bystanders could have idly stood by as a fellow human was killed, the story line quickly became exaggerated. The crowd supposedly egged Martell on. Bystanders allegedly laughed at Deletha's plight. Detroiters such as Tiffany Alexander and Harvey Mayberry came to be seen as heartless. In *The Des Moines Register,* columnist Donald Kaul damned the whole city: "Detroit makes people crazy." Criticism flooded in from as far away as Europe and Asia. Police had a difficult time finding people to testify in court against Martell, because anyone who came forward was immediately asked the most obvious question: Why didn't you do anything to help?

For years after the incident, Tiffany Alexander asked herself the same question. And she wasn't alone. Why did Harvey Mayberry, Lehjuan Jones, Raymont McGore, and Michael Sandford not stand up to Martell Welch, when each believed in his heart that it was the right thing to do? Is it possible that everyone on the bridge that night was a callous coward? When asked, each person came up with a reason they had not acted. "There was nothing I could do, being a woman and him being a big man," Alexander said, but she knew it wasn't true. Even if people had been afraid to physically intervene, what would it have taken to call the police right away? And even if people had been afraid to intervene on their own, surely they could have confronted Martell as a group?

Did Deletha Word have the misfortune of spending her final moments surrounded by a uniquely callous selection of humanity? One piece of evidence suggested otherwise: The bystanders were stricken with guilt afterward. On learning that Deletha was the mother of a thirteen-year-old girl, Tiffany's anguish caused her to burst into action. She decided to step forward, identify Martell from a police lineup, and testify against him in court. Yes, she told police, she had seen the assault begin and had seen it end. After Deletha had plunged to her death, the four friends in Tiffany's car had driven a little farther on the bridge, pulled a U-turn, and passed Martell's car again. Deletha's assailant was on his way home. He was so close that Tiffany could see him mopping perspiration from his brow with a towel. No one else in Tiffany's car wanted to have anything to do with the trial and the adverse publicity. But Tiffany stuck to her decision, even though it meant harassment whenever she left her house. She started wearing a wig to keep people from recognizing her as one of the cold-hearted bystanders on the Belle Isle bridge.

What do you think happened on the bridge that night? From the outrage that followed, you would think Deletha had been surrounded by the only people in the world who would not help a victim in distress. Everyone else swore they would have come to her aid. Children in schools told reporters they would not have sat idly by. The right course of action was obvious: Step forward, do something, think for yourself. If Tiffany Alexander, Harvey Mayberry, Lehjuan Jones, Raymont McGore, and Michael Sandford had not been eyewitnesses to a horror but victims themselves, surely they would have expected others to use their heads a little better.

This was my own view of the tragedy when I first heard about it as a reporter. It was not until I started learning about the hidden brain that I realized there was an entirely different way to think about what had happened. The more I learned, the more I came to see that Mayberry, Sandford, McGore, Jones, and Alexander did not really have insight into their own behavior. My research into the tragedy of the Belle Isle bridge led me—unexpectedly—to a beautiful September morning in New York in 2001.

Six years after Deletha's death, a young equity trader at a financial services investment bank in New York went to work on a sunny Tuesday morning in September. Bradley Fetchet had been at Keefe,

Bruyette & Woods for less than a year, but his talent had already been noticed. There was another Brad at the firm already, so the twenty-five-year-old Bucknell graduate was given the moniker Fetch. Each day, his mother told me, Fetch took special pride as he stepped into work on the eighty-ninth floor of the South Tower of the World Trade Center. It is not surprising that Fetch came to think of the firm as special. The employees of Keefe, Bruyette & Woods prided themselves on their camaraderie. They thought of themselves as more than colleagues—the firm felt like family. New recruits, in fact, were often literally family—many came to the firm by way of recommendations from relatives at the company. Tied together by blood, outlook, and social ties, the employees formed an unusually cohesive group. On September 11, 2001, the seven-thirty morning meeting at the firm was particularly well attended. As the meeting broke up about an hour later, people drifted back to their desks, chatting with one another before the start of trading at nine o'clock. That was when they heard a terrible muffled noise. It was as if an earthquake had struck. It was eight forty-six A.M. According to an account of the event pieced together by the man who would later become the new head of the firm, the muffled explosion brought Joe Berry, the chairman of the company, running out of his office. "Jesus Christ," he shouted. "What the hell was that?"

If the architecture of the Belle Isle bridge produced a situation where Deletha Word's options for physical escape were tragically limited, the muffled explosion that Fetch and the others heard created a similar situation. What mattered in this case, however, was not the physical structure of the tower but the architecture of time. Fetch and his friends did not know this, but their own lives were in deadly danger. They had just one opportunity for escape—a sliver of a window had been opened by an event hundreds of miles away. Earlier that morning, United Airlines Flight 175 from Boston had seen its takeoff delayed by fourteen minutes at Logan airport. That delay created a small opportunity for Fetch and his friends to survive, but of course the employees of Keefe, Bruyette & Woods did not know that. When Fetch and his friends heard the explosion in the North Tower that Tuesday morning, they did not know the United Airlines plane was sixteen minutes away from crashing into their building. The impact of the United plane would tear a diagonal gash in the South Tower that would stretch from the seventy-seventh to the eighty-fifth floor. Virtually every person who was still in the building above the zone of impact would die.

In the overwhelming tragedy that was enveloping the United States, hardly anyone noticed that something strange happened at Keefe, Bruyette & Woods that morning—a puzzle. The investment banking firm was actually spread over two floors in the South Tower, the eighty-eighth floor and the eighty-ninth floor. Escape routes from both floors would be severed by the impact of the United Airlines plane. But when the survivors were accounted for, it turned out that nearly every employee on the eighty-eighth floor escaped and survived. Fetch and nearly everyone else who worked for the same company on the eighty-ninth floor stayed at their desks and died. John Duffy, who became CEO of the firm after the tragedy—and whose son was among the employees who died—told me that 120 employees were spread over the eighty-eighth and eighty-ninth floors that morning. Of the sixty-seven people at the firm who died, sixty-six worked on the eighty-ninth floor. Only one person who died worked on the eighty-eighth floor, and, as we will see, that death was the result of a conscious act of courage.

Accounts pieced together from telephone calls made from the eighty-ninth floor and accounts from a few survivors show that Fetch and the others did not know that the explosion they heard was caused by a plane crash—the North Tower was not directly visible from the firm's trading area in the South Tower. But from their perch in the sky, they saw smoke and thousands of pieces of paper drifting across the sky. One employee would later say it looked like a ticker tape parade. Confusion broke out. People raced to windows for a better look. Senior staff recalled what happened during the terrorist attack on the World Trade Center in 1993. Those who tried to leave got stuck for hours in elevators. The emerging school of thought in disaster management was that rather than trying to get everyone out of a big building like the World Trade Center, it made sense for people who were not affected by a problem to stay inside their workplaces, rather than wander out into danger. This wisdom had filtered down to every old-timer in the building.

Put yourself in the shoes of the people on the eighty-ninth floor. You have no idea what is happening. A muffled explosion from an adjoining tower, smoke, and drifting pieces of paper is all the information you have. The idea that nineteen hijackers have taken control of four airplanes and aimed them at the nation's most prominent landmarks, including the building where you work, is not just beyond the realm of comprehension. It is beyond the realm of imagination. Fetch and his friends also had one nervous eye on the clock—trading on the stock market was to open in a few minutes at nine o'clock.

Chairman Joe Berry dispatched someone to check with building officials about what to do. Meanwhile, families, friends, and colleagues who heard about the explosion on television started calling to make sure their loved ones were okay. The calls had the unintended effect of keeping employees at their workstations.

Meanwhile, the United Airlines plane, after initially going southwest through Massachusetts, Connecticut, and New Jersey, pulled a lazy U-turn over Pennsylvania. A subsequent re-creation of its flight path showed that the plane drifted southeast at first, then made a ninety degree left turn at the New Jersey border and headed northeast toward Manhattan.

Some of Fetch's colleagues wandered over to windows that offered a good view of the North Tower. Others determinedly settled into their desks to get ready for the start of trading—and advised their slacker friends to do the same. Officials in the building finally announced over the public address system that people in the South Tower could stay where they were rather than risk exiting the building, where they could get hit by falling debris from the North Tower.

Fetch saw the burning North Tower from a window with a good view. The sight shook him up. He saw someone leaping from an upper floor and falling hundreds of feet. It was horrible. He didn't realize that something even worse was about to happen. United Flight 175 was plunging ten thousand feet a minute, aimed at the southern tip of Manhattan. Fetch did what anyone else might do in his situation, what most of the people around him were doing. He picked up the phone. He called his father at work. After a brief conversation, he hung up. The United plane was only moments away. Fetch dialed another number. He wanted to reassure his mother that he was all right. Mary Fetchet was not in, so Fetch left her a message.

"He said, 'I want to tell you the plane hit tower two and I am in tower one and I am alive and well,'" Mary Fetchet recalled in an interview. "He said, 'It was pretty frightening because I saw someone fall from the ninetieth floor all the way down.' There was a long pause. He cleared his voice and said, 'Give me a call. I think I will be here the rest of the day. I love you.'"

Seconds later, Fetch's building shuddered violently with the impact of United Flight 175. Virtually no one on the upper floors knew that one stairwell in the building survived the crash. Nearly everyone above the zone of impact who did not escape within the sixteen-minute window perished.

What happened on the eighty-eighth floor of Keefe, Bruyette & Woods? The employees there had the same culture and camaraderie as their colleagues on the eighty-ninth floor. They knew the same things about the building. They experienced the same confusion when they heard the explosion in the North Tower. They had the same doubts about what to do. Friends and family were calling people on this floor, too. People here had heard the frustrated accounts of those who'd tried to get out of the building after the 1993 attack. The announcement telling people to stay put reached the eighty-eighth floor as clearly as it did the eighty-ninth floor. Some people on the eighty-eighth floor jumped up when they heard the explosion from the North Tower. They looked at one another in horror. One man, J. J. Aguiar, ran through the floor screaming at people to leave. But as we have seen, there were plenty of other forces prompting people to stay. Given all the evidence, why did the people on this floor evacuate en masse?

It is important to emphasize that it is only in hindsight that we know that the people on the eighty-eighth floor who ran down the stairs after hearing the first explosion did the right thing. Toward the end of his suicidal descent, Marwan al-Shehhi, the terrorist at the controls of the United Airlines plane, dropped more than twenty-five thousand feet in a few minutes. The plane was traveling at nearly six hundred miles per hour at the moment of impact. If the nose of the plane had been tilted just a fraction of a degree in one direction, everyone on the eighty-ninth floor might have survived, too. If the plane had struck one of the lower floors, some of those who fled the eighty-eighth floor might have been just as unlucky as the people who stayed at their desks on the eighty-ninth floor.

If the explosion in the North Tower had been the result of an accident rather than terrorism, a scenario that seemed far more plausible during those first sixteen minutes, then the people who stayed in their offices on the eighty-ninth floor might have ended up looking like the wise ones, while the people who ran outside might have been hit by falling debris. The point is not that employees on one floor made the "right" decision while the employees on the other floor made the "wrong" decision.

The point is that on each floor virtually everyone reached the *same* decision.

But wasn't every employee at Keefe, Bruyette & Woods that morning making decisions on his or her own? Wasn't every employee exercising judgment? If all the people were making deliberate and individual decisions to evacuate or stay, shouldn't we expect to see a similar balance of decisions on both floors? Many people on the eighty-ninth floor should have decided to leave, while many people on the eighty-eighth floor should have stayed. That, emphatically, is not what happened. Nearly everyone on one floor left. Nearly everyone on the other stayed. Could every employee on the eighty-eighth floor have independently reached one conclusion, while nearly every employee on the eighty-ninth floor independently reached the opposite conclusion? The odds of this happening purely by chance are similar to the odds that you'd find one particular grain of sand among all the beaches in the world.

Studying the decisions of individuals has not told us why people on one floor escaped while people on the other floor stayed. Could our approach to the puzzle have been wrong? Rather than focus on the details of why people stayed or left, perhaps we ought to step back—

the evidence, after all, shows a *mass* decision to leave one floor, and a *mass* decision to stay behind on the other. Trying to understand mass decisions by studying individuals is like photographing a panoramic scene with a zoom lens rather than a panoramic lens. The details keep us from seeing the larger picture. All we see is chaos and caprice—or what a scientist would call noise.

What happens if we step back? We see something quite different. If you happened to be part of the group on the eighty-eighth floor, you ran for the stairs because everyone else was running for the stairs. If you happened to be part of the group on the eighty-ninth floor, you stayed because nearly everyone else was staying, too. It is crucial to note that the people on the two floors, just like the bystanders on the Belle Isle bridge, did not explicitly think about their actions this way. No, every person *felt* they were making autonomous decisions. But the evidence shows that the decision that made the difference between life and death that morning was not made by individuals. That decision was made, for lack of a better term, by groups. Group decisions provide us with a signal. The details about individuals—who did what, who felt what, who thought what—is noise.

Three years before the 2001 attacks, a sociologist named Beningo Aguirre published an extraordinary paper in an obscure journal called *Sociological Forum.* Although the paper spoke directly to their situation, the information in it was nothing that the employees of Keefe, Bruyette & Woods could have been expected to know. Aguirre sent out questionnaires to people who were in the World Trade Center during the 1993 attack, when terrorists detonated a car bomb in the B-2 level of the parking garage. The explosion created a crater that was three-quarters of an acre in size, and seven stories in depth. It disabled the public address system and sent smoke pouring through air vents. Within minutes, the smoke traveled dozens of floors above the underground explosion. Aguirre wanted to find out how quickly people exited the buildings and what factors influenced their escapes. Remarkably, he found that it mattered little whether people were on an upper floor or a lower floor. In other words, being on the fortieth floor didn't mean that you necessarily took longer to get out of the building than if you were on the thirtieth floor. What really mattered was the size of the groups that people belonged to. The larger the group, the longer it took to escape. It took time for Aguirre to figure out why the size of groups made such a big difference. The sociologist eventually realized that during disasters, people unconsciously seek consensus with those around them. Groups seek to develop a shared narrative—an explanation for what is happening that is shared by everyone. The larger the group, the longer it took to arrive at a consensus.

People regularly make decisions that do indeed reflect their individual personalities and motivations. But when a disaster befalls a group, the behavior of the group itself, rather than individual decisions, is often decisive. Much of this happens at a subtle level, far below the level of conscious awareness, in the recesses of the hidden brain. In crises, we are hardwired to turn to groups for help and guidance. The ties that bind people together during crises explain why, when fires break out in big buildings, people perish or survive in groups. Fate comes in clusters. Entire families and floors survive, while other families and groups die together. When we try to understand such outcomes, we invariably focus on the thought processes of individuals—people such as Brad Fetchet or Tiffany Alexander—because our starting assumption is that human behavior is always the product of conscious thought and individual decision-making. But we thereby miss what is actually happening—the signal—in all the noise.

Observe for yourself what happens the next time a fire alarm goes off at your workplace or in any large public space—a subway car or department store. People will look at one another. They may ask one another, "What do you think is going on? Has this happened before? Is it a drill, a false alarm? Do I really need to shut down my computer and leave?"

Two years after the September 11 attacks, a fire broke out in a Rhode Island nightclub. A pyrotechnic display onstage went awry. A television camera in the back of the room was rolling, and the tape showed that as real fire erupted on the stage, people in the audience turned to one another. The fire set off a conflagration that killed ninety-six people within minutes. Nearly two hundred people were injured. The window of escape at the nightclub was even smaller than the window of escape at Keefe, Bruyette & Woods. People in the middle of the nightclub needed to act within seconds to have any chance of survival.

We assume that people inside a confined space will flow out evenly through all available exits during an emergency—because that is what conscious, rational, and autonomous creatures do. When a disaster claims many lives, we immediately ask about the number of exits that were available, about whether signs were clearly posted, and about whether precautions were taken to inform people about escape routes. Journalists write articles about building code violations, lawyers file lawsuits about shoddy construction materials, and policymakers review evacuation procedures. The Rhode Island nightclub fire demonstrated why these responses often miss the mark. Clear exits and evacuation drills are valuable, but they do not begin to address the role of the hidden brain during disasters: The first response of people who are trapped is not to review what they have been taught and make reasoned decisions, but to turn decision-making over to the group.

Trapped people seek consensus with those around them, even if acquiring such consensus wastes precious seconds. They follow one another, even if they know their comrades are going the wrong way. They help one another, even when such help is counterproductive. Rather than run to the nearest exit, they invariably try to leave a burning building the same way they entered it, which is why some exits during disasters remain unused, while crowds jam the main door.

We often think trapped people place narrow self-interest above the greater good. This stereotype is again premised on the assumption that we are rational creatures focused on self-preservation. In reality, people can undermine themselves—and reduce the overall survival rate—by trying to *help* one another. Rather than run, they wait to make sure *everyone* has decided to run. If some people are injured and cannot move, others feel obliged to stay by their side, even if they can do nothing to help. The strong and able-bodied stand solicitously at exits to help the frail and elderly—and exacerbate crowding. Heroism—driven by unconscious algorithms in the hidden brain that elevate group interests above individual interests in a crisis—often causes unnecessary casualties. Beningo Aguirre told me that when he studied the September 11, 2001, attacks, he found only one person at the World Trade Center who behaved the way disaster models predict everyone should behave: The man heard an explosion, reached under his desk for his tennis shoes, laced up, and ran.

The same patterns of behavior show up during larger-scale disasters. Reports from many coastal areas reveal that minutes before the 2004 tsunami in South and Southeast Asia struck, the sea began to recede. Fisherfolk in several countries gathered to discuss the phenomenon. They asked one another what was happening, not realizing the ocean was rearing its head like a cobra getting ready to strike. Like the people in the nightclub or the people in the World Trade Center, human beings given ambiguous warnings of disaster invariably turn to their friends and neighbors to seek consensus about what is going on.

If individuals explicitly ask themselves whether those they are turning to really know much more than they do themselves, it is easy to acknowledge the obvious: The person sitting in the cubicle next to you probably has no better information than you do. But the desire to arrive at a shared understanding of what is happening is an extremely powerful drive of the hidden brain in situations of grave threat. An alarm is distressing; the consensus of the group is comforting. Like many biases of the hidden brain, this one works well much of the time. Sticking with the group in our evolutionary history usually offered safety. Sure, it sometimes backfired, but our brains have evolved to tell us what works in aggregate, and our evolved instincts for survival are consequently blunt. When an alarm goes off, it triggers anxiety, and the hidden brain instructs you to turn to the group because groups provided our ancestors with comfort and safety more often than they exposed them to danger and risk.

In modern disaster situations, the comfort of the group regularly puts individuals at risk because threats are now so complicated that *none* of the members in the group knows what is happening. The point is not that groups always do the wrong thing. The point is that groups diminish our autonomy. Our comrades may not know what they are doing, but following them is much easier than going our own way. The group provides comfort, whereas going your own way triggers anxiety. But in disaster situations, anxiety is the *right* response; it is false comfort that is deadly.

I juxtaposed the story of what happened on the Belle Isle bridge with what happened to the employees of Keefe, Bruyette & Woods on September 11, 2001, for an important reason. When we think about these cases in hindsight, it is very easy to draw the conclusion that the people in Detroit were callous cowards, and that the people in New York who stayed behind in the office tower were fools. In fact, if you subscribe to the theory that individuals always make autonomous, deliberate, conscious choices, these are conclusions you must reach. Only cowards fail to do what they know is right, and only fools keep sitting at their computers when the 110-story tower next door is burning to the ground—right? If you study these situations in the context of the hidden brain, however, you arrive at a completely different conclusion. For better and worse, people like Brad Fetchet and Tiffany Alexander were decisively influenced by the people around them, who were in turn influenced by the people around them.

Our society does not believe the hidden brain exists, which is why we take only people's conscious minds into account when we design emergency evacuation procedures. It is rational to assume that when a fire alarm goes off at a workplace, people will get up and leave. But they don't. It seems implausible that in response to an alarm people who are working alone will jump up and run out of a building sooner than people working in large groups. But they do. In a rational world, larger groups should allow people to arrive at *better* conclusions because they collectively have a greater diversity of knowledge and experience. The problem is that in crises, individuals don't bring their disparate insights and ideas to the group; the group imposes conformity on individuals. When experts create models about how people should evacuate tall buildings in emergencies, they assume people will behave like water molecules and flow out smoothly from all exits, as long as the exits are clear. But the hidden brain's tendency to want to stick with the group means that humans in tall towers behave much more like molasses.

How does the new understanding of the hidden brain change how people should be taught to prepare for disasters? First, people need to be warned about their tendency to abdicate decision-making to groups. Offices with a large number of workers need to have more training in disaster preparedness than those that have fewer workers. It is a good idea to have trained members on staff who quickly understand that the reason everyone is sitting quietly at their desks as a fire alarm screams its head off is not that people have secret knowledge that the alarm is a drill, but that they are, in effect, paralyzed by their comrades. On the morning of September 11, 2001, many lives on the eighty-eighth-floor offices of Keefe, Bruyette & Woods were saved because one man—J. J. Aguiar—raced through the floor screaming at everyone to evacuate. Aguiar could not have known that a second plane was coming, so his judgment was really a gamble. But that is often the nature of leadership, and it had the profound impact that leadership exerts—it galvanized people into action. What happened to Aguiar? After literally forcing his comrades to escape, he went up the tower to get people on other floors to evacuate. He never made it out himself.

If even one person on the Belle Isle bridge had stepped forward to confront Martell Welch, there is no doubt in my mind that he or she would have instantly prompted many others to act, as J. J. Aguiar did on the eighty-eighth floor. Being the second person to step forward is infinitely easier than being the first.

You may think that the tendency of people to follow the herd occurs only during terrible tragedies, when people are under extreme pressure. It is true that crises strengthen pack mentality, but groups regularly influence us even in ordinary and trivial situations. People are less likely to answer a ringing telephone or answer a knock on a door if others are also in a position to respond to the phone or the door. People in groups leave smaller tips in restaurants than people eating on their own. Individuals are less likely to contact authorities about a problem if many people face the same problem—a burned-out streetlight, for example.

Some years ago, if you happened to be riding on some elevators in Seattle, Washington; Atlanta, Georgia; or Columbus, Ohio, you might have been an unwitting participant in an interesting experiment that showed how common group influences are in everyday life. Actors in elevators "accidentally" dropped some coins or pencils. If you were there, you might remember stooping to help the person pick up the items. Or, perhaps, you might remember not helping. (Most likely, you wouldn't remember the incident at all.) When the experiment was over, 145 actors had dropped coins or pencils before audiences that totaled 4,813 people. It was a mammoth undertaking, involving 1,497 separate instances where an actor dropped coins or pencils. What psychologists James Dabbs, Jr., and Bibb Latané were trying to find out was how often people bent down to help pick up the fallen items. When there was only one other person in the elevator with the actor, the chance that this person would help the clumsy stranger was 40 percent. In two of every five trials, in other words, an unwitting volunteer reached down to help. But as groups got larger, the likelihood that people would help began to shrink. When there were six other people in the elevator, there was still more than enough room to help pick up the items, but the chance that anyone would come to the aid of the stranger was only 15 percent.

Imagine the scene, if you will, in five out of every six of these trials. There are six people in the elevator with the actor. The butterfingered stranger drops a bunch of coins or pencils. They fall to the floor with a clatter. And then, as the elevator counts off floor after floor after floor, not one person moves a muscle to help. It is not as though people don't realize that someone needs help. They have to notice the stranger groping on the floor. Some people may feel uncomfortable and might silently wonder whether to get involved. But each person is surrounded by five others who are doing nothing. If the people knew they were being tested, virtually every one would instantly come to the aid of the stranger—what does it take, after all, to pick up some coins? But in the context of everyday life, where people are not thinking deliberately about how others are influencing them, going along with the group just feels like the natural thing to do.

The result is a paradox. Large groups ought to produce more people who are willing to help. Yet they usually produce fewer Good Samaritans. Our usual approach is to credit and blame individuals.

We conclude that those who pick up coins are helpful, while those who fail to help are callous. Our assumption is that people's decisions are always the product of conscious, deliberate choice. The purpose of this chapter is to reinforce the idea that even when it comes to the gravest matters of life and death, there is a layer beneath the level of individual autonomy where many of the really important decisions of life take place. Like so many other situations I describe in this book, the truly devilish thing about this process is that people such as Brad Fetchet and Tiffany Alexander *feel* autonomous. The machinations of the hidden brain, by definition, always remain hidden.

There is a way for us to lay bare the workings of the hidden brain in disaster situations, but it requires us to suspend our model of people as autonomous individuals. Let me show you what I mean through the example of a single employee at Keefe, Bruyette & Woods who worked on the ill-fated eighty-ninth floor. Like everyone else I interviewed at the firm, Will DeRiso was clearly above average in intelligence, social skills, and smarts. You don't get to work at a place like Keefe, Bruyette & Woods unless you are pretty bright. With Will's permission, however, let us stop thinking about him in the usual way for a few minutes. For the purposes of illustration, in fact, let us exaggerate the role of his hidden brain—let us imagine that he has *nothing but* a hidden brain. Instead of seeing Will as a smart and handsome young man with a smile that lights up a room, imagine him as a node at the center of a web. Connections radiate from him in every direction. A slender cord runs from his brain to Cold Spring Harbor, New York, where he grew up and his parents live. Another thread goes to South Bend, Indiana, where his brother the Catholic priest lives; another to New Jersey, where his sister lives, and still another to Long Island, to his other brother. If you'd mapped a diagram of Will's life in this way before the morning of September 11, 2001, you would have seen cables running to his gym, to the golf courses and beaches he liked to frequent, and to his high school friends.

Wherever Will went, new cables sprang up around him. Some stretched to acquaintances, others to strangers. Some were thick and strong, others slender. Some came into existence and snapped off within moments as Will passed someone he did not know on his way to work; others endured great absences and distances—the bonds of love, loyalty, and longing that make up a life. After graduating from Cold Spring Harbor high school, Will attended Notre Dame. He worked a couple of years for the Bank of America in Chicago before returning to Notre Dame to help coach the men's lacrosse team for nine months. He joined Keefe, Bruyette & Woods on July 31, 2000, following an introduction from a former Notre Dame lacrosse player. Will got married six weeks before September 11, 2001—he and his bride, Bridget, a schoolteacher, went on a honeymoon to the Caribbean island of Saint Martin. His web of connections—some weak, some strong—continued to multiply.

Christina Defazio and Jessica Slaven worked in the firm's back office group on the side of the eighty-ninth floor closest to the North Tower; the cords that connected Will to them were slender because he did not know them well. Cliff Gallant worked in the firm's insurance research group and had taught Will a lot of things—he was a good office acquaintance. Eric "Rick" Thorpe and Bradley "Brad" Vadas were close friends. They knew about Will's propensity for anxiety; college friends used to call him "crisis boy" for blowing things out of proportion. Rick and Brad regularly played practical jokes on Will. Sitting across from Will on the eighty-ninth floor was Karol Keasler, an event coordinator and administrative assistant. She had a bubbly personality and changed her hair color regularly from blond to brown and back again. Another nearby employee was Kris Hughes, an arbitrage trader—someone who helped find common ground between stock buyers and stock sellers. Will's job forced him to speak to countless people each day. He sold the research that people such as Cliff Gallant produced. Will needed to keep on top of what mutual fund administrators wanted to know; it was his job to supply them with a combination of what they wanted to know and what they needed to know. Like a scene from a science fiction movie, the hidden cables writhed and snaked about Will, growing and fading, but always encasing, enmeshing, embracing.

On Monday, September 10, 2001, Will moved desks. In his new location, he happened to be the member in his group that was closest to a little corridor that led to a solid metal door. The door opened onto a hallway, and then the stairs. Employees needed a pass to unlock that door.

On Tuesday morning, September 11, Will jumped onto a train from his home in Westchester around six-fifteen A.M., and then caught a subway from midtown Manhattan around seven. He attended the morning meeting at the firm and then drifted back to his desk. Like everyone else, he heard the explosion at eight forty-six A.M. It was more of a rumble than a boom, like an earthquake tremor, or the sound of workmen rolling something very heavy on the floor above.

As we go through the next moments, remember that we are not thinking of Will as an autonomous human being. We are seeing him instead at the center of a complex web of interconnections, with thousands of cables tugging him in different directions. If you prefer, think of Will as a cork bobbing on an ocean, passive, acted upon by every riptide and wave and drop of foam.

Karol Keasler yelled, "What was that?"

Another voice screamed, "Holy shit!"

After a moment, Kris Hughes, the arbitrage trader, exclaimed, "There was an explosion in the other building!"

"Oh my God!" Karol Keasler's voice was panicked. "Oh my God!"

The explosion itself was just outside Will's peripheral vision; the North Tower was really northwest of the South Tower. But when Will looked through a window that normally offered him a spectacular view of midtown Manhattan, he felt his stomach churn. The Empire State Building and all of midtown Manhattan had vanished. In its place was black smoke and thousands of sheets of drifting paper. It gave Will a sense of the magnitude of what had happened. The smoke and debris must have traveled fifty or a hundred yards from the other tower to so thoroughly obscure the view.

That is a hell of an explosion, Will thought. *I am glad I am not over there.*

Chaos erupted. People were jumping up. Fear leaped from one face to the next, like a contagion.

"Calm down! Calm down!!" Kris Hughes shouted. "It is in the other building."

Like a vacuum, the windows drew Will and Brad Vadas and Rick Thorpe. The horrific spectacle of the smoke and debris was irresistible. But as the tide of people drew Will toward the windows, a frantic knocking came from the door through the small hallway. It was a decisive moment.

I can't believe someone forgot their passkey, Will thought.

The desperate banging escalated, a connection that demanded his attention. Will didn't want to answer the door, but he happened to be the one closest to it. It placed an obligation on him. His connections with his friends pulled him toward the windows, but the plea from the door pulled him in the other direction. It broke him away from the tide. He went to the hallway and opened the door. As he left the main area of the floor, the connections he had to the people he left behind weakened. When he opened the door, new connections sprang out between him and the two ashen-faced women who stood outside in the hallway—Christina Defazio and Jessica Slaven.

Like a robot, Will repeated what Kris Hughes had just said: "Calm down. Calm down. It is in the other building."

Defazio and Slaven were so afraid they could not speak. And then Cliff Gallant came charging up the hallway from his office on another part of the eighty-ninth floor. He had been sitting with his back to the window when his room filled with a terrifying bluish light. It blasted him right out of his chair. He ran out into the research department screaming, "Get out!"

The bond between Will and Cliff sprang to life. There was a stairway exit right outside the door where Will was standing. Cliff Gallant and the two women made straight for it. Will glanced back once, still drawn by the weakening connections he had left behind. To his great good fortune, the architecture of the hallway that separated the door from the trading floor obscured most of the room he had left behind. He could not see his friends. And then four people from his own office, Bill Henningson, Jeff Hansen, Andrew Cullen, and Amanda McGowan come charging right at him in a pack.

When Will later reflected on that moment, he realized he made very little by way of a conscious decision.

"You do what you do," he said. "You are right there. You see people running down the stairs, you see people running right at you. You go down the stairs."

Will found himself running down the stairs so quickly after the initial explosion that he didn't see any other people besides his own group until they reached the eightieth floor. The Keefe, Bruyette & Woods employees paired off, and Will found himself with Cliff Gallant.

It was only when they got to the seventy-first floor that Will stopped his friend. It was partly because there were very few people in the stairwell, and the hidden brain makes us feel self-conscious when we do something that few other people are doing. And some of the old connections were drawing Will back to the eighty-ninth floor.

"Cliff," he said, "it is in the other building."

The news that the explosion had occurred in the North Tower came as a complete surprise to Cliff Gallant. "I thought it was in our building."

"No, it is in the other building," Will insisted.

Two connections snaking back to the eighty-ninth floor tugged at Will. If it turned out that this was not a big deal and no one else had run, Rick Thorpe and Brad Vadas would have a field day. This was the kind of episode that would ensure a full month of jokes at Will's expense. Something minor had happened and "crisis boy" had taken off like a rabbit.

Will persuaded Cliff to wait to see if others came trickling down. They stood in the stairwell. United Flight 175 was probably over New Jersey by this point. The minutes ticked by. No one else from the eighty-ninth floor appeared.

Will and Cliff sheepishly started climbing back up the stairs, drawn as ever by the cables that connected them to their comrades. They climbed two floors. They were right at the edge of the zone of impact of the coming plane.

It was yet another decisive moment. What saved the day was that people from other floors were now coming down the stairwell. They were strangers, and they formed only weak connections with Will's hidden brain, but there were many of them. Besides, it was getting difficult to climb against the tide of people. Climbing fifteen stories against that kind of traffic was crazy.

Will and Cliff turned around and went with the flow. They resolved to get out of the stairwell and take an elevator back up. Luckily for them, every door they tried was locked—the stairwell was now a tunnel leading them out of the building. Doors could be opened by anyone inside the building, but were locked against intruders trying to enter offices from the stairwell.

"We're going to go back and get laughed at so much for this," Will fretted.

Will and Cliff Gallant were in the stairwell on the fifty-fourth floor when they received the ultimate confirmation that they had overreacted. Building officials made the announcement that people in the South Tower could remain in their offices. There was a lot of noise in the stairwell, and the announcement was not heard clearly, but after people shushed one another, the announcement was repeated thirty seconds or a minute later. But by now the stairwell was so crowded it was impossible to go back up.

Just as Will was resigning himself to weeks of humiliation at the hands of his jokester friends, the United airplane crashed into the South Tower. The stairwell shook. It actually undulated like a snake. Will recalled seeing people on landings three or four floors above him. He clutched at Cliff.

This is it, he thought. *The North Tower has tipped over and hit the South Tower.* He was going to die. ·

There was no way he could have known at that moment that he was actually supremely lucky. The cables connecting him with friends and strangers had conspired to spring him from the trap in which he had been encased. His hidden brain had extricated him from the zone of impact. The South Tower would stand long enough for him to get out. Nearly every person from the Keefe, Bruyette & Woods office on the eighty-ninth floor who survived escaped within the first moments after the explosion in the North Tower. Those who stayed behind would have found it increasingly difficult to leave, because their hidden brains were anchored to dozens of other people who were staying put. It would have required an enormous and deliberate effort for an individual to overcome the strength of those ties, or for the group as a whole to reach a new consensus.

Many of the victims who stayed behind on the eighty-ninth floor were not racked by the kind of self-doubt that plagued Will. Once the United Airlines plane struck at 9:03 A.M., they had less than an hour to live.

CHAPTER 7

The Tunnel

Terrorism, Extremism, and the Hidden Brain

I want to return to Will DeRiso and the people trapped in the World Trade Center, and use this chapter to talk about the people at the other end of such tragedies—suicide bombers. What does our new understanding about the hidden brain tell us about religious zealotry and violence? Does unconscious bias play a role in the minds of terrorists? To answer that, I want to take you back to before September 11, 2001, to a tale that unfolded long before the term "suicide bomber" was even invented. It is a story that is not familiar to most people for the same reason that the strange patterns of death and survival on the eighty-eighth and eighty-ninth floors of the South Tower of the World Trade Center are unfamiliar to most people. Like the tragedy at Keefe, Bruyette & Woods, the story of Laurence John Layton is little known because it unfolded in the shadow of a much larger event—the infamous deaths of nearly a thousand Americans in 1978 at a utopian outpost in Guyana called Jonestown.

Laurence John Layton was still alive, but that was only because his mission went awry. His orders were to smuggle a gun aboard a passenger plane carrying a number of Americans, including a congressman. Once airborne, he was to shoot the pilot and turn the aircraft into an unguided missile. It would crash, and everyone would be killed, including himself. Layton did not think of himself as a terrorist. He felt his death was a necessary sacrifice, the only way to save his friends and family, and defend a dream he had nurtured all his adult life.

Layton was thirty-two years old, an X-ray technician with a receding hairline and bushy sideburns. He was not a member of the global jihad, and he did not come from a country rife with anti-American sentiment. Layton was born in College Park, Maryland, right outside Washington. He was the son of a U.S. government scientist and had been raised a Quaker.

The mission did not go as planned, but Layton did manage to smuggle a gun aboard the plane and did open fire at point-blank range. Upon his capture, he told police, "Yes, I shot the motherfuckers." Some days later, Layton took "full responsibility" for the deaths of the U.S. congressman and four other Americans at the Port Kaituma airstrip in Guyana. In a handwritten statement full of loopy J's, I's, and L's, Layton declared that no one had coerced him into the suicide mission. It was he who had "begged" for the privilege of being "allowed to bring down the plane."

A psychiatrist who interviewed Layton pressed him on the details of his mission: "The plane was supposed to go down? You were supposed to kill the pilot?"

"However, whatever way," Layton replied.

"To kill the pilot and make the whole plane go down?"

"Right."

Rebecca Moore and Fielding McGehee visited Larry Layton a few days after his capture. He was in a prison that encased two blocks in the middle of Georgetown, the capital of Guyana. The walls of the prison were twenty feet high and crowned with barbed wire. There was a low door through which the visitors entered. Moore and McGehee had come a long way from their home in Washington, D.C. They wanted to know why Layton had tried to bring down the passenger plane. They also wanted to know how his suicidal mission was linked to the deaths—a few hours later—of more than nine hundred Americans at Jonestown. Two of Moore's sisters were among the dead at Jonestown. News reports said the women had taken their own lives, but Moore believed that Carolyn and Annie had been murdered.

The couple from Washington stood in a little breezeway and watched the prisoner being brought from his cell. The visitor area of the Georgetown prison was just a low wall that came up to the waist. Completing the crude partition were three layers of mesh, cyclone fencing, and netting. Larry Layton came up to stand on the other side. It was difficult to see much more than his outline through the layers. But once or twice, as the breeze shifted the layers, McGehee thought he spotted Layton's eyes.

Layton was not a stranger to Rebecca Moore and Fielding McGehee. He had formerly been married to Carolyn, one of Moore's dead sisters at Jonestown. The Moore family and the Layton family had connections going back years. Their histories were intertwined with a church known as Peoples Temple and its charismatic leader, Jim Jones. Larry Layton's mother, Lisa, had died of cancer at Jonestown a few days before the mass suicide. His sister Debbie had been a high-ranking member of Peoples Temple. Debbie's defection from Jonestown had set in motion the events that led to the mass suicide of some nine hundred thirteen people in November 1978. Debbie's testimony that Jonestown was virtually a concentration camp prompted an investigation by Representative Leo Ryan of California. The congressman visited Guyana to figure out the truth about Jonestown. It was Ryan's party, swollen with defectors and returning to America, that Larry Layton was assigned to destroy.

The visitors from Washington were burning with questions, but they stepped carefully. They inquired after Layton's legal situation. The would-be suicide bomber had been arrested by Guyanese security forces after he and others had opened fire at the airstrip, killing the U.S. congressman and four others, and injuring several more. Layton said the Guyana court system was based on a defendant's ability to bribe his way out of trouble; a poor person could go to jail for ten years for stealing eighty-five dollars, while a rich man who committed murder could get off scot-free. The visit was soon over. The couple promised to come again. A prison official, Janak Seegobin, told the visitors that Layton had seemed disturbed when he'd first arrived at the prison. Recognizing that the prisoner was an intelligent man, Seegobin had offered him books on scientific topics, "to concentrate his mind." Layton was allowed to borrow two books at a time, then four. He devoured everything to do with psychology. He asked for a book on algebra. Seegobin confided to the visitors that he could not imagine Layton being responsible for any shootings. The prisoner seemed too gentle for that sort of thing.

What prompts a man to agree to kill the pilot of a plane he is traveling on? To strap a bomb to his chest and explode himself? Is religion to blame? Do the young Muslim men blowing themselves up in Iraq and Pakistan and other theaters of today's conflicts really believe that dozens of virgins will attend on them in the afterlife? For nonbelievers, followers of other faiths, and the vast majority of Muslims themselves, such beliefs seem fantastic. And if suicide bombers really seek nothing but death, it means they cannot be deterred.

There is an alternative explanation, but this does not give us many options, either. Are suicide bombers basically suicidal? Are they depressed people out to kill themselves, whose impulses are directed by terrorist masterminds into murderous channels? Might suicide terrorism be more about suicide than about terrorism? Ariel Merari once wondered if this was so. But then the Israeli psychologist set out to do what most commentators on terrorism do not do—he began to look for evidence. He collected detailed biographical accounts of suicide terrorists. He spent hours interviewing young Arab men and women in Israeli prisons, people who had planned to kill themselves but, like Larry Layton, had seen their missions go awry. And one by one, his preconceptions fell away.

Suicide terrorists are not crazy. If anything, Merari and other psychologists have found that these men and women seem to have fewer mental disorders than the general population. As a group, they are hardly more religious than everyone else. Large numbers of suicide terrorists do not come from religious backgrounds at all. Many are secular, even atheists. While some seek Rambo-style personal vengeance against groups that have wounded them, most have not directly experienced humiliation at the hands of their enemies. A considerable number come from wealthy and privileged backgrounds. They are college graduates and professionals, doctors, engineers, and architects. Nor do "psychological autopsies" of dead suicide bombers and psychological inventories of captured terrorists show that they are psychopathic automatons or nihilists. In fact, suicide terrorists on average seem more idealistic than their peers. They are often hypersensitive to guilt. Finally, the men and women Merari studied were not brainwashed simpletons who merely followed orders. They gave Merari thoughtful rationales for their behavior. Many of the would-be suicide bombers calmly told the psychologist that if they were released from prison, they would attempt another mission. They thought *he* was crazy for not seeing how their course of action was obvious.

As the psychologist's preconceptions fell away, he realized that we have misunderstood what motivates suicide bombers—and are therefore handicapped in our fight against them. Suicide bombers are not aberrational; large numbers of ordinary people can be turned into suicide bombers. The notion that suicide terrorists are mentally defective is also wrong. There is no clear psychological profile that predicts whether someone might become a suicide bomber. But there is a very distinct psychological profile of the *process* that produces suicide bombers. Merari likened it to a tunnel. Ordinary people go in at one end, and laser-focused suicide terrorists come out the other. At every stage of the tunnel process, individuals in the tunnel believe—as you and I always believe—that they have complete agency, complete autonomy. The tunnel is really a powerful system of manipulation, but the coercion is subtle. This is why suicide bombers rarely go to their deaths feeling coerced. There is no more powerful testament to the power of the hidden brain than the suicide bomber's tunnel. And it's a vivid example of how our false assumptions about human behavior and the brain exact a toll on our ability to make the right decisions as a society. Suicidal attacks remain a prime weapon of terror and insurgency, from Baghdad to Mumbai—and the recruitment of suicide terrorists extends deep into many societies, ensnaring children and women as well as countless young men. No matter how broad the pool of recruits turns out to be or how often our intuitions encounter disconfirming evidence, we are tempted to fall back on the notion that suicide bombers must be psychologically different from other people, and that they must be mindless automatons programmed to kill themselves and others.

Suicide bombers themselves tell us why they become suicide bombers. In notes and videos, they often say they are motivated by religious beliefs and political causes. These reports confirm our intuitions, so we rarely question them. But, as we've done with numerous other examples, we ought to distinguish between what people sincerely believe and what might actually be happening at an unconscious level in their heads. Suicide bombers may tell us that religious injunctions motivate their actions, but is this a fact or a *deduction* on their part to explain their behavior—not just to us but to themselves? Global data on suicide bombers, including data on terrorists from predominantly Muslim countries, show that religious belief is neither a necessary nor a sufficient explanation for suicide terrorism—*even when such violence is carried out in the name of religion.*

If the victims of terrorist attacks are unconsciously influenced by the psychology of large groups, the "peer pressure" of strangers, I believe the perpetrators of such attacks are unconsciously influenced by the psychology of small groups. It is small-group psychology—intense bonds of loyalty between small "bands of brothers"—that is common to suicide terrorism across the world, not religion or any particular political belief. Small-group dynamics don't explain only how ordinary people can be turned into suicide bombers; they explain how ordinary people can be prompted to do any number of extraordinary things.

The dastardliness of terrorist acts keeps us from seeing that the unconscious motivations of suicide terrorists are not unlike the motivations of many other groups, including those we consider heroes. Small-group psychology explains the behavior of the ordinary men and women in the uniforms of the New York police department and the New York fire department who calmly walked into the Twin Towers—and to near-certain death—on the morning of September 11, 2001. Small-group dynamics explain why ordinary people in military uniforms throw their bodies over live hand grenades and why soldiers volunteer for combat missions where the odds of survival are zero. Patriotism is the name we give to such behavior, but military commanders have known for generations that people don't give their lives for king, God, and country. That's what they *say*. In reality, ordinary men and women give their lives for the sake of the small group of buddies in the trench next to them.

Ariel Merari told me that when Japanese Vice Admiral Takijiro Onishi first sought kamikaze volunteers in the fading days of World War II, he lined up a squadron of pilots and said, "The only way we can save Japan is by sacrificing ourselves. I know it's too much to ask, so if any one of you doesn't want to do it, step forward."

"Of course," Merari added, "nobody stepped forward. It was group pressure. The people you were standing next to were people with whom you had fought. You valued their opinion. You didn't want them to think you were a coward."

Small-group dynamics have the power to overturn people's beliefs about what is and isn't rational behavior. To the extent that suicide bombers report being troubled by anything, they mostly report they are troubled about being held back too long. Kamikaze pilots worried that Japan was running out of fuel, and that there would not be enough gasoline for them to fly their one-way missions.

The power that small groups wield over individuals explains why in every historical instance that has produced suicide bombers, the supply of men and women willing to volunteer to kill themselves has exceeded the demand. Far from being subpar, many of these volunteers are talented. From the point of view of the manipulative groups that train and produce suicide bombers, why would you take the dumb and the deranged when you can have the smart and the skilled?

Suicide bombers belong to a very exclusive club, and the exclusivity of this club is one of its central appeals. The first step into the tunnel—the funnel that pulls ordinary people into the suicide bomber's world—is the ego-stroking notion that access to the tunnel is limited, that it is a reward for the most dedicated people, for those with rare talent. To enter the tunnel is to set yourself off from your peers, to be recognized as special.

———

Larry Layton did not start out wanting to be a suicide terrorist. If you had known him as he was growing up, you would have said he had precisely the opposite temperament of a suicide bomber. (Layton declined to be interviewed for this book, saying he did not wish to revisit painful memories. Details of his story were pieced together through interviews with his family and former members of Peoples Temple, records and documents seized by the FBI from Jonestown, accounts penned by survivors, court testimony, and a remarkable psychiatric evaluation of Layton that was conducted at the Guyana prison.)

Larry was the third child of Lisa Layton and Laurence Layton, a scientist for the federal government. Larry was deeply interested in nonviolence. He was raised a Quaker and internalized Quaker approaches to personal and political conflicts. When he was eleven, he refused to hit back as a bully tormented him—he simply stood with his arms extended and his fists clenched as the bully charged him again and again.

Larry "was perceived rather as a wimp," his brother Thomas would later remember in an account penned by multiple members of the Layton family and published as a book titled *In My Father's House*. He added, "Larry was always open, trusting, and obedient. Larry was the most Quakerly member of our family. His opinions and actions were based on moral and ethical principles. Perhaps being an underdog, he developed a sympathy for the downtrodden of the world."

Though he was not outgoing, Layton was interested in politics and became president of the Berkeley High School Young Democrats after the family moved to California from the Washington area. Layton wrote most of the articles for his high school student newspaper, *The Liberal*. He was passionate about the civil rights movement, and saw himself running for public office one day. "I was very shy around girls and had only one girlfriend in high school, she being a political nut like myself," he later observed.

The assassination of President John F. Kennedy prompted Layton to become disillusioned about the ability of politics to change the world. At the University of California, he started experimenting with drugs. Layton felt out of step with his peers, and his college years caused him to feel "further separated from straight society with its race for money, its power, and its lack of brotherhood."

In 1967, he married Carolyn Moore, a young woman who shared his sense of idealism. When he was called up by the draft to go to Vietnam, Layton declared himself a conscientious objector who opposed violence in principle. The draft board turned him down and told him to get ready for active duty. But Layton meant what he said about opposing violence in principle. In 1968, Larry and Carolyn Layton moved to Ukiah, California. They were, quite simply, "in search of utopia."

They did not know that an Indianapolis Bible-thumper had moved to nearby Redwood Valley in 1965. The Reverend Jim Jones picked the spot because he'd read a magazine article that said it would be among the nation's safest places in the event of nuclear war, which Jones believed was imminent. Shortly after Larry and Carolyn Layton moved to Ukiah, Jones sent missionaries to distribute cakes to new teachers in the area; Carolyn Layton was a schoolteacher. The couple learned that Peoples Temple was a multiracial group opposed to the Vietnam War and fervently committed to the civil rights movement. It was just the thing the idealistic couple was looking for. When the Laytons visited Jones's church, the preacher took Larry Layton aside and told him "intimate things about my life," he later recalled in court testimony. Jones said his psychic powers had revealed that Carolyn Layton had been out picking berries the previous day. The preacher also told Layton he had been suffering from a serious illness, but that contact with Jones had cured him. The charismatic preacher lavished attention and praise on the young man. He made it clear that if Layton joined Peoples Temple, he would be doing something special for humanity. Jones stroked Layton's ego, and told the young idealist that the cause needed his help. Layton, instantly under the spell of the leader he had long been seeking, believed it all.

The third time Rebecca Moore and Fielding McGehee visited Larry Layton in the Guyana prison, Layton seemed cheerful as he walked across the prison yard, but "nervous and agitated" once he arrived at the mesh partition. Layton told his visitors that "he couldn't wait to get away from this shit" and asked them to deposit some money in his prison account for essential supplies. He talked a little about the future.

Rebecca Moore listened politely as Larry Layton talked about his dreams of a life beyond prison. The would-be suicide bomber longed to be outdoors in a forest, by a stream, or on the beach. Moore was not sure her former brother-in-law could really function in the outside world. She did not have fears he was violent—if anything, she worried he was too much of a pushover. "He is definitely strange, although very sweet," she wrote in a letter to her parents after the meeting. "The police commissioner called him a crank."

Moore and McGehee still did not have their fundamental questions answered. Larry Layton had had so much to live for when he'd decided to go out and kill himself. Among other things, his beautiful wife had been five months pregnant. Why had he signed up to die?

From the beginning, Jim Jones railed against disloyalty. Shadowy groups were always supposedly plotting to undermine Peoples Temple because of its high ideals, and Jones was ever vigilant for traitors. The preacher's fulminations made sense to his rainbow congregation. Political idealists Robert Kennedy and Martin Luther King, Jr., were being assassinated. The FBI was bugging the phones of the president's political enemies. Police had infiltrated counterculture groups and killed antiwar protestors.

But Jones's message also resonated with the individual experiences of his congregants. Larry and Carolyn Layton had always felt out of step with society, and it did not take much to convince them that mainstream society was now trying to undermine their newfound friends. Larry Layton's sister Debbie was struggling with the recent discovery that her mother was Jewish. She had become hypersensitive to anti-Semitism, and it came as a relief to join the egalitarian world of Peoples Temple. Vern Gosney, another member, had not been able to rent an apartment because his girlfriend was black. Wherever the interracial couple went, they were turned down. Gosney finally snagged an apartment by taking his sister along. Shortly afterward,

Gosney's girlfriend died while giving birth—a doctor miscalculated the amount of anesthesia she was given. In a lawsuit that followed, the doctor said the patient's dark skin had made it difficult to see she was being starved of oxygen—had she been white, it would have been obvious she was turning purple. The jury agreed with the doctor. Stories like this enraged Gosney and the other members of Peoples Temple. Larry, Carolyn, and Debbie Layton came to accept that if they were not part of the solution, they were part of the problem. Larry Layton began working multiple jobs and turning over much of his salary to Peoples Temple.

"Being in Peoples Temple wasn't always pleasant, but one had the feeling he was really doing something to advance society," Layton would later write. "And there was a strong feeling of community—people of all races who really cared about each other."

For the first time in his life, Layton found himself surrounded by a small group of like-minded people—every member of Peoples Temple shared and validated his worldview. Layton had entered a tunnel—except it did not feel that way. It felt like he was among friends.

The same kind of tunnel vision that afflicted the members of Peoples Temple afflicts many other groups. After Layton's sister Debbie defected from Peoples Temple, for example, she found a new life in corporate America. As she developed the insanely busy habits of those on fast-track careers to financial success, she reflected that her business colleagues had a lot in common with the young friends she'd met when she first joined Peoples Temple. "Whether it is to treat the poor or to get a million dollars when you go public, the end goal is the same," she said in an interview. "All of your pain will be rewarded with something. That is why people become so myopic."

Like many groups that produce suicide bombers today, Peoples Temple provided humanitarian services for people that the rest of society had abandoned. Minus the endemic racism and disparities in the United States in the late 1960s and early 1970s, Peoples Temple would never have drawn so many recruits. Corruption, poverty, and hopelessness similarly fuel the supply of young idealists to terrorist groups today. Desperation makes small groups, cliques, and cults very attractive to people who have big dreams—but little hope of achieving them.

Tommy Washington was only seven or eight years old when family members drew him into Jones's fold. It was a wonderful community for a young black boy. Jones gave out nice gifts at Christmas, and Washington felt loved and accepted. The group's growing numbers gave Jones political clout, and he used his connections to help his flock. Jones encouraged Larry Layton to reapply to the Vietnam War draft board as a conscientious objector. The application was approved.

The preacher had different messages for different members. For those like Layton, who were interested in politics and ideas, the message was about socialism. For people who preferred their religion more theatrical, Jones would hurl the Bible onto the floor during sermons. After a stunned silence, he would offer himself to the heavens to be struck dead for his act of desecration. When no lightning bolt appeared, Jones would say that the reason God had not killed him was because . . . Jones himself was God.

The preacher conducted a stream of faith healings, and the testimonies of those he had "cured" were endlessly publicized. Jones would reach into people and pull out tumors; only a handful of his inner circle knew the tumors were prearranged pieces of boiled chicken liver. When the faith healings did not work, Jones would tell members that it was because they were insufficiently devoted—his power to help them depended entirely on how much faith *they* had in *him*. When people left his fold, bad things seemed to happen to them. Vern Gosney quit Peoples Temple right before his girlfriend died. Desperate and disconsolate, with a small baby he could not care for on his own, Gosney reached out to Jones. Peoples Temple welcomed him back, but Gosney still recalls the message he received: "This is what happens to you when you leave."

In 2004, a small group of men coordinated a series of bomb blasts in Spain, days ahead of national elections in that country. When police surrounded some of the perpetrators in a Madrid apartment a few

weeks later, the men blew themselves up. Al-Qaeda hailed the bombings, and investigators quickly began piecing together connections between the Spanish bombers and international terrorist organizations.

For Scott Atran, an anthropologist at the University of Michigan
who also studies terrorist groups at the National Center for Scientific
Research in France, the idea that al-Qaeda recruiters had picked and
trained the men, and coordinated the blasts, was ludicrous—although
that was the story line that was getting circulated. In detailed field
studies, Atran has seen that the pattern through which young Muslim
men join the international jihad is exactly the opposite of the conventional narrative that suggests shadowy recruiters from al-Qaeda are
spread out around the world in search of suicide bombers. The conventional explanation follows the telemarketer model—you aggres-
sively reach out to as many people as possible in the hope that some
tiny number will buy your product. Since one of the products
al-Qaeda sells is suicide, the conventional narrative has intuitive appeal, since most people do not want to commit suicide. It makes sense
that you would need an aggressive effort to recruit people for such un-
palatable work. It also makes intuitive sense that most people who
sign up for such missions would be poor and desperate—people with
few options—or those with personal scores to settle. Or perhaps they
are dim-witted young men ready to buy some fanciful story about virgins in the afterlife.

Let's take a closer look at these theories. A quick way to check the
veracity of the virgins claim is to put the question to yourself. Imagine
you could have the most mind-blowing sex possible—with sixty-four
virgins, if that is your fancy—the only proviso being that afterward,
you would be strapped tightly to a live bomb and exploded. Would
you sign up for such a deal?

"I ask people, 'Would you die for sex?' " said Marc Sageman, another terrorism researcher who relies on empirical evidence. "Women
laugh at that faster than men."

Sageman has built a database of hundreds of profiles of confirmed
al-Qaeda terrorists. Three-fourths are married, and two-thirds have
kids, plenty of kids—these are not sex-starved adolescents.

What about religious fanaticism? The group that brought suicide bombings into fashion in the modern era was the Liberation Tigers of Tamil Eelam, or LTTE, a predominantly Hindu group that fought for a separate homeland in Sri Lanka. But the group's central identity was built not around religion but around the Tamil language. It was Tamil culture and Tamil pride that LTTE cadres seemed willing to die for.

"Two-thirds of [suicide] attacks in Lebanon were carried out by secular organizations," added Ariel Merari, the Israeli psychologist at Tel Aviv University. "Religion is neither necessary nor a sufficient cause."

Many groups that produce suicide bombers do say that systematic humiliation is the root cause of their anger, but this does not mean that suicide bombers themselves have suffered such humiliation. "Lots of people have gut feelings that humiliation is important [in motivating suicide bombers], and we test things and we find most people's gut feelings are wrong," said Atran. "We find humiliation is inversely proportional to the willingness to commit violence. Humiliated people don't commit violence, but people do act in the name of others who are humiliated."

When Spanish authorities put some of the 2004 conspirators on trial, it turned out that most of the plotters were from a small neighborhood in northern Morocco. When Atran tracked down biographical information about the men, he learned that their favorite hangout was not the local mosque but the local café. Had al-Qaeda recruiters come looking for the Spanish bombers? No. It was the bombers who had gone looking for al-Qaeda.

"Bunches of guys get together and create a parallel universe," said Atran, who found the same pattern after interviewing the neighbors of Mohammed Atta, leader of the 9/11 attacks, and 9/11 organizer Ramzi bin al-Shibh. "They brought in twenty mattresses and stayed together. They were living in another world."

Atran went to Morocco, to understand the world from which the terrorists who attacked Spain had sprung. "I was in a barrio called El Principe in Morocco. I was sitting in this plaza and talking to kids about who their heroes are. They say Ronaldinho [the soccer star] and the Terminator and Osama bin Laden. The kids are weighing the pros and cons of becoming bin Laden or Ronaldinho. There are two cafés. I go to both of these cafés. The young men invite me over for tea, and Al Jazeera is on 24-7. The news is ten minutes on Iraq, five minutes on Palestine, and five minutes for the rest of the world. They are talking about gory images and how Islam is being attacked. One guy brings over his six-year-old son and says, 'If I can be a martyr, I swear I would.' They see this injustice and they have confirmatory biases, and anything else is blocked out. The kids listen to it. This is the way it is done, storytelling, war stories, schmoozing in the barbershop or café. There are no recruiters. No one says, 'Come join the jihad. I will give you money.' "

Atran discovered communities in Morocco that have produced dozens of young men who have volunteered to become suicide bombers in faraway places. He found the best predictor of whether a young man became a suicide bomber was not his religiosity, but whether he belonged to a small group where *others* had decided to become suicide terrorists. Within these small groups, becoming a suicide terrorist had become something of a group norm. Small "bands of brothers," Atran told me, hung out together, dreamed together, lived together. They married one another's sisters. They became one another's universe.

Among members of the Islamist group Jemaah Islamiyah, Atran has traced forty-five weddings where members of the group intermarried into one another's families. Small-group dynamics explain why investigators regularly find that the wedding videos of terrorists provide excellent information about potential collaborators.

The central feature of a tunnel is that it seals off the outside world. In our everyday lives, we are pulled in multiple directions. Conflicting responsibilities, clashing opinions, and the cacophony of a polyglot culture create stress in our lives, but they also keep us from seeing things in unidimensional terms. When people enter the suicide bombers' tunnel, they are deprived—either by design or by accident— of the usual tugs of the outside world. For people inside, the tunnel becomes the entire world. Small bands of brothers and sisters, who are intensely loyal to one another, can be brought together by different things—a political cause, a sports team, a shared history. We see examples of tunnel behavior all the time—when someone tattoos a sports team's logo on his forehead, for example. But like religion or history, sports only provides a vocabulary and an outlet to activate an underlying psychological process. Some tunnels direct people toward self-abnegation and public service, others toward violence; some tunnels lead people to workaholism, others to hedonism. The Chicago Bears fan who tattoos his team's logo on his cheek seems crazy to the rest of us. But the Bears fan is not technically crazy. The tunnel in which he lives has just taken him so far away from our definitions of normal behavior that the only way we can wrap our minds around what he has done is to call him crazy—but it doesn't get us closer to understanding the man or his motivations. When we think of suicide bombers as crazed and evil fanatics, we are applying our norms to their behavior. But inside the tunnel, the world has been turned upside down. Our norms no longer apply.

Masami Takahashi's father was thirteen years old when he signed up to be a kamikaze pilot at the end of World War II. The Yokarin Institute that trained Japanese suicide bombers was an elite school, and competition to enter the school was fierce. His father's fellow kamikaze recruits told Takahashi, a psychologist who eventually moved to Chicago, that the notion of dying for Japan had been dinned into every student. The only question was whether you would die in a glorious way or in a boring way. Thousands of young men eventually signed up for ever more exotic suicide missions, agonizing only about whether the war would last long enough for them to have their turn in the spotlight. Eventually, there were corps of suicide glider pilots and suicide torpedo operators—who had just enough oxygen to keep them alive underwater to steer a torpedo into an advancing battleship. Others volunteered to become suicide land mines, to be buried under the sand on beaches and kept alive long enough to detonate themselves once American tanks rolled ashore. The young men told one another endless stories about the heroes who had gone before them, and dreamed of the day they would similarly become heroes. While Shinto ideas provided some of the vocabulary for the missions, Takahashi discovered that his father and most of his father's friends, who were "not lucky enough" to go on suicide missions because the war ended, were hardly religious. Many were atheists, or

Christians, unlikely to be persuaded by Shinto ideas. They were also perfectly ordinary people who did not think they were doing anything unusual or heroic.

Ariel Merari found that by erecting monuments to suicide bombers and honoring their families, by setting up intricate rituals that confer meanings that are readily understood by everyone else in the tunnel, suicide terror groups create "psychological points of no return." For example, suicide bombers in Sri Lanka would enjoy the rare honor of a private meal with the shadowy leader of the LTTE before going out to detonate themselves. Today's suicide bombers know their families will be helped and honored once they are dead, and they themselves are honored before going off on their missions. The videos that groups such as al-Qaeda have suicide bombers make before they go out to die have propaganda value, but they are also a powerful psychological tool. Once you have boasted on videotape about what you are going to do—and reaped the psychic rewards of your group's adulation—not completing a mission means turning your back on the things that make your life meaningful. "Once the terrorist does this," said Merari, referring to the suicide bomber's videotape, "he's already dead—mentally."

The central insight of all this research is that suicide terrorism is only a special case of a larger phenomenon. The hidden brain's drive for approval and meaning, and the ability of small groups to confer such approval and meaning, is what is common to the world of the elite corporate executive and the young marine, the terrorist organization and the missionary order that sends idealistic people into harm's way. At a conscious level, brave soldiers, idealistic missionaries, and suicidal terrorists might tell you they are motivated only by patriotism, by service, and by religion. At an unconscious level, however, they are motivated by the same thing—the drive to be part of something larger than themselves, to see themselves as special, to be part of a group whose well-being and survival matter more than their own lives.

Once a terrorist group has established the idea that a particular cause is important and worthwhile, that joining a movement will set ordinary people apart from their peers, no one needs to go out and re-cruit people. *They* will show up on their own.

Marc Sageman put it simply: "People want to be suicide bombers because they are the rock stars of militant Islam."

The researchers Eli Berman and David Laitin have developed a theory about the groups that sponsor suicide terrorism. Since large sums of money are typically placed on the heads of terrorists, ordinary mem-bers stand to gain enormously by betraying their comrades. Berman and Laitin asked a simple but very interesting question: Why does this not happen very often? The reason, they concluded, is that terrorist groups behave much in the manner of exclusive clubs. People in ter-rorist groups have tremendous solidarity and can trust one another implicitly because they have been self-selected by rules that make it very difficult to get into the club in the first place. Unlike book clubs and gyms—associations where everyone can join but few people stay for any length of time—exclusive clubs go out of their way to *limit* membership. There is a high bar to join, and the dues are expensive, and even if you are wealthy, you might not be able to find a spot un-less you have close contacts among existing members. Clubs that erect social barriers or require applicants to go through prolonged periods of apprenticeship before they become full members effectively weed out candidates who are not fully committed and prepare the ground-work for the elite few who are chosen to develop intense loyalties to one another. The same thing happens with religious sects that impose years of penance and prayer before new recruits can become full members. This might be why ritual acts of hazing and cruel punish-ments for trivial offenses are meted out to new recruits in organiza-tions where group solidarity is crucial. It seems paradoxical that a terrorist organization—ostensibly an outcast group—should make things so difficult for people to become members, but Berman and Laitin convincingly argue that such rules are the only way these or-ganizations can survive.

Peoples Temple was a very exclusive club. It was true that Jones and others actively recruited new members, but it was also true that they made it really difficult for people to stay. Only die-hard believers were willing to put up with the insane requirements. While this meant that many people quit, it also meant that those who stayed were ever more cohesive and likely to be surrounded by others just like themselves. The tunnel was being sealed of leaks. Annalisa, another sister of Larry Layton, briefly flirted with the group, but dropped out. The authoritarian ways of Peoples Temple did not sit well with her. By contrast, Layton's mother, Lisa, got drawn in and stayed, finding in the group comfort and meaning that she did not have elsewhere in her life.

One technique Jones used to cement loyalty was sessions of ritual confession, where people given the honor of joining his elite planning commission acknowledged doing and thinking vile and horrible things. These "catharsis" sessions began with Jones or one of his aides bringing an accusation against someone. People who denied the charges were pilloried and screamed down, and relentlessly interrogated until they admitted their guilt. If you were a member of the elite circle, it was understood that you would strike the first blows against people you loved—any hesitation would ensure the group turned on *you* for putting a personal relationship ahead of loyalty to the group.

Sessions ran as long as twenty hours, with victims required to stand still as others tore into them. Very soon, members realized that the quickest way out of these sessions was to take the lead in castigating themselves. If someone leveled an accusation, it was best to admit to things that were far worse. This would be seen as a sign of loyalty and openness. So people admitted to impure thoughts, to illegal acts they may or may not have committed, and to just about every kind of sexual perversion. The sessions made people feel incredibly vulnerable; at various times, nearly every member was pilloried and humiliated and forced to submit to the will of the group. Many of the sessions were secretly taped for use as blackmail against members who might later stray from the group. The sessions had a powerful psychological effect—they underscored that loyalty to Jones came before all other relationships.

Members were often punished after their confessions. Sometimes, the punishment involved Jones having sex with the victim's husband or wife, after which both victim and spouse had to thank the leader for giving them absolution. Jones was rewriting the norms of human behavior within the tunnel; those who disagreed left, but those who remained implicitly agreed to relinquish the values of the outside world. The sessions sucked members deeper and deeper—the only way to explain the bizarre rituals to yourself was to reject all ideas from outside the tunnel. Ordinary expectations about human dignity and decency made the catharsis sessions unbearable.

Shortly after Larry and Carolyn Layton joined Peoples Temple, Jones seduced Carolyn. At a public session shortly afterward, he had Carolyn declare that Larry Layton was an inadequate husband and lover and that she wanted a divorce. Larry Layton was speechless, but before he could regain his footing, Jones assigned him a new partner, a young blonde named Karen Tow. Outside the tunnel, such interference in people's personal lives would have been grounds for fights and lawsuits, or at least a parting of ways. Inside the tunnel, these manipulations cemented the conviction that Jones ran not only the organization but the personal lives of all its members.

In time, as Layton fell in love with Karen, Jones seduced her as well. When Layton admitted to Jones that he was upset, Jones put him on the floor for a catharsis session. Something had to be wrong with Layton for him to not realize that Jones slept with the women in *their* interest. Layton was made to stand still as the congregation lit into him. All the people he loved and admired reminded him of every occasion when he had ever done anything wrong. Then they started to beat him up—physical punishments were increasingly becoming part of the catharsis sessions. Soon, he was bleeding. When he tried to fight back, he was castigated for being a coward and abandoning nonviolent principles.

Men and women alike were forced to confess they wanted to seduce Jones. Usually these confessions followed episodes where Jones had forced himself on them. After raping Layton's sister Debbie, Jones told her that he had sensed that she needed a sexual relationship with a divine presence. As he had done with countless others, Jones made a public announcement afterward that Debbie had forced him into sex. The usual barrage of accusations and calumny descended on the young woman for bothering Jones with her trivial needs. During a visit to Los Angeles, Jones raped Larry Layton, too. Jones told Layton that the pain was training for the day when government agents would come and imprison members and torture them. Jones later told a congregation of nearly a thousand people what had happened between him and Layton. Larry Layton later said in court testimony, "It was the most painful and horrible experience I had ever had, and that—and then to be humiliated in front of the congregation afterward was just—it just destroyed my self-worth."

Everything inside the tunnel was turned upside down. There were times when Larry Layton was not sure whether he hated Jones or loved him. "I blamed myself for the things that happened to me. And although a part of me hated Jones, I—I came to think it was just evilness in me that I hated him." Jones convinced Layton that he "had been a horrible person in another lifetime and that's why these things were happening to me. And plus he—he would use the whole congregation. It was not just like he would turn against you. The whole congregation would like scream at you, and yell at you, and, you know, everybody would get up and give instances where I had, you know, mistreated them or done something wrong."

In addition to the psychological elements that go into constructing the suicide terrorist's tunnel, many groups cut off physical contact between recruits and the outside world. As Peoples Temple flourished in California, Jones went to extraordinary lengths to cloak his group in secrecy. When journalists threatened him with exposés, Jones launched his followers on their final step to total seclusion. Through much of the 1970s, Jones had been preparing an escape to Guyana, where he had leased thousands of acres of land and begun work on a utopian outpost. Fueled by paranoia about CIA and FBI threats, and actual threats of exposure from journalists and officials who were starting to take a closer look at his activities, Jones and a large number of followers decamped for Guyana in 1977. They took with them many incriminating confessions from the catharsis sessions to blackmail members left behind in America who might speak ill of the group. Jones also moved a large supply of guns and ammunition to Guyana.

Larry Layton, for all his years of service and obedience, was not invited to come along to utopia. A few months later, however, his sister Debbie—who had moved with Jones to Guyana—defected from Peoples Temple, bringing word to the United States that Jonestown was little more than a concentration camp. On the day Jones learned that Debbie had vanished, he summoned Larry Layton from California. Layton's family tried to stop him, but he was dead set on following his orders. Besides obedience, there were family ties that drew Layton to Guyana—his mother was in Jonestown and was suffering from cancer.

Layton's wife Karen was in Jonestown, too. Layton entered Guyana on May 15, 1978. In the following weeks, as Debbie Layton tried to warn U.S. officials that Jones was making preparations for a mass suicide, Larry and Lisa Layton systematically debunked Debbie's claims to the media and questioned her credibility.

According to a transcript of one conversation with a reporter for the *San Francisco Chronicle*, Larry Layton said, "I am not surprised about what she is saying. She had been stealing thousands of dollars from me and others. . . . I imagine she is probably still on drugs." Lisa Layton chimed in, "Seniors are treated beautifully here. We are socialists, and socialists treat their seniors very beautifully." Larry Layton jumped in again and reprised the familiar techniques that had been used in the catharsis sessions. "I would appreciate being able to say just a couple of words to refute these mountains of lies printed by my little sister. . . . She is a thief! And that is the reason she is attacking us, because she stole money from her mother. That is why she is telling these ridiculous lies. And the reason they are being printed is because we are socialists."

Jones set up armed guards to patrol his utopia. During the night, people in Jonestown heard gunfire, and Jones would tell them in the morning that his guards had fended off attacks by mercenaries employed by the CIA. Sometimes he had followers stay up all night armed with machetes, to take on the invading hordes. He ranted about conspiracies, and planted people who tried to induce other members to defect. People grew afraid to discuss their concerns about Jonestown with one another, since their confidants might have been working for Jones. As he had done from the start, Jones continued to provide services for people, continued to minister to their spiritual needs, and claimed to heal their illnesses.

Larry Layton pleaded with Jones to heal his mother's cancer. Lisa Layton was in terrible pain, partly because there was little medical treatment available at Jonestown. But Jones said that Debbie's defection and her loss of faith had left him unable to help the Layton family. Jones had told people for years that it was *their* faith in *him* that allowed him to cure them. Larry Layton was crushed. He could do nothing but watch as his mother died, racked with pain. In public speeches, Jones spent hours railing against Debbie Layton for betraying them all. Larry Layton felt intolerably guilty. Everything that was wrong at Jonestown seemed to be his fault. Richard Janaro was assigned to the same cabin as Layton that September. Layton was unshaven and largely silent, Janaro later recalled. "I'm all right," he would snap. "Leave me alone."

All of the paranoia that Jones had nurtured erupted when Representative Leo Ryan arrived in Guyana with an investigative team in November 1978. Within the tunnel that was Jonestown, it was the ultimate confirmation that enemies would never leave the idealists alone. On November 17, Ryan's party entered Jonestown and conducted interviews with residents. Many told him that they would not dream of leaving. "For a lot of you that I talked to, Jonestown is the best thing that ever happened to you in your lives," Ryan said in a speech, and the statement was met with a standing ovation. Tensions were running high the following day, however, as it became clear that fifteen people wanted to leave. There were nearly a thousand Americans at the camp, and the defectors comprised only a tiny fraction, but for Jones and others it was confirmation that they had been fatally betrayed.

Larry Layton finally saw his chance to redeem himself. After everything that had happened, the death of his mother, his sister's defection, and his own sense of guilt, he finally saw a way to turn himself into a hero. Layton asked Jones for permission to join the defectors, and to blow up their departing plane. "Well, I can go in there with dynamite, you know," Layton would later recall about his conversation with Jones. "He said, 'No, we don't have the means anyway.' I said, 'Well, I can use a gun,' but he still was negative on it." But after conferring with some aides, Jones agreed to the plan. One of the leader's mistresses, Maria Katsaris, emerged from a meeting with Jones and told Larry Layton, "It is okay. You can go ahead and use a gun."

Layton told Representative Ryan that he wanted to defect, too. The other defectors were suspicious. But the congressman allowed Layton to come along, and made arrangements for Layton to be searched before he boarded the plane. Survivors recall Layton was deathly silent as the defectors were transported to the Port Kaituma airstrip five miles away. One recalled him being in an almost "trance-like state."

Was Layton thinking fearfully about his impending death? That makes sense only from *outside* the tunnel. No, Layton was afraid that his mission would go awry. For many years, Jones had told his followers that the number sixteen was unlucky. As Layton rode to the airstrip, he realized that with his addition, the party of defectors now numbered sixteen. It was a bad omen. There was worse to come. Layton had expected there would be only one plane at the airstrip that would carry the congressman and the entire party, one airplane that he could destroy, and thereby wreathe himself in the glory that had eluded him all his life. But after the party got to the airstrip, two planes arrived. Since more defectors had signed up than Ryan had expected, the congressman had ordered a second plane.

"When I found out there were two planes, I was really terrified, because I knew that whatever I did would be a waste," Layton later said. "But then I knew—I felt like, well, I have to go on. . . . I feel like I volunteered. I do not feel like—you know, I felt like what I was doing was right. And—but I was terrified because a lot of things went wrong. Like sixteen was always an unlucky number for our group. And sixteen people were getting on the plane. . . . I felt like everything was going bad, very wrong."

Jones and Katsaris had anticipated the problem. Right before Layton was dispatched, Katsaris told him, "If there are two planes, make sure you get on the first plane."

Layton pushed his way forward and demanded to board the first plane, a six-seater Cessna. While the other defectors were assembling on the airstrip, Layton snuck aboard. Representative Ryan ordered Layton off. The defector could not have been on board for more than a few seconds. He was searched, found clear, and allowed to reboard. He sat in the second row behind the pilot. Vern Gosney sat beside him, and Temple members Dale Parks and his sister sat in the back row. Another member, Monica Bagby, sat in front next to the pilot.

A flatbed truck arrived at the airstrip and stationed itself close to the second plane. Layton knew that other Jones loyalists had been dispatched to the airstrip on that truck, but he did not know what they had been instructed to do. "I mean, I thought I was going to be on the plane and that was the end of it," he would later say.

"You expected the congressman to be on that plane also?" the psychiatrist who later interviewed him asked.

"I expected everybody to be on that plane," Layton replied.

Layton's plane began taxiing. But as defectors began to board the second plane with the congressman, the flatbed trailer swerved into the path of Layton's plane, and gunmen on the trailer opened fire on Representative Ryan and the others.

"I didn't know these guys were coming out," Layton would recall. "Well, I remember some people coming out in a truck. But the first I heard was, Boom! Boom! Boom!"

Vern Gosney, sitting beside Layton, started screaming. "They are killing everyone! They are killing everyone!"

Oh hell, Layton thought.

Their plane had still not gotten off the ground. Layton was still intent on crashing his plane—even though it no longer made any sense. He started yelling at the pilot, "Get it off the ground, get it off the ground."

But the Cessna was blocked. The men on the trailer concentrated their fire on the defectors on the second plane.

When Vern Gosney turned around, he saw Larry Layton was holding a gun.

At point-blank range, Layton shot him. He pointed the gun through the front seat and shot Monica Bagby. Then he whipped around and placed the gun at Dale Parks's chest. He pulled the trigger.

Parks fell back in his seat. It took him a moment to realize that he was still alive. The gun had misfired. Parks leaped forward and wrestled Layton for the gun.

Gosney, despite being injured, helped Parks subdue Layton. The would-be suicide terrorist was not a big man, and he certainly was not much of a fighter. Parks grabbed the gun. He whipped it around, pointed it at Layton, and pulled the trigger. The gun misfired again.

The men on the flatbed trailer killed Representative Ryan and four others. There was wild chaos on the airstrip. The passengers on the Cessna deplaned. Shortly afterward, Guyanese police arrested Layton. He made no effort to escape.

He signed a confession that said, "I, Larry Layton, take full responsibility for all the deaths and injuries that took place at the Port Kaituma airstrip. I had begged the Bishop Jim Jones that I be allowed to bring down the plane but he disapproved. My reason for supporting this was because I felt those people were working in conjunction with CIA to smear the Peoples Temple. . . . I went to the airport intending to bring down the plane. But when the shooting started, I also started shooting."

Layton was not responsible for all the deaths at the airstrip. The people he shot, Monica Bagby and Vern Gosney, were injured, but neither was dead. It was the men on the flatbed trailer who had killed the congressman and others.

In the months and years to come, people would puzzle over why someone like Larry Layton would agree to become a suicide terrorist, and why he claimed responsibility for things he had never done. Later, at trial, defense and prosecution lawyers would clash over whether the airstrip confession was coerced. But from within the perspective of the tunnel, both Layton's actions and his confession made total sense.

Layton was not trying to take on blame that did not belong to him. Within the warped mental framework of the tunnel that was Jonestown, Layton was trying to take *credit* that did not belong to him.

Five miles from the airstrip, after Layton had left on his suicide mission, Jones issued a prophecy that the plane carrying the congressman and defectors back to America was going to crash. He claimed it was another of his psychic revelations.

"There's one man there who blames, and rightfully so, Debbie Blakey for the murder of his mother, and he'll stop the pilot by any means necessary," Jones said, referring to Debbie Layton's married name. "He'll do it. That plane will come out of the air. There's no way you fly a plane without a pilot."

Jones gave a long, rambling speech that ranged widely from animal rights to human rights abuses by Chilean dictator General Augusto Pinochet. He warned his flock that Ryan's visit was only the tip of the spear, that enemies were gathering to kill them all and torture the children. His paranoia had reached the point that he believed that Leo Ryan and the defectors would escape from the doomed plane via parachutes, come down over Jonestown, and open fire on the children.

"What's gonna happen here in a matter of minutes, is that one of those people on that plane is gonna, gonna shoot the pilot," Jones told his audience. "I didn't plan it, but I know it's gonna happen. They're gonna shoot that pilot and down comes that plane into the jungle, and we had better not have any of our children left when it's over, 'cause they'll parachute in here on us. . . . So my opinion is that we be kind to children and be kind to seniors and take the potion like they used to take in ancient Greece, and step over quietly because we are not committing suicide. It's a revolutionary act. We can't go back. They won't leave us alone. . . . When they start parachuting out of the air, they'll, they'll shoot some of our innocent babies."

The speech was taped, and later recovered by the Federal Bureau of Investigation. It features the voices of several people in the audience, who declare they will do whatever Jones asks of them.

In their final meeting with Larry Layton before they left Guyana, Rebecca Moore and Fielding McGehee were allowed to see the prisoner face-to-face. It was a short meeting. Moore embraced Layton, and McGehee shook his hand.

In a letter to a family member of one of those who had died at Jonestown, Rebecca Moore, who later became a professor of religious studies at San Diego State University, summed up her visit. "I went to Jonestown thinking, hoping, my sisters had been murdered. I found out two things. One, they hadn't been murdered. They chose to die. They made their choices. And two, Jonestown wasn't such a terrible place. Jones was crazy, true. But people were committed to Jonestown, to the ideals they had. . . . There were few murders, if any: the children certainly were murdered. They had no choice. The others— they could have taken their chances with the guards, and a few did. Why were only two persons shot? I think it was because people could not bear to go on living knowing their life as a community was at an end."

In the Guyana prison, Layton gave every indication he was still inside the tunnel. He "feared being murdered in prison so he carved C-I-A on his stomach so that if he was killed, the rest of the world would know who was responsible," said Stephan Jones, one of Jim Jones's sons who was also imprisoned in Guyana.

When Layton heard about the mass suicide, he immediately assumed it was because he had failed to carry out his mission properly. If he had crashed the plane, everything would have turned out all right. He had failed, and so the community he had been trying to protect had been destroyed.

Shortly after Layton's mission and the mass suicide, a New Jersey psychiatrist named Hardat Singh Sukhdeo visited Guyana. He interviewed Layton on multiple occasions and made recordings of the conversations. "I just—I couldn't accept, you know, that Jones had done that," Layton told Sukhdeo at one point. "He was—that time period of my life, before I realized what a monster he was, he was like—like a supreme being to me."

"I looked upon him as like a savior," Layton went on. "Not as a god creator, but as a savior. You know, like somebody that comes from a more highly evolved—well, maybe the most highly evolved

being in the universe that has come to this planet to—straighten—
bring in socialism. In a sense, you know, I saw him as the only god
there is."

Layton was released from the Guyana prison because authorities
were reluctant to prosecute crimes conducted by an American against
other Americans. Layton was extradited to the United States and
stood trial in California. Since his victims Vern Gosney and Monica
Bagby were traveling in a foreign country and presumably under the
jurisdiction of foreign laws, the case around Layton centered on
whether he had conspired to kill Leo Ryan, who, as a member of Congress, was entitled to protection under U.S. laws even while traveling
overseas.

After multiple trials, Layton was sentenced to a lengthy prison
term. He became a model prisoner. But the infamy of Jonestown and
the fact that he was the only person convicted in its aftermath meant
he was always turned down for parole. Shortly after the September
11, 2001, attacks, Layton came up for parole again. It was probably
the worst time in the history of the nation for a suicide terrorist to be
asking for clemency.

But in a last minute twist, the man that Layton had shot, Vern Gosney, heard about the parole hearing. Gosney was now a cop in Hawaii. He bought an air ticket on his own and flew in for the hearing.

The paranoia and psychological tunnels that produced the September 11 terrorists, Gosney said, were built from exactly the same
kind of cloth as Jonestown. "That is what Jim Jones was talking
about, being willing to die, suicide bombers, being willing to die for
your cause," Gosney told me in an interview. "I didn't do anything
overt to kill anyone, but I started to see how I could have very easily
been in Larry's position. We were all subject to the same indoctrination and mind control, and he was just as much a victim as I was."

Gosney's emotional testimony on behalf of his "brother" Larry
Layton turned the tide at the parole hearing. Layton was released
shortly afterward and now lives in Northern California.

While he was still in prison in Guyana, Layton once mused about
what he had learned. How had a community that had been founded

on the highest ideals lost its way so badly, and how had a man who'd started life as a Quaker become a suicide terrorist?

"Where did things go wrong?" Layton asked himself in a letter he wrote back home from the Guyana prison. "First, when discipline became so austere that people were afraid to speak their minds. Second, religious states of mind and politics don't mix well. The advance of democracy has coincided with increased secularization of religion. Third, power corrupts absolutely."

"There is a lot I will never know about Peoples Temple," Layton said. "The only thing I can say is that it started out looking like a civil rights movement, and Jim Jones started out looking like Martin Luther King. Obviously, things turned out differently."

About obeying Jones's summons to go to Guyana, he wrote, "I was a fool to leave California, but then I was a fool long before that."

As he sat in his prison cell in Guyana, it slowly became apparent to Layton that the world he had inhabited for so long was not the real world, that it was only a tunnel that had appeared to be the whole world. For years, Layton had falsely believed he was being hunted and persecuted, and that family members who tried to warn him about Jones were his enemies. Now, with the whole world against him, Layton found that there were still people like Rebecca Moore and Fielding McGehee who were willing to travel long distances to stand by his side and wave the family flag.

"If there is one thing that jail teaches you, it is appreciation for freedom," Layton wrote. "If there is one thing that being vilified and deserted teaches you, it is appreciation for those who stand by your side when it appears the world has turned against you. So much for my paranoia."

CHAPTER 8

Shades of Justice

Unconscious Bias and the Death Penalty

This chapter focuses on an issue that has been widely explored in the media: racial disparities in the criminal justice system. New research into the hidden brain provides surprising information about the nature of these disparities.

I am about to describe two murders that took place some years ago in Philadelphia; both crimes were solved and the court cases produced convictions. As you read these accounts, keep your eyes open for clues that tell you which of the men convicted of murder got a sentence of life in prison and which man got the death penalty.

It was a lovely April morning in South Philadelphia. Raymond Fiss left his home at seven-thirty carrying a brown bag—lunch his wife, Marie, had packed for him. Fiss was a heavy man, two hundred sixty pounds crammed into a five foot eight frame. He slid into his silver and black convertible, and drove away. It was the last time Marie would see him alive.

Fiss had a routine on Saturday mornings. Right before he reached the small beauty shop he owned at 2701 McKean Street, he tooted his horn outside a nearby home. This was the home of Catherine Valente, a septuagenarian who liked to get her hair done on Saturday mornings; she also did odd jobs for Fiss. That morning, Fiss wanted Valente to get the rollers ready before his other customers arrived. The beautician drove on, parked outside his salon, picked up his brown paper bag, and went to unlock the door.

Angelina Spera was sitting in front of her bedroom mirror and had just finished combing her hair. Her house was across the street from the Fiss beauty salon. Spera got up to go downstairs to make some coffee, but lingered a moment by the window. She saw Fiss, who had owned the salon for twenty-one years, being accosted by a black man. She watched as Fiss opened the storm door and unlocked the main door of the salon. Spera heard him tell the accoster, "Get the hell out of here!"

The man pushed Fiss into the salon. The moment they disappeared from sight, Spera raced to the telephone and called the police. She took the phone to her window to keep watch.

Inside the salon, Fiss and his assailant went past chairs and hair dryers. The salon was tiny, about nineteen feet by seventeen feet. There was a small bathroom; it had just a toilet and a sink. We do not know what words transpired between the two men, but we do know that at a range of a little more than three feet, the man shot Fiss. Burning its way through the blue jacket Fiss was wearing, the .38 caliber bullet left a grayish residue. It blasted into the beautician's chest, broke his sixth rib, was deflected by the bone, bruised his right lung, and tore his esophagus. It also tore his liver and sliced through his aorta. Dark blood surged into Fiss's chest, and into the tunnels of tissue that the bullet had excavated. Having done its worst work, the bullet then shattered Fiss's tenth thoracic vertebra, passed between his tenth and eleventh ribs, and came to rest just beneath the skin of his left back. The beautician fell to the ground. His legs protruded through the bathroom's doorway. His eyes were open, but glazing.

Catherine Valente arrived at the salon just in time to hear a pop that sounded like a car backfiring. The lights were not on inside the salon, but it was sunny outside and some natural light had entered the space. She saw a black man inside the salon. He half turned toward the back of the little room, and mumbled, "I'll be back, I'll be back." He pushed past her and exited. From the building across the street, Angelina Spera did not get a good look at the man's face, but she saw that he was carrying a brown paper bag. The man unlocked the beautician's convertible, jumped into the car, and drove away at high speed.

By the time police reached the beauty salon, Fiss was dead. Catherine Valente, who found the body, was in shock. Yes, she told police, she had seen the assailant, but no, she didn't think she could identify him.

"Would you be able to recognize this man if you saw him again?" the police asked her, according to a statement she signed at her home later that day.

"I don't think so," she replied.

Angelina Spera also told police she would not be able to identify the assailant.

The killer had taken the money Fiss had on him—about thirty dollars. The murder incensed the community; crime was on the rise in Philadelphia. Three days after the murder, a meeting was called at Saint Edmond's parish hall. Residents demanded two housing projects in the neighborhood be closed, and asked authorities to keep black "outsiders" away from white neighborhoods. There was intense pressure on the police department to crack the case, but the trail was cold. The man who'd killed Fiss had vanished.

Six days after the murder, Catherine Valente was sitting by the television as the twelve o'clock news on Channel 6 got under way; the picture was on but the sound was off. She saw a mug shot of a man accused of robbing a jewelry store.

"That's him! That's him!" she shouted to her daughter. "He's on television, he's on television!"

On the same day that South Philadelphia residents were accusing authorities of not doing enough to protect them from crime, two black men showed up at Gentile's Golden Nugget jewelry store at 1910 East Passyunk Avenue in Philadelphia, about one and a half miles from the beauty salon where Fiss was murdered. The owner of the jewelry store, Vincent Gentile, buzzed them in. A third man was close behind. The men were interested in gold charms. Gentile had the charms in a locked case. The men inquired about a King Tut charm, and the jeweler told them it cost five hundred fifty dollars. They asked to see it. Gentile fetched his key.

The moment he opened the case, the jeweler felt something pressed against his back. He turned around slowly to see that it was a gun. Between them, the robbers appeared to have two guns. They prodded him toward the back of the store, where Gentile lived in a private residence. As he was being marched past a showcase, Gentile surreptitiously pressed a silent alarm to alert police. One of the men warned Gentile not to touch anything, and the jeweler assured the robbers that he would comply with their instructions.

Three people were sitting at a table in the back of the store. One was a store employee; the others were Gentile's friends. Holding them at gunpoint, one of the robbers warned, "Don't look at us or we'll kill you." The trio looked quickly away. In short order, the jeweler found himself handcuffed to his employee, Rose Madera, while his two friends Abner Zeigler and Matthew Greco were handcuffed to each other. All the victims were forced to lie facedown on the floor. Gentile felt someone rifle through his pocket; a ring on his finger was removed. The victims lay still for five or ten minutes, as the robbers ransacked the store. Suddenly Gentile heard running footsteps and a voice shouting, "The cops, the cops are outside!"

The robbers ran toward the back of the store, through a parlor and a kitchen, and into a yard. They disappeared down an alley at the back. Gentile could not get up, so he asked his friends to buzz in the officers.

Philadelphia police officer Kenneth Rossiter was on patrol that day in South Philadelphia when he responded to a radio call from a fellow officer. In the backyard of a home about a block and a half from the jewelry store, the other officer had found some dropped jewelry. Rossiter met up with the other officer and they knocked on the door of the house, and on the windows, but no one answered. Some neighbors called out that they could see someone fleeing, and the officers took off in pursuit. Rossiter spotted a man running about a block away. The man turned north, ran behind a bank and through a parking lot, and ran north again. Rossiter ran a parallel route, and as he arrived at an intersection, he saw the man make a throwing gesture, as if he were discarding something. The man raced west, with Rossiter and the other officer in pursuit. They lost sight of him again. But close to the intersection of Hicks and Morris streets, about three large blocks from the jewelry store, Rossiter spotted the man sitting on a step. He had neither gun nor stolen merchandise in his possession. The officers placed him under arrest.

Police took the man back to the jewelry store, where Gentile identified him as one of the robbers with a gun. In the area where Rossiter had seen the man fling something away, police later recovered a .38 caliber revolver from under a parked car.

The photo of the man Rossiter arrested was the one that Catherine Valente saw on television two days later. Ballistics tests showed that the gun found was the same gun that had been used to murder Raymond Fiss.

The arrested man was identified as Ernest Porter, and prosecutors charged him with murder. Porter denied the charge. A single fingerprint lifted from the door of the beautician's shop was said to match Porter's left thumbprint. At the murder trial, Officer Rossiter conceded he had lost sight of the running man several times, and that the man he had arrested had no evidence on his person linking him with the robbery. There were no fingerprints on the gun. But prosecutors put Vincent Gentile on the stand, and the jeweler emphatically identified Porter as one of the robbers. Prosecutors used Gentile's testimony to link Porter to the man who threw away the gun, and used the gun to link Porter to the murder of Raymond Fiss.

"Mr. Gentile, I'd just like to ask you, are you positive that this defendant in the white striped shirt is the defendant who was in your store with the handgun that day?" the prosecutor asked at one point in Ernest Porter's murder trial.

"Yes, it was," Gentile replied.

Porter's public defender mounted virtually no defense. The jury took only forty-five minutes to find Porter guilty of the murder of Raymond Fiss.

Go ten blocks west of where Fiss was shot, and you get to the Schuylkill Expressway. Follow it west as it curves past central

Philadelphia, past the art museum and the boathouses that light up at night. Hop onto West Girard Avenue, and then go west on Lancaster to Lebanon Avenue. If you'd made the six-mile trip in 1992, you would have arrived at the Love Pharmacy at 6525 Lebanon Avenue. The Love Pharmacy was owned by Thomas Brannan. He was sixty-four, and a very gentle and popular man. He often opened the pharmacy after regular hours—including all hours of the night—if people needed emergency medications. He had standing instructions to his employees—if they were ever robbed at gunpoint, no one was to offer resistance. Lives and safety were more important than money to Thomas Brannan.

On a Thursday morning that November, two young black men ambled into the Love Pharmacy. Brannan's sister, Patricia Gibson, was working in the store. One of the young men told her he was suffering from stomach cramps. Gibson suggested he try the medication Donnagel. The young man's friend suggested Pepto-Bismol. The men argued with each other, as they took in the layout of the pharmacy. One of the men asked Gibson what time the pharmacy closed. She said seven o'clock. The men left.

Sharon Brogan went to the Love Pharmacy that evening to pick up a prescription. She entered the store around six-thirty, but then remembered she had forgotten to bring a medical card. She lived nearby, so she turned around to go home and get it. As she exited the store, she noticed four young black men standing near a Cadillac in front of the store. When she returned to the store a few minutes later, the men were no longer outside the store; they were inside. One of them stood at the door. Brogan tried to get in, but the young man told her the store was closed.

A voice in the background shouted, "Get her in here!"

The young man grabbed Brogan and pulled her inside. A holdup was under way. The man at the door went through her pockets and took her checkbook. Brogan saw the cashier Maureen Quinn in the back, while another woman, Diane Copes, lay facedown on the floor.

The leader of the robbers asked Brannan for a prescription drug; the pharmacist told him pharmacies in Pennsylvania did not carry that drug. Quinn, the cashier, perhaps remembering Brannan's instructions to be cooperative in the event of a holdup, led the robber to a cabinet where all controlled substances were kept under lock and key. Misunderstanding what Quinn was doing, and believing she was contradicting her boss, the robber asked Brannan why he had lied.

The robbers made Quinn push the NO SALE button on the cash register. All the store employees were now on the floor, lying facedown as the robbers ransacked the pharmacy's money and drugs. They took a bottle of the narcotic Percocet, ten bottles of Xanax, about sixty money orders, and approximately four hundred dollars in cash.

Then the women in the store heard a shot—it came from the robber standing over the prostrate body of Thomas Brannan. The pharmacist had been offering no resistance; he was shot in the back as he lay facedown on the floor.

Brogan heard one of the other robbers exclaim, "What did you do that for?"

The robbers quickly exited. Quinn called police. Brannan was not dead, but he was dying.

The pharmacist told medics his stomach was on fire. Gentle to the last, he made a quip when someone checked on him a moment later: "I've had better days."

Five days after Brannan's murder, someone tried to cash one of the stolen money orders from the Love Pharmacy. The cashier, Mitchell Wolf, called Traveler's Express, the bank that owned the account, and then the pharmacy, which was listed as the issuing agent. When Wolf heard a recorded message on the answering machine that the pharmacy had been closed because of a murder, he called authorities. Police, meanwhile, were following up on a tip from a man who claimed to have heard something from one of the robbers—the tipster said the man who shot the pharmacist was called Arthur Hawthorne. The tipster identified Hawthorne in a photograph. Hawthorne was arrested eight days after the murder; he threw a telephone at police officer James Westray when the cop burst through the door. Hawthorne tried to grab Westray's shotgun. The police officer reversed the gun and slammed it into Hawthorne's head, and knocked him to the ground.

The other robbers were quickly rounded up. One of the four, David Sheppard, said Hawthorne and another young man had asked the others to help pick up a prescription. He claimed he had not known a robbery was planned until it was under way. Sheppard said he had remonstrated with Hawthorne in the getaway car about shooting the pharmacist. "It was fucked up, because the guy gave up everything and there was no reason to shoot him. He was an old guy."

Police showed a photo array that included Hawthorne to Sharon Brogan, the customer who had been pulled into the pharmacy as the robbery was getting under way. Brogan identified photo number six as the man who was standing over the pharmacist when he was shot. It was Hawthorne.

The same day, Diane Copes, who had had to lie facedown in the pharmacy, also identified Hawthorne as the man who had shot Thomas Brannan. Maureen Quinn, the cashier, also independently identified Hawthorne as the murderer. "Number six looks like the man who grabbed Tom, and that's the man who shot Tom."

Hawthorne's ex-girlfriend turned over a tape to police on which the robber had said he was going to have to leave her for a while and go away. And Hawthorne's sister said her brother had incriminated himself when she'd asked him if he was involved in the killing.

"Shut up. You talk too much," he had said at first.

"You must have had something to do with that. You're sitting there looking all stupid," she'd retorted.

"Yeah," Hawthorne had admitted. "I killed that man."

The crimes I have just told you about involve a number of other factors. At the time of his murder trial, Ernest Porter faced other robbery charges, and a rape charge. Arthur Hawthorne had allegedly robbed two other stores in July 1992; when police officer Robert Dunne arrived at the scene of the second robbery, he found himself staring into a 9 mm semiautomatic gun. At point-blank range, Hawthorne pulled the trigger. The gun clicked twice but did not fire. In October, Hawthorne again pulled a gun on police; both times, he was released on bail. Both men had long and troubled emotional histories. Porter had been in psychiatric care since he was four; Hawthorne came from a dysfunctional family, where drugs ruled his life from an early age.

In 2006 Stanford University psychologist Jennifer Eberhardt and three other researchers, Paul G. Davies, Valerie J. Purdie-Vaughns, and Sheri Lynn Johnson, conducted an analysis of why some violent crimes produce death sentences while others result in life imprisonment or lesser terms. Eberhardt and her colleagues examined a database of more than six hundred cases in the Philadelphia area, cases in which the crime committed was serious enough to warrant the death penalty. From this group of cases they extracted the photographs of all the black defendants who had been convicted of murdering white victims. The group included Ernest Porter and Arthur Hawthorne. They asked a large group of independent people who knew nothing about the cases—not even that they were looking at criminals—to rate the faces on one measure: the degree to which they looked stereotypically black. Whether or not race has any meaning as a biological construct, people had no trouble identifying stereotypically African features: thicker lips, broader noses, curlier hair, and darker skin tone. Take a look at the two images in Figure 2. These are pictures of volunteers, not criminals. See if you have any trouble telling which face looks more stereotypically African.

Now look at the two images in Figure 3 on page 177. The picture of Arthur Hawthorne is on the left, and Ernest Porter is on the right. Do you have any trouble telling which face looks more stereotypically African?

Figure 2. Stanford psychologist Jennifer Eberhardt showed that people are quickly able to pick out features that are stereotypically African. These two men are volunteers.

Figure 3. Stanford psychologist Jennifer Eberhardt has studied whether the features and skin tone of convicts influence the severity of their sentences.

Once the psychologists had obtained ratings for all the defendants, they compared the sentences of those who looked more African than average with those who looked less African than average. Without any other information, without knowing anything about the crimes or the extenuating circumstances, without hearing arguments by prosecutors and defense teams, without having a chance to think about who made up the juries, you would think it would be impossible to guess which criminals got the death penalty. You would be wrong. Defendants who looked more stereotypically black than average were *more than twice as likely* to receive the death penalty as those who looked less black. If you split the convicts into two groups, the "less black" group stood a 24.4 percent chance of getting the death penalty. The "blacker blacks" had a 57.5 percent chance of being sentenced to death.

Porter's conviction involved a far more circuitous case than Hawthorne's conviction. Porter was identified by the jeweler Vincent Gentile in connection with a robbery. Police then linked a gun thrown by a man fleeing the robbery to the Fiss murder. There were no eyewitnesses to the murder, and no fingerprints on the gun. The only person who got a glimpse of Fiss's killer—the septuagenarian Catherine Valente—said on the day of the killing that she would not be able to identify him. In the other case, there were more than half a dozen people who saw Hawthorne kill Brannan, and several others who provided corroborating evidence. Raymond Fiss had had an altercation with his assailant before he was shot; by contrast, Brannan had offered no resistance and had been lying facedown on the floor when Hawthorne shot him in the back. But it was Porter who got the death sentence and Hawthorne who got life in prison.

It is important to note that Eberhardt's research does not tell us that Porter should have received a life sentence or that Hawthorne should have been sentenced to death. But what it does tell us is that there are systematic differences in the way people with Ernest Porter's skin tone and features have been evaluated in the Pennsylvania criminal justice system. Whatever our view of these cases in particular, and of the death penalty in general, we can agree that such results are disturbing.

When the Pennsylvania Supreme Court refused Ernest Porter's appeal in 1990, Supreme Court Justice James T. McDermott told Porter that to escape the jaws of justice required extraordinary luck. Waxing eloquent from the bench, McDermott said, "Those who bring a criminal purpose to the daily lives of others, as did the appellant here, must pass through that sticky web of the ordinary round of things. To alter them to fit a criminal purpose requires more than malice and a gun. It requires that the passerby, the late or early riser, the sleepless or ill neighbor, the returning party goer, house painter, roofer, locksmith, cement crew, sudden fire, clocks running slow or fast, and the other quotidian needs and purposes that tie us to the earth synchronize with their single purpose. As the appellant was to find, they rarely do."

McDermott was wrong. Chance, in the role of skin tone and facial features, plays a very large role in deciding the fate of men such as Ernest Porter.

There are a host of other examples in the criminal justice system that reveal an appalling lack of consistency. Some kinds of crimes are much more likely to be solved than others. Some criminals get the book thrown at them; others get away with lighter charges. Prosecutors in urban areas are less likely than their counterparts in rural areas to seek the death penalty for cases involving crimes of equivalent seriousness. Where violent crime is common, there appears to be a desensitization effect that prompts urban prosecutors to unconsciously rate these crimes as less egregious than their rural counterparts do. A variety of reports suggest that police (and the mass media) are much more interested in crimes involving white victims than in crimes involving victims who are people of color. Also, Eberhardt found that the bias against darker-skinned convicts in death penalty sentencing was limited to cases involving white victims, and did not extend to cases where victim and perpetrator were of the same race. Something about black-on-white crime activated unconscious stereotypes that linked criminality with race in the minds of jurors.

What explained the behavior of judges, juries, and lawyers in the murder trials that Eberhardt studied? Some judges and juries and lawyers could have been deliberately biased, but it is implausible that large numbers of them were overtly bigoted. It would have taken only a single juror, remember, to overturn a death penalty sentence. What are the odds that large numbers of juries that handed all the additional darker-skinned convicts the death penalty had comprised twelve people with unrelenting bigotry in their hearts?

There is a better explanation for the data, a simpler explanation. Juries that decided to send all those extra people with Ernest Porter's skin tone to death were convinced they were doing the right thing. If you spoke to these juries, you would not find them packed with bigots. You would find upstanding people who were firmly convinced they were doing the right thing—much as Frances Aboud's preschoolers thought they were doing the right thing in associating words such as "cruel" and "bad" with some faces rather than with others.

Like in many other areas where the hidden brain influences us without our awareness, there is one fundamental problem that is rarely addressed when we think about racial disparities in the criminal justice system. Like deciding which people to hire for jobs, or guessing which stocks to buy, the criminal justice system is based on the idea that human behavior is the product of conscious intention. We believe that juries that want to be fair are fair. We believe good intentions equal good outcomes. The assumption—the false assumption—is that biased outcomes result from deliberate bias and that such errors can be overcome by setting up a confrontational system where prosecutors and defense attorneys keep one another honest.

Why do we hold so resolutely to this assumption in the face of all the evidence to the contrary? For one thing, it is easier. We are programmed to trust our memories, judgments, and perceptions. When we feel we are acting fairly, it is easy to conclude that we must in fact be acting fairly. Besides, the alternative is terrifying. If we accept the possibility that people—well-intentioned people—can be unconsciously biased into doing the wrong thing even when they explicitly feel they are being careful and fair, we must acknowledge that our system of justice is not just prone to occasional error but that it is designed to fail regularly. The jury system, after all, enshrines the personal intuitions of twelve human beings as the word of law. Given the unconscious errors that jurors, judges, and prosecutors—and even defense attorneys—are vulnerable to, gross failures are inevitable, just as buildings based on a child's understanding of physics will inevitably fall. Re-imagining our system of justice based on the new understanding of the brain and behavior is a daunting undertaking. It isn't surprising that we prefer to hold on to the myth that the good intentions of honest people can keep unconscious biases at bay when it comes to decisions involving the lives and deaths of other human beings.

I began my reporting of this chapter with an assumption of my own. All the people that Stanford psychologist Jennifer Eberhardt studied were convicted of serious crimes; her study focused only on sentencing disparities between convicts based on their skin tone and features. I assumed, going in, that Ernest Porter and Arthur Hawthorne were guilty.

As I studied the murder of Raymond Fiss and the arrest and conviction of Ernest Porter, however, I discovered a series of troubling issues. The behavior of lawyers, witnesses, and police officers made me wonder whether Porter may have been a victim of unconscious racial bias not only during the sentencing phase of his case, but from the very moment he was arrested.

It turned out, first of all, that the police had interviewed two people who provided an alibi for Porter at the time of the Fiss murder. The police appear to have shared that information with Porter's defense lawyer, because he mentioned these witnesses in his opening statement to the jury. Inexplicably, they failed to appear as witnesses. Both said later that they would have testified if asked. The witnesses were the parents of a young woman named Meredith Barbour, whom Porter was dating. He was often over at her place. Meredith's mother, Harriet Barbour, and her stepfather, Jesse Dawson, Jr., were interrogated by police right after Porter was arrested. Both independently said that Porter had come over to their house the night before the Fiss murder and watched a Philadelphia 76ers basketball game. Both said Porter was still in the house the next morning—past the time when Fiss was murdered.

The judge who presided over Porter's murder trial was Albert Sabo, who would come to be called "the king of death row." In a quarter century on the bench, Sabo sentenced more people to die than any other judge in the country, according to Robert Dunham at the Philadelphia Federal Defender Office. By the time Sabo retired, his rulings single-handedly accounted for 40 percent of all of Pennsylvania's death row inmates from Philadelphia—and Philly accounted for half the death row inmates in the state. A disproportionate number of Sabo's convictions involved defendants who were people of color. The fact that Sabo sentenced so many people to die does not automatically mean those sentences were flawed. What does raise serious questions, however, is that three-quarters of Sabo's death row convictions have run into trouble during the appeals process—higher courts have found problems ranging from prosecutorial misconduct to improper jury instructions. A federal district court has ruled that Sabo's instructions to the jury in the sentencing phase of the Ernest Porter trial made it difficult for the jury to take mitigating factors into consideration.

Prosecutors in the Porter trial struck off eight potential jurors who were black. These potential jurors included longtime residents of Philadelphia. One was a former army veteran. Another man had seen a close friend killed and a cousin's wife raped—the kind of juror who is usually willing to impose harsh penalties. The black potential jurors expressed no reservations about the death penalty. By contrast, white jurors dismissed by the prosecution during jury selection were clearly conflicted about the death penalty.

"People like to say death penalty cases are the worst of the worst," said Michael Wiseman at the Philadelphia Federal Defender Office, which has represented Porter and other death row inmates who have seen verdicts brought into question by higher courts. "They are usually the product of a prosecutorial judge, an incompetent lawyer, and an impaired defendant."

Errors in the case surfaced the very moment police arrested Porter. He tried to tell them that his name was not Ernest Porter at all but Theodore Wilson. When the issue came up during trial, the court stuck to the wrong name—in the interest of convenience. (I have retained the name of Ernest Porter in this account because that is the name under which Wilson currently sits on death row. It is not his name, but it's the name under which the state of Pennsylvania plans to have him executed.)

Porter's lawyer did virtually nothing to challenge the circuitous nature of the prosecution's case, and the defense called no witnesses of its own. The gun that police discovered was not in Porter's possession at the time of his arrest, and was found several days after the Fiss murder. There were no fingerprints found on the weapon, even though police said it had been discarded by Porter as he'd fled the botched jewelry store robbery. More than one robber at Vincent Gentile's store had had a gun, but the defense did not explore the possibility that the Fiss murder weapon may have belonged to one of the other robbers. The officer who arrested Porter, moreover, did not see Porter throw a gun away; he saw him make a throwing gesture as he ran, and police later found a gun under a car in the area.

Officer Kenneth Rossiter testified that he was certain the man he arrested was the man he had pursued in a lengthy chase, but the officer did not actually see Porter's face until he found him sitting on a step in an alley. Until that point, Rossiter saw only the back of a running man—and the running man was a block or more away. The police officer acknowledged that he had lost sight of his target several times during the chase, and that he was about half a block away when he saw the running man make a throwing gesture.

"Were you able to see positively what it was that this person discarded?" the prosecutor asked Rossiter during Porter's trial.

"No. Not positively, no," Rossiter replied.

Rossiter did not see Porter leave Vincent Gentile's jewelry store; the police did not get access to the store for several minutes after the robbers fled because they had to be buzzed in. And it was only after Catherine Valente identified Porter on television—after telling police on the day of the murder that she would not be able to identify the killer—that the police linked the jewelry store robbery with the Fiss murder. Porter had been in trouble with the law before, and his fingerprints were on file, so it is not clear why police—who said they'd picked up a fingerprint from the beauty salon and were under intense pressure to crack the case—did not link Porter to the crime before Valente did. Neither Valente nor Angelina Spera, the witness who watched the beauty salon from the building across the street, saw Fiss's killer touch the exterior of the beauty salon's front glass door as he entered or exited—but this was where police said they found Porter's thumbprint.

Vincent Gentile's testimony identifying Porter as one of the jewelry store robbers and Valente's identification of him as the man leaving the beauty salon were central to establishing the chain of links in the prosecution's argument. But right after Porter was arrested, the police showed Valente a photo array that included Porter and several other men, and asked her to try and identify the beautician's killer. She declined to look at the photos. In court, Valente said she was positive Porter was the man she'd seen leaving the Fiss beauty salon, but at no time did she ever pick Porter from a lineup or photo spread.

The prosecution could have linked Porter to the murder even if Catherine Valente's testimony and the fingerprint were called into question. Vincent Gentile identified Porter, officer Rossiter saw Porter throw something away that was later found to be a gun, and the weapon was linked by ballistics experts to the Fiss murder. But without a direct way to link Porter to the beauty salon, each of these links was essential to the prosecution's case.

Much rested on the testimony of Vincent Gentile, who was a respected member of the community. But in 2006, with Porter still on death row—and still maintaining his innocence—Gentile made an extraordinary admission: "On April 30, 1985, my Philadelphia jewelry store was robbed. Ernest Porter was subsequently arrested and charged with the robbery. When I later saw Mr. Porter at the preliminary hearing for the robbery, I did not recognize him. I told a woman who worked in the court that Mr. Porter was not the person who robbed my jewelry store. She said that defendants always look different once they are in court and that the evidence showed that he was the one who robbed my store. Once I was told he was guilty of the robbery of my store, I did whatever the prosecution wanted, which included testifying about the gun at Mr. Porter's homicide trial as well as at the robbery trial. However, in my heart, I knew that Mr. Porter was not one of the men who robbed my store."

Eberhardt's study pointed a finger at juries who sentenced men such as Ernest Porter to death, but it seems clear that jurors were not exclusively to blame. I cannot help but wonder whether darker skin tone and features not only unconsciously predispose juries to view some convicts harshly, but also unconsciously bias police, prosecutors, and even defense attorneys to weigh some lives more lightly than others.

Ernest Porter has been on death row for nearly a quarter century. I interviewed him several times at the close-security prison near Pittsburgh that houses most of Pennsylvania's death row inmates. Access to the area where prisoners talk to visitors was controlled by a series of five remote-controlled doors. Fences that seemed at least thirty feet high crisscrossed the prison; they were topped with loops of shiny barbed wire. Guards kept watch from turrets. Visitors were patted down, made to walk through metal detectors, and sniffed by dogs. I was separated from Porter by a solid glass window; we communicated using telephones. He was always in an orange jumpsuit and always had his wrists handcuffed in front of him. Porter had short curly hair, and a mustache. Deep furrows lined his forehead.

He did not seem particularly interested in Eberhardt's thesis that racism plays a role in death penalty sentencing. "There's nothing new about this," he told me on one occasion, as I tried to explain what the psychologist had found. "Wake up. You live in America."

Porter said the prosecution had initially offered his lawyer a deal— a guilty plea in exchange for life imprisonment.

"I said, 'You have to be crazy,' " Porter told me, as he explained how he'd expected the trial to show he was innocent.

A number of medical and psychiatric experts over the years have documented that Porter suffered from a range of mental problems, including delusions and mental retardation. (Porter's defense lawyer presented no medical experts to testify about his mental health, even though the lawyer had access to extensive files detailing Porter's impairments and his horrific history of sexual and physical abuse as a child. Even if Porter were found guilty, the mitigating information may have headed off a death sentence.) Porter seemed severely impaired to me. His moods were variable; a broad smile could be replaced by a hostile glare in the briefest flash. He was suspicious of everyone. He told me that he expected police to kill Vincent Gentile for retracting his testimony. He worried that his lawyers at the Federal Defender Office in Philadelphia did not have his best interests at heart. He believed prosecutors engaged in a conspiracy with police to have him framed.

He spoke in jerks and stops. He left many sentences—and many thoughts—unfinished. He constantly repeated the phrase "here it is" as conversation filler. He told me it took him hours to understand what his legal papers said; composing a simple note in response was an arduous challenge.

Porter's account of events on the day of his arrest is light-years from what prosecutors alleged. He told me that he had stepped out to catch a bus and had been caught up in an indiscriminate sweep of African American men by police hunting down the jewelry store robbers. He said he knew nothing about any guns, jewelry store robberies—or dead beauticians. Porter believed the Philadelphia police framed him because an angry public had wanted someone in its crosshairs, and he was a perfect fit for every preconception of a dangerous criminal.

"You need only a few of these cases to run for public office if you are like Ed Rendell," Porter told me, referring to the city's then district attorney, who is now the Democratic governor of Pennsylvania. It is ironic, but the man who helped put Porter on death row might be the only person to stand at the eleventh hour between Porter and a lethal injection.

Porter's legal case is in a strange limbo. A federal district court upheld a plea filed by the Federal Defender Office that said Judge Sabo's jury instructions during the sentencing phase were flawed, and the federal district court ruled that Porter should not be executed. But the court simultaneously upheld Porter's guilty conviction after prosecutors argued that the case stood regardless of Sabo's poor instructions and Gentile's retraction. Porter's lawyers went to the federal appeals court for the third circuit to argue that Porter ought to be exonerated; the state of Pennsylvania, meanwhile, appealed to the same court to argue that Porter was guilty and that he deserved to be executed.

Porter remains on death row as of this writing, pending the outcomes of these cross appeals. Each day, he told me, he wakes early, exercises, and has a "birdbath" in his sink. After breakfast, he spends a couple of hours outdoors, locked in a cage with another death row inmate. The cage is about eight feet high, seven feet long, and five feet wide. He gets a basketball, but is told that it is a security violation if the ball slams against the cage. He spends the rest of the day and night in his cell. On weekends, Porter spends twenty-four hours a day in his cell. He gets to shower on Mondays, Wednesdays, and Fridays.

Porter told me his cell is eight feet long and six feet high. It has a solid door and two small windows. (The prison declined my request to visit Porter's unit.) When Porter places his ear at a vent, he indistinctly hears the voice of the inmate in the next cell. He told me he talks at length to the walls and the floor.

Porter reiterated his innocence repeatedly, but conceded his account was unlikely to be believed. If his version is true, it would imply a conspiracy involving several members of the Philadelphia police department, all the way from fingerprint experts to homicide detectives, with possible collusion from prosecutors. I have asked myself many times whether I believe Porter, and I must say I am not convinced. But perhaps that is the wrong question. The real point is not whether I believe Porter's claims but whether I believe the prosecution's claims. Is the case against Porter as airtight as we would like a case to be before we execute someone? I have a difficult time saying the answer to that question is yes.

Porter painted a picture of city and police misconduct that seems unbelievable—except that ten days after he was arrested in 1985, the same city and police department bombed their own town. With permission from the mayor, police dropped a bomb on the rooftop of a small radical group known as MOVE. The fire that resulted burned down sixty-one houses and killed eleven members of the group, including five children. Over the span of two decades, the city of Philadelphia has spent upward of forty million dollars investigating the events that led to the bombing, paying settlements to victims, and rebuilding. The city block the police so recklessly razed was in predominantly black west Philadelphia.

"My whole life is wasted for crimes I never even done," the man the state of Pennsylvania calls Ernest Porter told me. "You go to sleep with death on your mind and you go through your day with death on your mind. It's enough to drive you crazy."

CHAPTER 9

Disarming the Bomb

Politics, Race, and the Hidden Brain

n 1994, the psychologist Anthony Greenwald at the University of Washington was exploring links between unconscious mental associations and attitudes. I've talked about such associations before. Our hidden brain notices discrete things that regularly appear together and associates them—every time we see one thing, it prompts us to expect the other, too. We associate insects with stings and annoyance, rattlesnakes with bites and danger, and a garbage dump with disgust. There is nothing mysterious about this. Over the course of our lives, we have seen innumerable links between insects and stings, snakes and danger, and garbage and rot.

Greenwald guessed that if he gave people a word, they would be faster matching concepts that were associated with that word than concepts that were not associated. It should be easier to bring "America" to mind when someone said "baseball" than when someone said "badminton." Greenwald designed a word association game. He put the names of a number of flowers in a list with the names of various insects, and then threw in a number of positive and negative words such as "beauty," "love," "nasty," and "ugly." Unsurprisingly, he found it very easy to group "roses" and "tulips" with "beauty" and "love," and "cockroach" and "beetle" with "nasty" and "ugly." When he put all the words in a single list and timed himself as he put a check mark next to all the flowers and the positive words, he completed the task a little faster than when he tried to check off all the flowers and the negative words. Every time his hidden brain heard "rose" or "tulip," it automatically provided him with the positive associations that people usually have with flowers. When he encountered "beauty" and "love," he checked them off quickly. When he encountered "nasty" and "ugly," his conscious mind had to connect the unrelated concepts—and resist the hidden brain's answers. Predictably, this took longer. So far, the test had not told Greenwald anything he didn't know. Who needs a test to find out he or she associates flowers with beauty?

But Greenwald did not stop there. He replaced the names of the flowers and insects in his list with typically Caucasian names such as Adam and Chip and typically African American names such as Alonzo and Jamal, and then tossed in a bunch of pleasant and unpleasant words. He tried to play the same association game. Since he didn't consciously associate either Caucasian or African American names with positive or negative concepts, he assumed he would associate all the names with pleasant and unpleasant words at the same speed. He was wrong. He found it was as difficult to associate "white names" with unpleasant words as it was to associate flowers with unpleasant words. But Greenwald's hidden brain effortlessly associated "black names" with words such as "evil" and "poison." It was as if his hidden brain equated white names with positive concepts and black names with negative concepts. Greenwald was horrified. He didn't think of himself as a racist, and he didn't know what to make of his performance.

He got in touch with a colleague, the psychologist Mahzarin Banaji. Without telling her what the test was about, he asked her to play the word association game on her computer. Banaji found she had results identical to Greenwald's. She effortlessly associated white names with positive concepts and black names with negative concepts. *That's ridiculous,* she thought. She knew she was no racist. She was a professor who spent lots of time teaching *other* people how to watch out for prejudice. Since Greenwald's test required Banaji to tap computer keys with her left or right index finger, Banaji figured the weird results had to do with whether someone was right-handed or left-handed, so she reorganized the test on her computer. All of a sudden, it was now her other hand that effortlessly grouped black names with negative words and white names with positive words. Banaji changed the order in which the names were presented. It made no difference. Her hidden brain simply found it easier to associate "Alonzo" and "Jamal" with "evil" and "poison," and "Adam" and "Chip" with "dream" and "heaven." Banaji sat back in her chair and stared. She felt small in a way she had never felt before.

This is the origin of a psychological test for unconscious bias that has revolutionized the scientific study of prejudice in the last decade. Greenwald dubbed it the Implicit Association Test, or IAT. Millions of people have taken the free Internet tests that he and Banaji have made available over the Internet—at www.implicit.harvard.edu. If you take what is known as the race bias test today, you'll see white and black faces instead of names, since this provides more accurate results. Hundreds of thousands of people have been disconcerted by their scores. Large majorities of Americans—including substantial numbers of African Americans—find it easier to associate white faces rather than black faces with positive concepts. Overwhelming majorities find it easier to associate men's names rather than women's names with careers and professional activity. The tests detect things that seem absurd. Many Americans are quicker to associate the British actors Hugh Grant and Elizabeth Hurley with being American than the tennis player Michael Chang and the television personality Connie Chung. It is as though their unconscious minds associate whites—even whites who are foreigners—as American, and Americans who are people of color as foreigners. In one set of tests before the 2008 presidential election, psychologists found that many voters unconsciously associated former British prime minister Tony Blair with being more American than Barack Obama. If you'd asked volunteers which one, Blair or Obama, was American, of course, they would have looked at you funny. If people knew—at a conscious level—that Obama was American and Blair was foreign, why did their unconscious minds have the opposite associations? With every variation of the test, volunteers responded exactly as Greenwald and Banaji had to that first test: with disbelief.

If the only thing the Implicit Association Test did was to make people feel bad about the unpleasant associations in their heads, the test would not be very useful. Ultimately, we're interested in people's behavior, not in "thought crimes." But over the past decade, many experiments have shown that results on the Implicit Association Test predict people's behavior in real-world settings. In tests conducted before the 2008 presidential election, for example, the speed at which people unconsciously associated Obama with being American predicted whether they supported the biracial candidate in both the Democratic primary and the general election. People who unconsciously saw Obama as less American than Hillary Clinton and John McCain were less likely to vote for him. This was so even if—when explicitly asked—they stated Obama was every bit as American as his competitors.

It is useful to situate all conversations about race in their proper context: Voting against Obama did not automatically make anyone a racist. And race bias was just one factor in how people thought about politics. Race bias in the 2008 presidential election may have pulled the country a few percentage points in one direction. The bias would not have made a difference to the way most people voted, but it could have tipped people on the edge one way rather than the other. The bias affected both Republicans and Democrats. At an unconscious level, not seeing Obama as American exerted a subtle tug on people. It made them less likely to want to see him elected president. Remember, we are *not* talking about people who consciously thought of Obama as a foreigner with a doctored birth certificate. We're talking about people who never would've said aloud—or even to themselves—that they disliked Obama because he was foreign. But when they thought about the candidates, Obama may have just felt a little different. Hillary Clinton, John McCain, and Sarah Palin may have felt a little more "like one of us." Once people felt that way, they could easily have come up with reasons to support their intuitions. You can always find things about a candidate to like or dislike.

How do we know that unconscious attitudes about Obama preceded the conscious justification of those attitudes? In the experiment, it was people's unconscious attitudes—as revealed by Greenwald's test—rather than their conscious views about the issues, that better predicted whether they voted for Obama or preferred another candidate. The idea that we provide ourselves with explanations to justify our conclusions is counterintuitive because it certainly feels as though our conclusions are the product of careful thought. Here is an analogy that might help—this is not an original idea of mine. Let's say you kick a soccer ball into the air. Imagine that as it flies, the ball suddenly acquires consciousness. How would it explain to itself why it is flying? It has no knowledge or awareness of having been kicked. But since it knows that all effects have causes, it tells itself that it is a ball that decided to fly, because that's the most plausible explanation. In the same way, once the hidden brain whispered to these voters that Obama was different, they quickly came up with plausible ways to explain to themselves why they didn't like the candidate—his views on health care, perhaps, or the economy.

These results are upsetting and embarrassing. We know we are decades away from Selma and Birmingham, from those bad old days when women were not allowed to vote. We've changed, haven't we? Banaji once told me that the embarrassment she and others felt after doing the Implicit Association Test was a good thing. It showed that people not only believed they were not biased, but that they did not *want* to be biased.

Banaji, Greenwald, and another psychologist named Brian Nosek at the University of Virginia have studied the results of hundreds of thousands of volunteers who have taken the Implicit Association Test on the Internet. The psychologists have created a map of America that shows the peaks and valleys of bias, the places where unconscious racial prejudice is highest and where it is lowest. Nosek has found, for example, that people in the second congressional district of New Jersey, which is nestled between the Delaware Bay and the Atlantic Ocean, have higher average levels of race bias than those in the twenty-seventh congressional district in the Deep South of Texas, which includes the towns of Corpus Christi and Brownsville. Volunteers in Alabama's first congressional district, centered around Mobile, show higher unconscious racial bias than those in the ninth congressional district of California, which includes Oakland and Berkeley.

Nosek overlaid his map of unconscious anti-black race bias on a map of electoral outcomes in all congressional races. He found a remarkable association between bias scores and political views—the higher the unconscious race bias scores in a congressional district, the more likely the district was to elect a Republican. (The psychological research into the relationship between racial bias and political outcomes in the United States has focused mainly on bias against blacks. Ongoing research is exploring the effects of bias against other minorities.)

If racial bias had nothing to do with politics, and if the implicit association test was meaningless, as some of its critics have argued, there ought to be no correlation between bias scores and political orientation. But Nosek saw a very clear pattern. On average, districts with the greatest racial bias were more likely to vote for conservatives, and districts with the lowest racial bias tended to vote liberal. The difference, it should be emphasized, was a matter of degree. Large numbers of people in the Bay Area revealed the same anti-black or pro-white attitudes as people in Mobile, Alabama. But on a sliding scale, some areas showed greater levels of bias than others.

This doesn't mean that you can look at a district's race bias scores and automatically predict whether the district will elect a Republican or a Democrat. As I said, bias is only one factor in people's political views—and it is far from being the most important factor. Some of the districts with the lowest bias scores—such as the second congressional district of Idaho, which includes the towns of Idaho Falls and Pocatello—are strongly Republican, while some districts with high bias scores—such as the first congressional district of North Carolina—elected a Democrat in 2006 and 2008.

There are places where race bias appears to be irrelevant to election outcomes, and places where it seems to play a substantial role. But of the ten congressional districts with the highest bias scores among white voters, eight were won by Republicans in the 2008 elections, and only two by Democrats. The ten districts with the lowest bias scores revealed the opposite pattern—seven were won by Democrats and only three by Republicans.

Race bias scores predicted not only whether liberals or conservatives got elected, but what kind of liberals and conservatives got elected. Fully half the districts with the lowest bias scores elected people of color. Only one district with the highest bias scores elected a person of color (and he was a Democrat). Five of the seven Democrats elected in the districts with the lowest bias scores were Asian, Hispanic, and African American. All the Republicans elected in the districts with the highest bias scores were white.

In two of the districts with the highest bias scores—the first congressional district of Alabama and the ninth congressional district of North Carolina—control of the seat switched from one political party to the other in the middle of the civil rights movement. This was part of the dramatic shift in the American South away from the Democratic party in the 1960s, owing to the Democratic party's support of civil rights legislation that guaranteed voting rights and dismantled legalized segregation. The first congressional district of Alabama elected Democrats from 1877 to 1963—eighty-six years—but elected a Republican in every subsequent election through 2008. The ninth congressional district of North Carolina had elected a Democrat for twenty-two straight years before 1963; starting in 1964, the district elected Republicans for more than four straight decades.

Since we are talking about science, we ought to examine the research with a skeptical eye. Is the link between racial bias scores and political orientation merely a correlation, or is there a causative connection? If you see a lot of people holding umbrellas and wearing rain boots, it would be wrong to say that wearing rain boots causes people to hold umbrellas. The two things are related, but one does not cause the other. Both are caused by something else, the fact that it is raining. Could an unrelated third factor be responsible for both racial bias and political orientation? Second, isn't it possible that the connection between race and politics is better explained by simple demographics? People of color tend to vote for Democrats, so there ought to be a connection between diversity and whether a district elects a Republican or a Democrat. What does racial *bias* tell us that the racial *makeup* of a district does not?

The question about correlation and causation cannot be answered with certainty. It is possible that the connection between race bias and political conservatism is only a correlation. The only way to prove causation is to conduct the kind of experiment that is impossible in real life: You change some people's unconscious racial attitudes and see if their political orientation fluctuates in response. If it does, you know that racial attitudes are influencing how people think about politics. Nosek believes the relationship flows in both directions—race bias contributes to conservatism, and vice versa—and that both might also be influenced by other factors. People who are sensitive to threat, for example, tend to adopt conservative views and are also suspicious of people from other groups.

The second question—the interaction between racial bias and racial makeup—has a clear answer. The demographic makeup of a district seems to act like a switch that sometimes brings racial bias into play, and sometimes eliminates it from the equation. Anti-black race bias does not seem to play much of a role in districts that have very few black people. It is only when a district starts to show an element of diversity that unconscious race bias seems to influence voting decisions. In other words, everyday contact between whites and blacks appears necessary to make bias salient—to bring into play racial attitudes that lurk beneath the surface. Remember the study by Jennifer Eberhardt into sentencing disparities? The sentencing disparities showed up only in cases involving black-on-white crime, not in cases involving same-race crime.

In the same way, the presence of blacks in a congressional district seems to make race bias relevant to the voting decisions of whites. But when there are a very large number of blacks in a district, the connection between race bias and political orientation among white voters is drowned out by the fact that blacks tend to vote for Democrats, and so districts that have a lot of blacks invariably end up electing Democrats. White voters in congressional districts where racial minorities make up more than, say, 40 percent of the electorate certainly tend to vote Republican—the presence of minorities makes race relevant to the voting decisions of whites—but the tidal wave of people of color voting in the other direction renders that bias irrelevant.

So, again, when there are few or no minorities, race bias doesn't seem to have much of an effect on political outcomes—the "switch" is turned off. And when there are lots of minorities, the effect of racial bias is again irrelevant because the tendency of whites to vote Republican in these areas is canceled out by the tendency of blacks and other minorities to vote for Democrats. Race bias seems to tip congressional seats only in districts where you have both high bias scores among whites and a minority population that is sizable enough to be visible in everyday settings but not so large as to control the congressional district's electoral destiny. Nosek estimated that race bias accounted for no more than 10 percent of the political variation in the country overall—hardly decisive, except in close races. Even this relatively small effect, however, produces clear patterns nationally between racial attitudes and voting outcomes.

Many conservatives plaintively ask why psychologists don't spend more time analyzing the voting behavior of people of color. Nearly all African American voters, for example, voted for Barack Obama in the 2008 presidential election. People of color, in general, vote overwhelmingly for Democrats. Isn't this a bias, too? It certainly is. I don't think it is an unconscious bias, however. Many people of color enthusiastically supported Obama because they wanted to elect the first nonwhite president. This is emphatically not the case with unconscious race bias and conservatism—white voters tell us that race has nothing to do with their political views. If most research focuses on the biases of white voters, it is also because these biases matter more. There are more white voters in the United States than voters who are people of any other race, and a bias that affects whites is likely to be consequential in a way that a bias among a minority group is not. History also tells us what to focus on. We have never had a female president, so it would be silly to spend time studying why some voters may be biased in favor of women instead of asking why voters are biased in favor of men.

Making connections between racial bias and politics always gets people upset. But if you look at this data calmly, you can say two things. One, the race bias data does not provide liberals with a cudgel with which to bash conservatives. Yes, it is true that, on average, districts with higher bias scores tend to vote Republican and districts with lower bias scores tend to vote for Democrats, but the fact is that race bias is surprisingly common across political orientations. A large majority of Americans, including substantial numbers of African Americans, hold negative associations with black faces and positive associations with white faces.

But it is undeniably true that there is a steady association between higher racial bias scores and a conservative orientation, on this and other psychological tests. We do not know whether race bias makes people politically conservative, whether conservatism tends to prompt people to adopt racially biased attitudes, or whether some third factor causes both. But if you are a patriotic Republican who passionately believes in the American ideal that all people are created equal, these results ought to be disconcerting.

In the 1980s, the Democratic pollster Stan Greenberg identified a group of voters in Macomb County, Michigan. They were blue-collar workers—often union members—who had been staunch Democrats for decades. They voted their pocketbooks, and it was the Democratic party that defended their economic interests. But starting in the mid-1960s, a substantial number of these voters switched parties. Greenberg found that in the 1980s, these voters supported Ronald Reagan, and Greenberg dubbed them Reagan Democrats, a term that has endured. Every four years, the national and international media descend on Macomb County ahead of presidential elections to see what the Reagan Democrats are up to. A few years ago, the plaintive book *What's the Matter with Kansas?* asked why so many blue-collar folks were voting Republican, when their economic interests lay with the Democratic party. Author Thomas Frank concluded, in large part, that these voters were influenced by hot-button cultural issues such as abortion, gay rights, and guns.

Frank argued that the Reagan Democrats ought to vote their pocketbooks by supporting labor rights, progressive taxation, business regulation, health care reform, and other policies traditionally championed by the left. Republican politicians typically ask voters to vote their values—often defined by evangelical Christianity—ahead of class and pocketbook, particularly when it comes to issues such as abortion and the role of religion in public life. This is all perfectly acceptable grounds for disagreement. Liberals can disagree with someone who votes for president using abortion as a litmus test, and conservatives can disagree with voters who do not place religious values at the core of their political beliefs—but both sides have to acknowledge that these are all legitimate ways to determine one's political choices. However, many Democratic pollsters have argued that the Reagan Democrats' switch in political allegiance was not made on legitimate grounds. Rather, the switch was driven by an issue that we can all agree ought to be illegitimate in politics: racial bias.

Let's start with what polls and electoral data tell us: If only white people could vote in U.S. presidential elections, the Republican candidate would always win. Democrats did not capture the majority of the white vote in a single presidential election between 1964 and 2008, including during back-to-back wins by Bill Clinton in the 1990s and Barack Obama's "landslide" victory in 2008. Successful Democratic presidential candidates manage to split the white vote, or get close, and then win a majority among people of color. White men in particular have overwhelmingly drifted away from the Democratic party, and this trend more than any other has produced Republican victories in two thirds of the presidential elections held between 1964 and 2008.

If only white men were allowed to vote in elections in the United States today, it would be a complete waste of money to conduct an election at all. Pollsters will tell you that it is inconceivable for Democratic presidential candidates to win or even split the votes of white males. When successful Democratic candidates manage to split the overall white vote, it is usually because they reduce the magnitude of their loss among white men and gain an advantage among white women. For all of the talk of Barack Obama's "post-racial" win in the 2008 presidential race, he would have *lost* in a landslide if the election had been limited to white voters. Obama won only 43 percent of the white vote nationwide and less than a third of white voters in the South. According to the National Election Pool exit poll, conducted by Edison/Mitofsky, only 28 pecent of Southern white men voted for Obama. Such numbers usually portend defeat for Democrats; Obama overcame his poor showing among white voters by racking up mammoth support among younger voters and people of color.

But the fact that whites—and white men in particular—tend to vote Republican is not sufficient to conclude that racial bias is at work. If you were to talk to the blue-collar voters of Macomb County who moved away from the Democratic party, most would emphatically tell you they were not motivated by racial animus. To many, even the suggestion would be offensive. And it is not as though Republican politicians make overt pleas to racial bias. Very often, race is never even mentioned in campaign materials, stump speeches, and party platforms. Most presidential elections, moreover, have featured two white males running against each other. So how do we know that the charge of race bias is not a fiction dreamed up by Democratic partisans who are unhappy that a group of voters have drifted away from their column?

Let's look at the issues that many of these blue-collar voters themselves cite to explain why they drifted away from the Democratic party over the last quarter century. These voters gravitated toward conservative candidates *before* gay marriage and abortion became hot issues. Concerns about crime, welfare, and affirmative action topped their list of concerns starting in the 1970s, and it is these issues—along with more recent concerns about drugs and illegal immigration—that have provided Republican candidates with their most potent electoral weapons. Affirmative action has an explicitly racial component to it, so let's leave it out of the discussion. But there is nothing inherently racial about welfare or crime, is there? You have white families on welfare and black families on welfare, law-abiding whites and law-abiding blacks, white criminals and black criminals. Who can disagree that there ought to be less crime and fewer people dependent on public assistance?

Conservatives have long provided a rational—if debatable—argument against welfare. They've argued that it provides perverse economic incentives for broken families and that it encourages laziness. If single mothers with children can get welfare while married mothers with children do not, does this not create an incentive for mothers to have their children raised in single-parent households? If you tie the size of a family's welfare check to the number of children a single mother is supporting, doesn't it create a perverse incentive for her to have many more children than she could raise successfully? And since welfare programs are directed primarily at the poor, doesn't the regular arrival of a check from the government discourage the poor from working? If welfare recipients were to go out and get even a moderately well-paying job, the check would stop. These are the familiar talking points of the anti-welfare argument. Here is how the conservative Heritage Foundation puts it: "Higher welfare payments do not assist children; they increase dependence and illegitimacy, which have a devastatingly negative effect on children's development. It is welfare dependence, rather than poverty, which has the most negative effect on children."

Whatever your political views, and regardless of whether you agree with the Heritage Foundation's thesis, all sensible people ought to be concerned about the potentially perverse effects of an ostensibly high-minded program.

In all of this discussion, voters and politicians emphatically tell us that race plays no role in their feelings about welfare. But is this true? This is precisely the kind of question that social psychologists have studied for decades. When people say bias plays no role, there are good reasons to believe they are telling pollsters what they believe to be true. They are not saying race is irrelevant when they secretly know it matters; in their hearts, these voters likely feel no racial animus. But that does not tell us what is going on in their hidden brains.

What kind of a mental image springs to the minds of these voters when you speak to them about welfare or crime? If race bias plays no role, it ought to be just as likely for white welfare recipients or white criminals to come to mind as black welfare recipients and black criminals.

Researchers have conducted a number of experiments along these lines. The basic idea behind the experiments is very simple. You divide a group of white voters at random into two groups and give them campaign materials criticizing welfare—using the race-neutral arguments of the Heritage Foundation. One group, however, hears about the problem through the use of an illustrative white family on welfare; another hears about the problem through an illustrative black family on welfare. If the debate around welfare is only about personal responsibility, dignity of work, and economic fairness, it should make no difference that one group sees a black family while another group sees a white family. The issue has nothing to do with race, so you would expect there would be just as many people in each of these groups who are persuaded that welfare is—or isn't—a problem. On the other hand, if race is an issue—never explicitly mentioned, but a factor in the hidden brain—then the group that hears about the issue through an illustrative black family should end up being more critical of welfare than the group that hears about the problem through an illustrative white family. The same would go for crime. If lowering crime is a race-neutral issue, as it ostensibly ought to be, it ought to make no difference if you make a pitch about the importance of reducing crime to one group of voters using an illustrative black criminal and a pitch to another group of voters using an illustrative white criminal.

Martin Gilens at Princeton University once conducted an experiment along these lines. He asked a number of white Americans about their views on welfare. He then gave them an example of a woman in her thirties who had a ten-year-old child and was on welfare. Gilens told some volunteers—picked at random—that the woman was black, and told others that the woman was white. He asked all the respondents their overall views on welfare. Gilens found that volunteers had about the same level of negativity toward the white welfare mom as toward the black welfare mom—which seemingly supports the Heritage Foundation's argument that opposition to welfare is race-neutral. But Gilens found that negative attitudes toward the black welfare mom played a more powerful role than negative attitudes toward the white welfare mom in driving people's overall views about welfare. Seeing the benefits of welfare accrue to a black woman made volunteers significantly more hostile to welfare as a whole than seeing benefits accrue to a white woman. Gilens also found that volunteers told about a welfare mom whose race was not identified automatically tended to invoke an image of a black woman rather than a white woman, even though there were more whites on welfare than blacks. More African Americans are on welfare as a proportion of the overall black population than is the case with whites, but if I sit a welfare recipient behind a screen and ask you to guess his or her race, it is absolute numbers that count, not ratios. Since there are more whites who receive welfare than blacks, the odds are that the person behind the screen will be white. Why do so many people believe the person will be black?

Gilens eventually concluded that unconscious racial attitudes were the single most important determinant of welfare views among his white volunteers. It was not that their opinions about self-reliance and individualism did not matter; they did. But if you took a group of people with the same views about self-reliance, hard work, and personal responsibility and talked to them about welfare, they were much more likely to automatically visualize a black person than a white person. Thinking about a black person, moreover, prompted many more people to decide they were against welfare in general, because negative opinions about blacks on welfare were more potent than negative opinions about whites on welfare.

What does this mean if you are a political strategist or a politician who is hoping—cynically or instinctively—to take advantage of racial bias? It means that all you have to do is talk about welfare in general, and voters' hidden brains will do the rest for you. This does not mean that every politician who expresses a concern about "welfare queens" is motivated by race bias. The insidious thing is that it is impossible to tell whether a given politician is raising a concern about welfare because of his or her ideological beliefs about self-reliance or because he or she is trying to exploit racial bias—or both. Short of conducting an experiment, it is similarly impossible to tell if a given voter's views stem from a belief in self-reliance or from racial bias, or both. You can instantly see why this is a potent political tool. Racial appeals can now be embedded in a conversation that ostensibly has nothing to do with race.

The same phenomenon is true with crime. George H. W. Bush's use of the "Willie Horton" ad in the 1988 presidential election is widely credited with his demolition of Democrat Michael Dukakis. Horton was a convicted murderer in Massachusetts who raped and stabbed a Maryland woman while on a weekend furlough. Dukakis, as governor of Massachusetts, inherited the furlough program from a prior governor and eventually shut it down, but Bush painted him as being slow to dismantle the program and therefore soft on crime. Much was made of the ad because it lingered on the image of Horton's black face, and Bush was accused of exploiting racial bias. But the photo was just the icing. It's hardly necessary to show a black man's face to evoke the image of a black criminal in the minds of white voters; all you have to do is talk about crime in general and their hidden brains will supply a picture of a violent black man.

Many other issues work the same way. Everyone can agree that the drug trade has devastated communities, but if talk about drugs unconsciously and automatically evokes an image of black people smoking crack rather than white people snorting cocaine or if people have greater fears about drug dealers who are black or brown than about drug dealers who are white, you can exploit race bias without ever making a reference to race. Ditto for illegal immigration. If talk of "illegal aliens" brings a Hispanic person to mind rather than a white immigrant, or if Hispanic illegal immigrants conjure a more threatening and malevolent picture in our minds than white illegal immigrants, you can appeal to race bias without ever mentioning—even to yourself—that the real problem you have with illegal immigration is brown people.

The psychologist Robert W. Livingston once told volunteers about a crime in which a Milwaukee woman had been severely injured following an assault by an illegal immigrant. Some volunteers were told the criminal was from Canada and named David Edmonds. Others were told the criminal was from Mexico and named Juan Luis Martinez. Livingston asked his volunteers to play juror and decide on an appropriate prison sentence. The volunteers recommended a longer prison sentence for the Mexican, even though both fictional illegal immigrants had committed exactly the same crime.

Once people's attitudes are influenced by bias, even their basic perception of facts can change. In 1982, at a time when Ronald Reagan was drumming up concerns about welfare, a CBS/*New York Times* survey asked people this question: "Of all the people who are poor in this country, are more of them black or are more of them white?" More than half of all Americans believed there were more poor black people than poor white people in the United States. African Americans at the time constituted 28 percent of Americans who were poor, according to U.S. Census Bureau definitions of poverty.

In a more recent survey of Illinois voters some years ago, when the issue of welfare reform was very hot, more than 60 percent of respondents overestimated—by a factor of 100 percent—the number of Americans who were on welfare. One in three volunteers grossly overestimated the number of African Americans on welfare, and two in five overestimated the size of welfare payments that families received. Ninety percent of the respondents greatly overestimated the amount of the federal budget spent on welfare. The errors were not small. There was not one factual question related to welfare where the majority of respondents got the right answer, or even came close. Americans believed that welfare recipients were more numerous, more lucratively compensated, and more likely to be black than the facts warranted. Those who made the largest errors, and believed the most inaccurate facts, were often the most confident about the accuracy of their views. It was all the doing of the hidden brain, of course—and a gold mine for politicians willing to exploit such bias.

"All of us can agree there are issues that are not matters of preference but matters of fact," Mahzarin Banaji once told me. "The reason this is powerful is, it shows our minds will not just distort our preferences, but distort facts."

I believe that, like bias among Frances Aboud's preschoolers, voters can end up with racial bias in adulthood without ever intending to be biased, without anyone deliberately instilling bias in their hearts, and with everyone trying their utmost not to be biased. I am not suggesting that political campaigns do not explicitly exploit racial fears by talking about welfare, crime, and illegal immigration; they do. But the reason those campaigns work is that when you talk about those issues, it is minorities who automatically spring to the minds of many voters.

Why do so many Americans automatically think of a black criminal or a black welfare recipient when they think about crime and welfare? The fact that disproportionate numbers of African Americans *are* poor and *do* get in trouble with the law does not explain why so many people automatically bring blacks to mind during discussions of crime and welfare. As the Illinois survey showed, many people don't merely think more blacks *as a proportion of the black population* receive welfare than do whites, they overestimate the absolute number of blacks on welfare. If the perception of black poverty and criminality is out of line with the statistical evidence, where does it come from?

Part of the answer has been well-explored: Media representations of criminals and welfare recipients are often skewed. Media coverage regularly reflects existing stereotypes—the black murderer seems more newsworthy than the white murderer—and the heightened news coverage of certain crimes in turn strengthens the stereotype.

But I believe there is a more important explanation, and it is rather mundane. (As I said at the start, we seek dramatic explanations for dramatic phenomena. Much of the hidden brain's power, however, lies in the fact that its influence is subtle and mundane.) Even if media coverage were not biased and the proportion of people on welfare and in trouble with the law were absolutely identical among all ethnic groups, large numbers of Americans would still mentally inflate the number of minorities who are poor or violent and undercount the number of whites who are poor or violent. Minorities have a disproportionate risk of being linked with negative associations *for no better reason than that they are minorities.*

You can show this in everyday settings that are less emotionally charged than welfare and crime. Divide a group of one hundred people into two groups, A and B, with eighty of them assigned to group A and twenty of them assigned to group B. Make everyone in group A wear red and everyone in group B wear blue—so that every person's group membership is visible and easily identifiable. Tell all the people about ten instances when members of these groups took an unauthorized cookie from the cookie jar; eight of the cookie stealers were from group A and two from group B. If you later ask people in group A to guess the *total* number of cookie stealers in each group, they are likely to overestimate the number of cookie stealers in group B and underestimate the number of cookie stealers in group A. They may even feel that there are a larger number of cookie stealers in group B than in group A. When you mention cookie stealing to someone from group A, a person from group B can come more readily to mind. People in group A, in other words, can greatly overestimate the number of cookie stealers in group B for no better reason than that group B is smaller than group A—and everyone belonging to groups A and B are clearly identifiable.

Aberrational things done by people in a highly visible minority group stick up in our minds more dramatically than aberrational things done by members of a majority group. The technical term for this phenomenon is an illusory correlation. If you ask people in Thailand whether Thai men or white male tourists from the United States are more likely to be child molesters, they can easily tell you that there are more American pedophiles than locals. That's because, in Thailand, white males are a highly visible minority. Aberrational things that they do will be more memorable to Thai people than aberrational things done by locals.

There is experimental evidence to back up what I have just told you. Researchers once divided volunteers into two groups. Both were shown a fifteen-minute excerpt of a local TV news program. In the middle of the newscast, right after a commercial break, the volunteers saw a story involving a violent crime. The story featured a photograph of a suspect. Without the volunteers' knowledge, researchers digitally altered the complexion of the suspect so that some volunteers saw a suspect who appeared white while others saw a suspect who appeared black. Every other detail of the crime story remained identical.

As with the welfare study, the experiment showed that viewers shown the photo of a black suspect ended up more worried about crime than those shown the photograph of a white suspect. But that was not all. Volunteers shown a white suspect did not associate criminality with whites as a whole, but volunteers shown a black suspect tended to associate criminality with blacks as a whole. (Gilens similarly found that his volunteers didn't think that black welfare recipients were lazy; they thought *blacks as a whole* were lazy.) This is how illusory correlations work: When two unusual events take place simultaneously, our hidden brain subtly biases us to see the events as linked, even if they have nothing to do with each other. The consequences of this bias can be gigantic, but the underlying phenomenon is mundane and shows up in innumerable everyday contexts. If you happen to have stomach upsets on two mornings because of something you ate, and you also happen to be catching flights on each of those days, your hidden brain will bias you into believing that flights bring on stomach upsets. If the error were limited to believing that those two flights brought on a bad stomach, it would be one thing. But the bias causes you to believe that *all* flights bring on stomach upsets.

How can we defend against such bias in politics? The troubling thing is that most voters—and perhaps most politicians—do not understand where their attitudes and beliefs and facts come from. At an explicit level, people may talk and think only about issues. They worry about crime, illegal immigration, and drugs. There is nothing biased about this. It is perfectly legitimate to want to see less crime, to want to see immigration laws enforced, and to want to control the abuse and trafficking of narcotics. Critics of tough immigration, drug, and crime policies would be wrong to suggest that these concerns stem entirely from racial bias. In the absence of racial bias, concerns about crime and drugs and illegal immigration would hardly disappear. But race bias prompts people to think differently about these issues, and prompts a few more people in every hundred to adopt stances that they might not have adopted otherwise. It also poisons our ability to honestly debate these issues, or even agree on basic facts. And because appeals to unconscious bias do not have to be spoken about or even thought about deliberately, the manipulation is almost completely immune to refutation. How do you refute something that ostensibly does not exist?

"When explicit claims about race are made, they can be rebutted; but when blacks are linked with crime, welfare, or drug use only implicitly, such links are less likely to be challenged," Gilens once wrote. "Thus, a subterranean discourse on race in U.S. society emerges, based largely on misleading images and chosen to influence voters by inciting fear or indignation. Rarely does one hear public figures make the explicit claim that irresponsible black mothers are the 'problem' with welfare or that violence-prone black men are the reason our streets are unsafe at night. But since they are not being made, such claims are not refuted. The public is left to draw its own conclusions, based on existing stereotypes and biased media coverage, and the conclusions drawn are exactly what one would expect."

A few months before the 2008 presidential elections, the secretary-treasurer of the AFL-CIO, Richard L. Trumka, told colleagues about an encounter he'd had with an old friend in his hometown of Nemacolin, Pennsylvania. The Democratic primary race between Senators Hillary Clinton and Barack Obama was in high gear.

"I ran into a woman that I had known for years—she was active in Democratic politics back when I was in grade school—back when Abe Lincoln was born," Trumka joked at a union convention. Then he grew serious. "We got to talking, and I asked her if she'd made up her mind who she was supporting, and she said, 'Oh, absolutely. I am voting for Hillary. There's no way I'd ever vote for Obama.' I said, 'Why is that?' She said, 'He is a Muslim.' I said, 'Actually he is a Christian just like you and I, but so what if he's a Muslim?' Then she shook her head and said, 'Well, he won't wear that American flag pin on his lapel.' I looked at my lapel and said, 'I don't have one, and by the way you don't have one on, either, but come on, he wears one plenty of times. Besides, it takes more than wearing a flag pin to be patriotic.' She said, 'Well, I don't trust him.' I said, 'Why is that?' And she dropped her voice a bit. She said, 'Because he is black.' And I said, 'Look around this town. Nemacolin's a dying town. There's no jobs here. Our kids are moving away because there is no future here. And here is a man, Barack Obama, who is going to fight for people like us, and you want to tell me that you won't vote for him because of the color of his skin? Are you out of your ever-loving mind, lady?' "

Trumka's comments were widely circulated. Polling by unions was finding that Obama's race was playing a role in the minds of many members. "I think race bias does play a role," Karen Ackerman, the research director of the AFL-CIO, told me about a month before the 2008 election. "We see it among union voters and in certain demographics—retirees and veterans, older voters."

The Democratic pollster and political consultant Celinda Lake told me she started to worry when polls taken by white pollsters and black pollsters among rank-and-file union members in battleground states started to come back with different answers. White union members told black pollsters they were going to vote for Obama, but told white pollsters that they were going to vote against Obama. Lake feared that many people were hiding their true feelings to black pollsters so as not to appear racist, and expressing their true intentions to white pollsters. Other polls showed that while nearly three quarters of voters said they would be comfortable voting for a black man, fewer than half thought their neighbors would be comfortable doing so.

I drove to northwestern Pennsylvania about three weeks before the 2008 election. The state had emerged as one of the major battlegrounds of the election. Polls showed Republican candidate John McCain struggling, but Democrats and Republicans agreed that if McCain was to thread the needle to victory, he would have to win Pennsylvania. If the Republican was to have any chance in Pennsylvania, he would have to win big in the suburbs and small rural and blue-collar towns such as St. Marys, which sits at the edge of Appalachia in the northwest part of the state.

St. Marys is part of Pennsylvania's fifth congressional district, which is so sparsely populated that it occupies nearly a quarter of the land area of the entire state. (Pennsylvania has nineteen congressional districts.) The fifth congressional district is overwhelmingly white and strongly Republican. On Brian Nosek's national race-bias map, it scores high on racial bias. People from this district who have taken the implicit association race bias test tend to show higher levels of racial bias than about 75 percent of the congressional districts in the United States.

As I drove off the interstate and onto the local roads that led to St. Marys, I was acutely conscious, in ways I usually do not think about, that I was a person of color. It did not help that, in the matter of a single hour, I got pulled over twice by police cruisers. In the first case, I had pulled to the side of a road to look at a map. When I glanced up, there was a cruiser behind me with lights blazing. The cop gave my car a quick once-over and sent me on my way.

In the second case, I was following a couple of slow cars on a two-lane road. I glanced at my speedometer; the cars were going around forty-five miles an hour. The speed limit was fifty-five. On a clear stretch of road where passing was permitted, I overtook the vehicles, stepping hard on the gas to get around them as quickly as possible. The cop who pulled me over a few moments later said the cars I had overtaken had been going sixty-five miles an hour, and that he had tracked me going ten miles per hour faster than that—twenty miles above the speed limit. I felt rattled.

When the cop returned after checking my driving record to give me a speeding ticket, I told him, defensively, that I was an extremely safe driver who had never received a moving violation in nearly two decades on the road. "Frankly," he snapped, "that surprises me." I thought about that afterward. The cop had known me barely a minute. In that narrow window, how had he formed a general conclusion about me that would cause him to feel surprise at the two decades of accumulated evidence in my driving record? What might have happened if the driving data had not existed and the cop had had only his intuition to guide him?

The Republican vice presidential candidate Sarah Palin held a rally in Pennsylvania that same day. Videos taken outside the rally by Obama supporters showed dozens of Republicans yelling comments straight into cameras: "Barrack HUSSEIN Obama," "Go back to Kenya," and "The only difference between Obama and Osama is the B.S." The comments might have been isolated and amplified by selective editing, but they did seem to evoke widespread laughter among the all-white crowd. An older man carried a monkey with a headband. "This is little Hussein," the man said, laughing. Others yelled, "Obama bin Laden," "Go back to Africa," and "Born in Kenya, citizen of Indonesia!"

Then there was, "We need a Muslim president!"

"If he gets in office, he's not going to have a cross section of America in his Cabinet. It is going to be Al Sharpton, Reverend [Jeremiah] Wright, Jesse Jackson."

"This isn't an Oprah show."

When McCain and Palin were pressed by journalists to address comments being made by their supporters at rallies, including occasional recommendations of violence against Obama, the candidates said the comments were restricted to a small minority that in no way spoke for the majority.

Union members belonging to the local Communications Workers of America in St. Marys were canvassing union households the day I visited. I had arranged to walk around town with a fifty-four-year-old organizer named Rosann Barker, a heavyset white woman with a square face, short bobbed hair, and an affable attitude. Barker worked for the Northwestern Pennsylvania Area Labor Federation based in Franklin, and lived outside Erie. She had driven a couple of hours that morning to St. Marys. Barker told me she didn't think race was a big factor in her part of the state.

I also met Rick Zimmerman, the president of Local CWA 502 in St. Marys. He wore a T-shirt and, like nearly every other male union member I met, blue jeans. "I don't see any Obama signs—maybe people are tearing them down at night," he told me with a grin. "They say St. Marys is a prejudiced town. We don't have many colored people around here."

Barker and I set off to one neighborhood. She had a list of union household addresses, and planned to knock on doors and give people her union's views of the candidates. Canvassing is a tiring and generally unrewarding business; there are long stretches of locked doors and impassive faces, interspersed with threatening bulldogs and people who enthusiastically support the candidate you want to see elected. The actual targets of canvassing efforts—people who are undecided or against your candidate but still amenable to persuasion— are few and far between.

I introduced myself as a journalist to every person I met. Linda Emerett, who was sweeping her driveway with a long broom, told us that she thought all politicians were a bunch of crooks. "I wanted Huckabee," she said, referring to the Republican presidential candidate Mike Huckabee, a favorite with evangelical voters. "It felt like he was more in tune with the person who goes out and sweeps the driveway. The others talk down to us. They use words that I sometimes think, 'What the "h" are they talking about?' I think Obama is telling people what he thinks they want to hear. They've got forked tongues."

Mark Flacinski, whom I met on the street, said, "I don't think Obama is the answer. I don't think McCain is the answer, either, but I think he is the best of two evils."

Every person I met who was younger than forty said they were for Obama. Nearly every person older than sixty said they were undecided or for McCain.

Other groups of union members had fanned out across St. Marys. One voter told union canvasser Terry O'Connor that he thought Obama was a Muslim. Another told O'Connor he was not going to vote for Obama but was going to vote a straight Democratic ticket for all other offices.

"We're in Appalachia, and this is the Bible Belt," O'Connor told me, as if this were sufficient explanation. "The problematic ones are the rural white voters, fifty to sixty and up. We're going to win a lot of them, but open-mindedness is not something they are known for. . . . I don't mind people voting for McCain because of abortion, but not because people think Obama is a Muslim."

Gary Bittner, a union organizer who works in twenty-eight of Pennsylvania's western counties, told me, as he chain-smoked cigarettes, that there was a "cultural" issue related to Obama. "They are scared of what they don't know. I tell them, 'What's important to you—your job, health care, pension benefits?' "

Bittner said that Obama's race was often an undertow in conversations. I asked him to give me an example.

"It gets said, but not in polite conversation," Bittner replied. "Let's say there is a text message going around saying, 'Barack Obama will get shot eight minutes into his presidency.' There are people who find that funny."

At the American Legion later that day, I engaged an older white man in conversation. His name was Don Joatt and he was seventy-three. He was a lifelong Democrat who always voted a straight party ticket. But he said he was uncomfortable about Obama.

I asked him what issues were of concern to him in the election. Joatt said the economy and jobs were his principal worries. He said he disliked free-trade agreements that were bringing in a flood of cheap imports. As a result of imports from China, Joatt told me, the lightbulb factory he had worked at for thirty-seven years had seen its workforce shrink from sixteen hundred employees to three hundred fifty.

"I really don't know which way to go," Joatt said. "I've been a Democrat all my life, but I don't know what to think about this election. Tax-wise and everything else, I don't know what to think."

I asked him whether he knew which presidential candidate was more in favor of the free trade that he vehemently opposed. Joatt said he thought that McCain—who had vocally insisted that he was a much fiercer advocate of free trade than Obama—was more sympathetic to the cause of protectionism.

"I am not sure about Obama," Joatt said. "I am not sure if I can trust him. . . . If Hillary had stayed in the race, I would have voted for her."

Zimmerman took me to the home of a colleague, a sixty-eight-year-old white woman who had worked at his union for forty years. The woman came barefoot into her yard to talk to me. We stood below a maple tree, as her dog—a cross between a cocker spaniel and a collie—wandered about. Two large flags hung from her porch—an American flag and a Vietnam POW-MIA flag. When I talked to her, the woman agreed to be identified, but she called me urgently a day later to request I not mention her name.

She said she was born in St. Marys and had always lived there. She was a lifelong Democrat, and despised the Republican candidates in the 2008 election. Among other things, she thought the government had no business telling women what to do with their bodies—she was fiercely pro-choice. She loved everything about Hillary Clinton. But when Obama won the Democratic nomination, she said she could not bring herself to support him.

"From what I see, the blacks get entries into college and free loans—Latinos, too," she said. "I am opposed to affirmative action."

She told me she had been concerned that if Obama won the presidency, the interests of white people would be cast aside: "I was worried I would have to go to the back of the bus." She acknowledged that Obama's race was a concern.

But then, she told me, she had a talk with her sister, an Obama supporter. The sister convinced her that Obama would not send white people to the back of the bus. She said she was reluctantly coming around to the idea of voting for Obama.

I asked her what her sister had said about Obama that had changed her mind.

"My sister said, 'You don't understand—he is white, too. He has a white mom and white grandparents.' That had a lot to do with it."

As you can see from these conversations, race bias is never completely implicit or completely explicit. Sometimes it lies beneath the surface; you think it is there, but you can't be certain. Other times, you don't have to think at all.

Days before the election, the canvasser Rosann Barker and I had another conversation. She sounded distressed—a large number of signs had appeared overnight in her residential community. The signs consisted of just four words printed on a small sheet of paper: VOTE RIGHT VOTE WHITE. Elsewhere, she told me, in a riposte to Obama's "Change You Can Believe In" slogan, signs said, CHANGE MEANS: COME HELP ANOTHER NIGGER GET ELECTED. Barker's voice choked. She said she had raced around the neighborhood taking down the signs.

"I didn't think it was so prevalent, but boy, the billboard signs and these laminated pages—it shows that in the rural community I live in, there is a race problem," she said. "It is my community, the place where I live. More than a hundred of these signs had to be taken down. I never dreamed someone would go to that extent. I knew there was prejudice but didn't think it was to that extent."

The Chicago O'Hare Hilton hotel is located within the complex of the busiest airport in the United States. From airport terminals, short walkways put you under the ten-story hotel, which has a façade of black metal and tinted glass. On September 27, 2008—one day after the first 2008 presidential debate between Senators John McCain and Barack Obama—a small group of people from all over the United States flew into Chicago for a secret meeting at the airport Hilton.

Room 2020 in the west wing of the Hilton had been reserved for the day. On a small plaque affixed outside the room were printed the words "Center for Social Inclusion." The room's interior was occupied by a large rectangular conference table and a dozen black leather chairs. Through the window, you could see shuttles from the Marriott hotel and National Car Rental company sweeping by the passenger arrival areas at the airport. From time to time, red and white trains going between terminals rumbled by in opposite directions on an elevated track.

The meeting had been organized on short notice—barely a week and a half had gone by since the group had informally coalesced through emails and conference calls. The people at the meeting were among the country's foremost thinkers on issues related to bias and politics. When Obama became the first African American candidate to be nominated by a major political party, these experts decided they wanted to apply what scholars had learned about prejudice to combat bias in the election. From Washington, D.C., came Todd Rogers and Celinda Lake, Democratic party pollsters and consultants. From Los Angeles came Jerry Kang from the University of California. From New Jersey, Rachel Godsil of Seton Hall law school. From Atlanta, Drew Westen, a political psychologist and Democratic party consultant. From Philadelphia, Camille Charles, a sociologist at the University of Pennsylvania. There were several other community activists, political organizers, and academic researchers. Other experts who could not make it to Chicago called in and participated through a speakerphone.

The group had been summoned by John Powell, a legal scholar at Ohio State University. If talk about welfare, illegal immigration, and crime were coded ways to talk about race, Powell wanted to come up with ways to deactivate such bias. The first way—the traditional way—was to uncover the bias. You combat subterranean bias, in other words, by bringing it to the surface. The Obama campaign had chosen a different route: Race was rarely to be made explicit, and the campaign never made a fuss about racism. Even in the face of explicit racism—thousands of people openly said that they would never vote for a black man—Obama stayed relentlessly positive. When people hurled racially tinged epithets at Obama at rallies; when some Republican party leaders openly questioned the biracial candidate's religion, background, and patriotism; when Hillary Clinton publicly declared that "Obama's support among working, hard-working Americans, white Americans, is weakening . . . ," the campaign responded with the same uplifting messages of unity that Obama had honed since his famous speech at the 2004 Democratic National Convention. Rather than accuse anyone of racial bias, the campaign preferred to call people to their better angels, to remind Americans that they were above racism.

Obama's strategy had been successful. He had won the Democratic nomination. But Powell feared there would come a time when the strategy would no longer work. Powell's team had heard that Republicans were planning a major attack in the late fall drawing on excerpts from Obama's books where he talked about using drugs as a young man and having devoured Marxist and feminist literature, and the speeches of Malcolm X. Powell reached out to the Obama campaign but was met with resistance. "Initially I tried to get the campaign to do it, and they were of the opinion that it wasn't necessary," Powell told me. "My response is, 'If you are right, great, but what if you are wrong? You should have something ready. If you don't need it, no sweat, but if you want something and don't have it, you are in trouble.' . . . They are not taking advantage of the research in the last thirty years. They think [talking about race] is necessarily divisive. They don't realize people are very conflicted."

Mahzarin Banaji called in to the Chicago meeting from Harvard. The psychologist had long been a proponent of fighting unconscious bias by dragging it into the open, by making implicit biases visible. But in this situation, she felt Obama was doing the right thing. All politicians, she told me, had to emphasize the bond they had with voters, and it made sense that Obama should stay clear of the subject of race. The bond that a member of a minority group has with most voters cannot be the thing that marks him as a minority.

The group discussed different ways in which campaign advertisements have exploited race bias. In the 2006 Senate election in Tennessee, African American candidate Harold Ford was the target of an ad that played on miscegenation fears. The ad featured a young white woman who claimed to have met Ford at a Playboy party, and ended with her seductively whispering, "Harold, call me." One anti-Obama ad showed the candidate's grinning face morph into the face of a wolf. A conservative group linked Obama with Kwame Kilpatrick, the disgraced black mayor of Detroit, who had recently been ejected from office on criminal charges. As the ad listed the various charges against Kilpatrick, it showed footage of Obama standing with Kilpatrick and praising him. The ad advised voters to learn who Obama's friends were. (Kilpatrick's skin is much darker than Obama's, and the ad deliberately darkened Kilpatrick's complexion even further to play on the unconscious biases of white voters against dark-skinned black men, according to sociologist Camille Charles at the University of Pennsylvania.)

Toward the end of the day, I asked the group around the table how Obama might be vulnerable to unconscious bias. Powell, who wore a beard speckled with gray, said that Obama was not vulnerable in the way African American leaders usually are. Obama could not be depicted as threatening. But he was vulnerable to suggestions that he was an outsider and foreign; his middle name was Hussein, and he had spent long stretches of his childhood in other countries. It was the "He's not one of us" message that Powell was worried about.

"The primary target is the Reagan Democrats," Powell told me. "People who belong to unions, who in Ohio voted for [Democratic Governor Ted] Strickland. Strickland won by a huge margin. It helped [that] his opponent was a black Republican. You don't have to convince them that unions are good, or governments have a role, and wouldn't it be great to have health care."

If he lost, Powell concluded about Obama, it would be because people who agreed with Obama on the issues did not want to vote for a black man. "It will be because of Democrats."

The pollsters, consultants, and psychologists around the table in Chicago decided to devise a series of anti-bias messages and get them out to voters in battleground states. The group wanted to "inoculate" voters against divisive appeals. They planned to come up with a series of ads to get people to think about the role of race in the election. One would involve shoving an actual elephant into a diner as patrons chewed their food and took nervous glances at the behemoth. As the elephant flapped its ears, a message would say, "Let's talk about the elephant in the room."

There was only one time in the 2008 election when the Obama campaign's strategy to neutralize the subject of race came completely undone. It was during the Democratic primary, when comments by Obama's pastor, the Reverend Jeremiah Wright of Trinity United Church of Christ in Chicago, surfaced in the national media. Wright had often lashed out at white America in sermons about racial injustice, and Obama's opponents seized on the pastor saying such things as, "Not God bless America. God damn America!" The instant Obama found himself linked to Wright's inflammatory comments, his campaign stalled.

Reporters later dug up comments made by John C. Hagee, a pastor whom John McCain had embraced, who once said the Holocaust was God's plan to drive Jews to Palestine. And Larry Kroon, a pastor of Republican vice presidential nominee Sarah Palin, had said that God would "strike . . . the United States of America." On the same day as that first presidential debate, *The Washington Post* noted that "In the fine, new American tradition of presidential campaign 'pastor disasters,' Republican vice presidential nominee Sarah Palin might have one." It made intuitive sense that if Obama got into a heap of trouble because of his pastor's views, the same thing would happen to McCain and Palin. But that did not happen, and the people in Room 2020 of the O'Hare Hilton could have told you why. The real issue with Wright was not his militant and overheated comments but that contact with Wright unconsciously linked Obama to a notion toxic to many white voters—the angry black man who sought to make whites feel guilty about racism. There was no analogous identity archetype that Hagee and Kroon evoked—certainly nothing to rival the deep fears and anxieties that the angry black man conjured. It made sense that the McCain and Palin pastor controversies would sink like stones.

I found it interesting that even as the national media wrapped itself into pretzels about Wright's comments, many people of color found

Wright utterly unremarkable. Before he parted ways with Wright, Obama himself said he felt his church was not particularly controversial. Wright was certainly inflammatory and given to rhetorical excess, but this partly had to do with the theatricality of sermons in general and the style of the black church in particular. Obama once said Wright "is like an old uncle who says things I don't always agree with."

But if Wright had a tendency toward overblown rhetoric, most blacks had little problem with the emotional truth of his message: African Americans are 447 percent more likely than white Americans to be imprisoned and 521 percent more likely to be murdered. There is a five-to-one wealth gap between whites and blacks at birth, blacks live five years fewer on average than whites, and the black infant mortality rate is nearly one and a half times the white infant mortality rate. Wouldn't it be odd *not* to be angry? But once Wright's comments surfaced in the national media, and excerpts from his sermons were replayed endlessly on cable television, it was no longer possible for the Obama campaign to sell its "we are all Americans first" message. The America that Wright described felt like a cruel caricature to many whites. Which version of reality, Obama's opponents asked, did the candidate endorse? Hillary Clinton sat down for a lengthy interview with Bill O'Reilly of FOX News, and agreed with the conservative commentator that Obama had some explaining to do. Where the country had seen in Obama only a quiet, well-spoken Harvard-educated lawyer, the Wright episode raised questions about whether Obama was secretly the kind of militant black activist that many whites abhorred.

Obama's first instinct was to let things blow over, but Wright—who could be described as Obama's friend in only the loosest sense of the term—held a televised meeting at the National Press Club in Washington, where he fought back against his critics, argued that they were motivated by racism, and charged that the attacks on him were attacks on the entire black community. Wright addressed his comments to a crowd of supporters, and they gave him a standing ovation. The press conference put Obama in an even more difficult bind;

shortly afterward, Obama renounced his ties with Wright and then did something he almost never did before or after in the 2008 campaign: He explicitly talked about race.

In a now famous speech in Philadelphia, Obama presented a picture of race relations very different from that presented by his former pastor. He played conciliator, and explained to white people why black people were often angry, and explained to black people why white people were resentful of being reminded endlessly about the legacy of slavery. The country had come a long way since the days of Jim Crow, Obama reminded his black audience, but the country also had a long way still to go.

The speech was psychologically astute—and precisely what a psychologist who studies the hidden brain would have recommended. The researchers Richard P. Eibach and Joyce Ehrlinger have shown that a central reason whites and blacks in America have very different impressions about the state of racial progress is that whites unconsciously compare the state of race relations with the past. Compared to the days of slavery, the country *has* made enormous strides in race relations, and many whites find it incomprehensible that blacks do not regularly acknowledge the progress that has been made. Eibach and Ehrlinger found that blacks, on the other hand, unconsciously compare the status quo with an idealized future where discrimination does not exist; for the young black man or woman who suffers subtle forms of discrimination in the workplace, it isn't much consolation to say things were worse two hundred years ago. From this perspective, many blacks cannot understand why whites would downplay the reality of their everyday experience. Each side had a point, Obama effectively told his audience, and each side had more in common with the other than either believed.

Without overtly looking like he was doing so, Obama also reminded white voters that he was half-white. "I can no more disown him than I can my white grandmother," Obama said about his former pastor. The speech was made at the National Constitution Center, and Obama used the occasion to draw the country's attention to the document that bound the nation together. Rather than speak on behalf of any group, Obama spoke on behalf of everyone.

The Philadelphia speech was a huge political success, and it revived the Obama campaign. Obama never seriously addressed the subject of race again, and in fact took great pains to avoid the subject altogether. For all the historic significance of an African American man reaching for the presidency, one of the ironies of the Obama campaign is that it was largely mute when it came to the subject of race. At the Democratic National Convention in Denver, which was held on the forty-fifth anniversary of the famous 1963 March on Washington, with an African American man on the presidential ticket of a major party for the first time in history, John Powell pointed out to me, with some bitterness, that Obama never mentioned the words "race," "Martin Luther King," or "civil rights" in his acceptance speech. The documentary shown about his life, Powell added, was "heavy on white people." It emphasized his mother's side of the family—his white side—far more than it did his father's side, even though in his book *Dreams from My Father* Obama emphasized how important it was for him to find his identity as a black man in order to become a leader.

Powell told me—and remember, this was a man who was working eighteen to nineteen hours a day to get Obama elected—that he found the Philadelphia speech politically brilliant but historically problematic. Rather than talk about the problem of race in America, Obama had talked about the problem of *anger* in America. Whites were angry with blacks, blacks were angry with whites. If everyone renounced their anger, we would all be better off. But Powell could not abide the idea that black anger and white anger were equivalent and somehow canceled each other out. If blacks were angry about slavery and segregation, discrimination and a lack of opportunities, whites were angry because they felt undeserving blacks were taking advantage of the system.

"Dr. King, in his most important speeches, talked about the importance of righteous indignation," Powell told me. "Obama understands that he is playing to a white audience. If he can be Tiger Woods and a nonthreatening black, he thinks he can get the support of white people."

Two undercurrents of discomfort ran beneath the table at the secret Chicago meeting. One had to do with the conflicting challenges of fighting bias and fighting to win an election. The people around the table knew that if they were against bias, they also had to be against the ageism and sexism that prompted voters to feel McCain was "too old" and that Sarah Palin was "yet another incompetent woman." By the end of the meeting, Powell said the goal was less about getting Obama elected and more about removing bias from the equation. As long as voters did not reject a candidate because of bias, it was perfectly legitimate to vote for or against anyone.

But there was another undercurrent that ran still deeper. When you found unconscious bias, there were two things you could do about it. You could fight it at an implicit level, as the Obama campaign was doing. Without ever making a fuss about racism, you could project counter-stereotypical messages that radiated calm and reassurance. The other approach was explicit—you called out voters who agreed with your candidate on the issues but were reluctant to vote for him because of racism. This would be the Martin Luther King, Jr., way, the path of "righteous indignation." The trouble was, calling people out on racism made them defensive. Even if you won the argument, you could lose their vote. The Obama approach was much more astute politically, but there was something disturbing about it. If the only way for a black politician to be acceptable to whites was to project an image of a nonthreatening black man—"the exception to the rule"—wasn't that implicitly an endorsement of the stereotype?

These concerns would be amplified as the group designed a series of ads and tested them among a large number of undecided white voters in battleground states. Celinda Lake ran the ads by five hundred men and five hundred women with blue-collar backgrounds, the people who told white pollsters one thing and black pollsters something else. Lake asked the voters what they made of each ad and how it made them feel. The psychologist Drew Westen measured how the ads changed unconscious attitudes toward Obama.

The elephant in the room ad was an example of how bias might be combated explicitly. Another ad targeted the hidden brain. It involved a blue-collar worker speaking directly into the camera. (One version featured a man, another a woman.) The speaker articulated many of the concerns about Obama that were being circulated in white working-class communities, that Obama would give preference to black people, and that he was an unpatriotic outsider. The idea, said Westen, was to openly acknowledge what people were feeling. But rather than dismiss such concerns as racist or wrong, as the union leader Richard Trumka had done with his old friend in Nemacolin, Pennsylvania, the ad gave people an alternative way to think about their feelings.

This was the text of the ad featuring a fiftyish white woman. The woman was identified as Sue Burton of Zanesville, Ohio: "A lot of people aren't quite sure about Barack Obama. He seems steady. He talks about things that matter to me—the price of gas and groceries, and health care we can count on. But then sometimes I get that feeling, you know, uneasy? I'm not really sure who he is. Does he really love his country? Maybe if he gets elected he's going to put the interests of black people above the interests of the rest of us. You know, I was talking with my mom about it. She and dad had the same questions about President Kennedy before he was elected. They had that same feeling. Uneasy. Maybe he'd put his Catholic faith before his country. I'm not prejudiced. I just want to know that he shares my values and cares about people like me. And I think he does. I think he loves his two little girls just like I love mine. I think he loves our country just like I do. It hasn't been easy for me. But I'm going to give him a chance. I am an American—and so is he."

The conventional way to counter an untruth is to confront it. Indeed, if you subscribe to the notion that people's conscious minds are all that matter, this is what you *should* do. Good information ought to drive bad information out of circulation. It's only when you think about politics with the hidden brain in mind that you understand why innumerable fact-checking websites and media articles ahead of the 2008 presidential election did little to prevent millions of Americans from believing blatant falsehoods about Obama. The "I Am an American" ad took a different tack. It set aside the conscious mind altogether and focused entirely on the hidden brain.

Rather than tell people that the allegations against Obama were false, the ad took the point of view of people who felt uneasy. It was an old lesson from therapy textbooks: Regardless of whether feelings were justified, they were real. You cannot eliminate feelings by denying their validity; indeed, denying them usually strengthened them. The "I Am an American" ad did not present refutations to the woman's beliefs or try to show that her feelings were unjustified or wrong. Rather, it was the woman herself who made the emotional decision to override her fears. She wasn't being *corrected*. She was being *courageous*.

The message tested well in focus groups, but some funders, Westen told me, were uncomfortable about a message that did not explicitly refute untrue insinuations about Obama. The notion of setting aside the conscious mind and focusing only on the hidden brain can be difficult to swallow.

"But if you refute it, it has a different meaning," Westen said. "My conscious concern about the refutation is it sounds contrived. This does not sound like a person who has struggled with this. It sounds like an Obama campaign worker."

The experts tested a number of other approaches. One ad called "Team USA" showed a girls' soccer match in progress with the soundtrack of "America the Beautiful" in the background. A series of adorable black and white children played together, intensely focused on the game, with smiles and camaraderie. It then showed a close-up shot of Joe Jacobi, a white Olympic gold medal winner in white-water canoeing, followed by a shot of a black woman, Teresa Edwards, a four-time Olympic gold medal winner in basketball. The ad then cut to an amateur men's basketball game, with players of all races engaged in intense teamwork. The ball swished through the basket, and the ad zoomed in on a black hand and white palm "low-fiving" in an acknowledgment of interdependence. A message on the screen read, "We're all on the same team. Team USA."

Whereas the ad with the elephant in the diner was designed to make people think, and perhaps make them feel uncomfortable, Westen told me the "Team USA" ad followed the model of the Obama campaign—to go for the lump in the throat. People wanted to feel good about themselves, and calling them to their better natures did this, just as calling them racists made them angry and defensive. The "Team USA" ad reinforced the racially inclusive impulses of voters.

In another ad, the camera cut seamlessly between two families, one white, one black. In both cases, the families sat on a couch, in identical positions, one child on the mom's lap while a little girl sat on her dad's lap. Both dads read aloud from the children's book *The Little Engine That Could.*

WHITE DAD: The very little engine looked up and saw the tears in the doll's eyes. And she thought of the good little boys and girls on the other side of the mountain

BLACK DAD: who would not have any toys or good food unless she helped. And then she said, "I think I can,

WHITE DAD: I think I can, I think I can."

BLACK DAD: And she hitched herself to the little train, and the little Blue Engine smiled

WHITE DAD: and seemed to say, as she puffed steadily down the mountain,

BLACK DAD: "I thought I could, I thought I could,

WHITE DAD: I thought I could, I thought I could,

BLACK DAD: I thought I could—"

"It is only a different voice and a different family, but they are sitting exactly the same way and doing exactly the same thing," Westen told me, shortly after he finished supervising the shooting of the ad with the black family. "The soundtrack to that is going to be a light piano or a female voice humming 'Amazing Grace,' and the only words that come up on the screen are *We are all God's children.* That is calling people to their better angels, to what their faith teaches them."

Westen thought the ad was especially effective because research showed that whites were drawn to images of black parents reading to their children—a message counter to the idea of disintegrated black families and disinterested black fathers. "When you pair 'hard work' with 'black,' you deactivate the stereotypes that make race so toxic, and when you add paternal responsibility to black dads, you do the same thing," Westen told me. "This is why people resonate to Cosby and Obama talking about taking responsibility for their children and father-absence being a disaster in the inner cities. You turn down the volume on one of the ways covert racism expresses itself."

The voters who participated in testing the ads were men older than thirty and women older than fifty who had not completed college. The results revealed how unconscious attitudes diverged from conscious attitudes.

Take the "All God's Children" ad with the black and white dads reading to their children. Westen shot and tested two versions of the ad—one had the black and white dads, and another featured a white family and two different black families, with one of the black dads darker than the other. In this second version of the ad, all the dads again read from *The Little Engine That Could,* and the cuts went seamlessly among the families. This ad, with two black families and one white family, scored very high in terms of voters' conscious responses. People really responded—consciously—to the idea of the black dads and the white dad reading the same children's book to their families in different homes. But Westen found that the ad had zero effect on people's unconscious attitudes toward Obama. The ad with the white family and just one black family—featuring the lighter-skinned black dad—generated less positive approval from voters at a conscious level but was far more effective at an unconscious level in changing people's willingness to support Obama. Without their awareness, something about the darker-skinned black dad rubbed voters the wrong way. Their conscious minds may have known we are all God's children; their unconscious minds did not agree.

The "I Am an American" ads with the blue-collar workers speaking directly into the camera about concerns that Obama was an outsider who would harm the interests of white people scored moderately well at the conscious level. But they were highly effective at the level of unconscious attitudes. The ad showing the female worker articulating her doubts and reaching an internal resolution was the most successful of all the ads that Westen and his group created.

Effectively, the group that met at the Chicago Hilton had come up with a series of tools. To be sure, the tools were crude, but they were the first real attempt made in the heat of a political campaign to turn down the volume on racial bias. As it turned out, none of the ads were aired before the 2008 election because the financial meltdown in the weeks before the election sent potential funders scurrying for cover. (Powell's team also found that many of the attack ads planned against Obama were never aired for the same reason.)

But the research showed that in order to combat conscious and explicit bias—people who shout racist things at rallies and put up VOTE RIGHT VOTE WHITE signs—ads of children playing together on a team, or black and white families doing identical things, are effective. To combat outright hatred, you want to call people to their better angels, and hope the lump in their throats can overcome the bile in their hearts.

But when it comes to unconscious bias—the gray monster lurking beneath the surface in a large number of voters—you need different tools. The "I Am an American" ad acknowledged the way many voters felt about Obama. Without telling them that they were wrong, it suggested an alternative route to channel their feelings.

"We are going back to the future to Freud," Westen told me. "There really is this dissociation he spoke about between the conscious and the unconscious, but we now have ways of measuring it. How do you detoxify race in elections so people cannot run the 'Call me, Harold' ad or the Kwame Kilpatrick ad or the Willie Horton ad? If you are vulnerable to such attacks, you have to measure both conscious and unconscious attitudes and develop strategies that address both."

I found the ads fascinating, but also disturbing, in that they sometimes placed what made political sense at odds with what made ethical sense. Which version of the "All God's Children" ad would you have chosen if you were a political consultant? You wouldn't have chosen the ad showing the darker-skinned black dad, because Westen's data demonstrated that it worked less well at persuading white voters than the ad that showed only the lighter-skinned black dad. In order to be politically effective, to get voters to support your candidate, you had to choose the ad that *went along* with people's unconscious biases against darker-skinned black men.

The same went for the "I Am an American" ad. When people spread racist lies about a black candidate, the obvious response was righteous indignation, but the more effective response was apparently to approach the problem sideways—to tell voters that the way they felt was understandable, but to ask them to "take a chance" on the candidate. Racist beliefs, in other words, were best left unchallenged if you wanted to persuade someone to vote for your candidate. I started to understand why Obama's approach had succeeded where so many other black politicians had failed; his campaign's conscious decision not to cry foul, not to voice the righteous indignation to which he was surely entitled, was the only way he could win.

I asked Celinda Lake about this after the election. She acknowledged that there was a tension between fighting stereotypes and trying to get a candidate elected. But she pointed out that if getting Obama into the White House involved making some compromises, it was also the case that Obama's election promised to reduce racism in the United States as nothing else could. The hidden brain learns through blind repetition, and Obama's election meant the country and the world would spend the next several years being bombarded with counter-stereotypical messages about a very smart, articulate, and charismatic black man—who happened to be the most powerful person on the planet.

"Having worked for a number of African American candidates," Lake said, "I don't care if I get someone elected by appealing to exceptionalism," the idea that that particular black candidate was the exception to the rule—an approach that could reinforce stereotypes. "I would like to end racism, but I [first] want to get Barack Obama elected."

Lake told me that David Axelrod, the political mastermind behind the Obama campaign, had helped a number of African American candidates get elected by relentlessly *not* focusing on trying to change people's underlying views about race and gender. When getting Carol Moseley Braun elected to the Senate, for example, pollsters once found that having Braun stand up and speak directly into the camera for an ad prompted voters to feel she was in their face—in a way they did not feel when a white man delivered exactly the same lines. It was clearly sexist and racist, and the path of righteous indignation might have said, "The hell with such biases—have Braun speak directly into the camera." But Axelrod, whose job it was to get Braun elected, suggested she sit behind a table and speak her lines. Voters immediately found the message more acceptable.

I don't know how to resolve the imperative of righteous indignation with the imperative to get your candidate elected. If the techniques of political consultants are sometimes icky, it should also be said that righteous indignation never got a black man elected president. It was Axelrod and Obama who found a way to make King's dream come true—by sidestepping controversy and turning down the temperature on race. Unfairness seems written into the DNA of politics, because voters consciously and unconsciously care about a host of factors that candidates cannot control. Political consultants will always try to find ways to win with the cards they are dealt—and that can mean exploiting both legitimate strengths and unfair advantages. Obama was clearly a gifted candidate. His calm, even-tempered style was a matter of natural inclination, and his adoration of his daughters was obviously sincere. Being a calm person does not automatically mean someone will make a good president, but the trait served Obama well in that a hot-tempered nature might have evoked the dreaded trope of the angry black man. Obama's visible love for his children helped disable unconscious stereotypes that link black men with disinterested fatherhood. Obama also happened to be biracial, and he used his links to whiteness to his advantage.

"Barack Obama had light-colored skin, and that made a big difference," Drew Westen said quietly after the election, during a conference call that brought everyone from the Chicago meeting up to speed on what the research had found. "Had he looked like Kwame Kilpatrick, it is not at all clear to me that he could have made it."

CHAPTER 10

The Telescope Effect

Lost Dogs and Genocide

The ideas in this book have been organized in concentric circles, where successive chapters have illustrated how the hidden brain influences our lives from very small issues to very large issues. We have examined the effects of the hidden brain among children and in intimate relationships, in disasters and in suicide terrorism, in the criminal justice system, and in politics. I decided to devote the final chapter of the book to the subject of . . . numbers. It sounds esoteric, but it is not. Consciously and unconsciously, the way we think about numbers influences the most important decisions we make as human beings.

Edward Shinnick was the head of internal affairs at the police department in Jersey City. He was married with two children, a respected figure in his northern New Jersey community. Shinnick loved being a cop, but was not entirely happy at internal affairs—few cops enjoy keeping an eye on their fellow officers. But Shinnick was articulate and verbal; when he was stressed at work, he talked about it at home with his wife, Michele, and with other friends. He was a cop's cop, a confidant to many fellow officers. He counseled colleagues through emotional upheavals and marital problems. He considered himself on police duty twenty-four hours a day, seven days a week. He carried his gun wherever he went. He never drank; he felt he had no right to be under the effect of alcohol when he was armed.

In May 2008, Shinnick put in his papers and retired. He was fifty-two years old. On May 28, a Wednesday, Shinnick visited his mother, who was in a nursing home. When he left, he gave a nurse his new cellphone number. He had lunch with an old buddy, a retired police lieutenant.

Shinnick did not come home that afternoon or that evening. It was not like him to be late and not call, but his wife Michele figured that he had probably gone back to the police department to meet some friends. She called around, but no one had seen Shinnick. By nine o'clock in the evening, at the urging of police, Michele filed a missing person's report. She went online and found that Shinnick had made a cash withdrawal from an ATM machine in Wyckoff, a short distance northwest of their home.

Shinnick had gone to Wyckoff and then had kept driving. He went all the way to Pennsylvania, to a Comfort Inn that he and Michele stayed in from time to time. Michele's cousin stayed in the Poconos, and whenever the Shinnicks drove back from a visit, they stayed at the motel. The Comfort Inn allowed dogs, and the Shinnicks were dog people. Ed Shinnick removed his E-ZPass from his car before he went on his trip; he knew Michele and his cop buddies would try to trace the car using the pass, and he did not want to be tracked down. He checked into a room at the motel.

Ed Shinnick had two guns with him, including his police service revolver. Inside the motel room, he aimed one weapon at his heart and the other at his head. He pulled both triggers simultaneously.

A cleaning lady found his dead body.

Michele Shinnick found the news incomprehensible. She pieced together the events of Ed Shinnick's last day. Why would a man planning to kill himself leave his new cellphone number at his mother's nursing home? The retired police lieutenant whom Shinnick had met for lunch was someone who used to teach cops about stress and the risk of suicide. Michele talked with him, and he told her that there had been no sign that Shinnick was contemplating suicide.

"If you were to make a list of the people most unlikely to complete the act of suicide," Michele Shinnick told me, "my husband's name would be number one."

Whenever someone takes their own life, our automatic response is to ask what was going on in their life. Taking one's life seems profoundly irrational, and we always look for evidence of mental disorder and stress, marital unhappiness, or a fall from grace. Shinnick had his share of troubles. He was not entirely happy at internal affairs, but he had just retired. Being a cop was certainly stressful—Shinnick had been standing at the harbor at Liberty State Park when the September 11 attacks took place. He saw the second plane hit the South Tower of the World Trade Center, and he helped count the dead in the days that followed. Shinnick had once been diagnosed with post-traumatic stress disorder after his car got stuck on some tracks. A train rammed his vehicle, and Shinnick was in and out of work the following year as he recovered from injuries. That was in 1993, fifteen years before he took his life. By the time of his death in 2008, the PTSD diagnosis had long faded from everyone's memory. On the plus side, Shinnick was a respected member of his community and a successful cop. He had a wonderful marriage and family. He had deep religious faith. Many people with much less going for them endure more difficult challenges and never contemplate suicide.

Michele Shinnick told me that four other police officers in the local area had taken their lives in the months after her husband's suicide. "It really is an epidemic."

That is no exaggeration. Suicide among police officers is under-reported; newspapers and local TV stations do not offer wall-to-wall coverage of police suicides the way they memorialize cops killed on the beat. The different kinds of attention paid to homicide and suicide obscure the fact that there are more than twice as many suicides among police officers in the United States as there are homicides. John Violanti, a research professor in the school of public health at the State University of New York at Buffalo, has spent years studying suicide among police officers. Contrary to popular notions about the risk of police work, Violanti and others have found that the risk of officers taking their own lives vastly dwarfs the risk that they will be killed in action. Drug wars and firefights; muggings, robberies, and assaults; murderers, rapists, and serial killers collectively pose a much smaller threat to your average cop than the risk that he will put his service re-volver to his head and shoot himself.

When scientists study epidemics, they don't study individuals. It is true that epidemics preferentially strike the vulnerable; a person with AIDS has a greater risk of catching the flu than a healthy person. But if you want to stop an epidemic, you don't go after individual patients or the idiosyncratic things that place individuals at risk. You go after the common factors behind the epidemic. You look for cures or vac-cines, and ways to halt the epidemic before it spreads. In the case of malaria, you stop an epidemic by preventing the breeding of mosqui-toes. Mosquitoes are the means—the vector—by which malaria is transmitted. You don't destroy the malaria parasite by curbing mos-quitoes, but destroying the vector keeps the parasite from infecting people. Mosquito eradication is a more effective way to stop a malaria epidemic than treating individual patients one by one with quinine. The difference between the two approaches—one broad scale and the other individualized—is the central difference between a public health approach to an epidemic and a medical approach.

When we probe the mental and emotional antecedents of someone who has committed suicide, we are implicitly pursuing a medical ap-proach. When we tailor interventions to individuals—counseling peo-ple who are stressed and asking what is going on in their lives—we are pursuing a medical approach. We are going after the problem of sui-cide one individual at a time. Every person is different from every other, because the constellation of symptoms, risks, and circum-stances is different for everyone. But is there another way to think about suicide, to think about it as a public health problem? Is there a kill-the-mosquitoes-to-halt-malaria approach to suicide?

John Violanti and other public health experts have asked them-selves what it is about police work that places officers at high risk for suicide. The conventional explanation is that police work is stressful. You don't know who lurks behind each corner when you are pa-trolling a beat, and you have no idea if the driver you pull over for speeding on a beautiful day is a drug dealer packing heat. But Violanti, like all good scientists, decided to put his intuitions to the test: He compared the risk of suicide in three stressful professions. He studied 8.5 million death certificates in twenty-eight states to find out the relative risk of suicide among police officers, firefighters, and military personnel. All three lines of work place people at personal risk and involve high stress; all involve unpredictable and long hours that can interfere with family life.

Violanti found that military personnel and police officers had a far higher risk of suicide than firefighters. Cops turn out to have about four times the suicide risk of firefighters. Black cops in the United States have nearly five times the suicide risk of black firefighters. White women who are police officers are twelve times more likely to commit suicide than white women who are firefighters.

The central difference among cops, military personnel, and firefighters, Violanti concluded, is that cops and military personnel carry guns. Nearly all police suicides involve the use of guns—the vast majority are service weapons. Guns don't make people suicidal, but they provide the impulse of suicide with a vector—in exactly the same way that the mosquito provides the malaria parasite with a vector. If cops were to check their guns at police departments when they left work, Violanti figured, a substantial number of police suicides might vanish.

Large numbers of police officers—and their family members—are also killed in accidental shootings involving service weapons. When you add together the number of police officers killed in accidents, the number of family members of cops who are killed in accidents, and the number of family members of cops who commit suicide, this pool of victims forms an even larger group than the number of police officers who commit suicide. No one knows exactly how often service weapons are implicated in all these deaths, but it is certain they are used frequently. If officers checked their weapons when they went off duty, it could reduce those deaths, too.

Violanti used to be a cop, and he understands how cops think. He knows the idea would never fly. Police officers such as Ed Shinnick think of themselves as being on call all the time. Even when they are off duty and in civilian attire, cops want to be ready to intervene in emergencies. Newspapers abound with stories of how off-duty police officers halted convenience store robberies because they were carrying their service weapons. Some police departments actually require police officers to carry a gun with them at all times. In Jersey City, Ed Shinnick was required to purchase his weapon. After he retired, the gun belonged to him.

Police officers think their biggest risk of getting killed comes from bad guys on the street. Hundreds of books, thousands of movies, and millions of pages of newsprint have been devoted to the general subject of cops and robbers. When was the last time you saw a movie or read a book about a cop committing suicide? Even if such a movie were made, you can bet it would never become the next *Die Hard.* Our intuitions tell us that cops are primarily at risk of getting killed in the line of duty. As a general rule, movies that contradict our intuitions—even intuitions that are demonstrably false—are movies that few people will care to watch.

The data on the relative risks of homicide and suicide are stark. Cops are only the most dramatic example of what happens when people have ready access to handguns. America's long debate about gun control has centered on the conflict between those who feel guns protect them from criminals and those who feel the availability of guns allows criminals to get their hands on weapons. Gun-control advocates say that the ready availability of guns in the United States makes gun-violence inevitable. Gun enthusiasts say, "Duh. The bad guys have weapons already and won't turn them in if we tighten gun laws. The only smart thing to do is to keep a gun in your home to defend yourself."

Neither side pays much attention to the *evidence,* which shows that people who have guns in their homes are at greater risk of being shot and killed than people who do not have guns in their homes. The risk does not come from homicidal maniacs or muggers or rapists. The risk comes from *people using their own guns to shoot themselves or their family members.* The gun debate in America should not be between those who argue that individuals have a right to protect themselves and those who argue that the interests of society should come first. The issue is whether people who live in homes with guns are safer as a result of owning a gun, and the answer, unequivocally, is no.

The combined risk of accidents, suicide, and domestic violence dwarfs the risk of homicide at the hands of a stranger. Each year in the United States, nearly twice as many people kill themselves as are murdered.

Only a small number of the four hundred thousand suicide attempts in America each year involve guns, but because people who shoot themselves usually kill themselves, gun suicides account for more than half of all *completed* suicides.

When the District of Columbia banned handguns in 1976—civilians were effectively prohibited from buying, selling, transferring, or possessing weapons—the suicide rate in the city of Washington, D.C., fell by 23 percent. The drop was immediate, and it was entirely because of a reduced number of handgun suicides. The researchers who conducted the study measured suicide rates before and after the handgun ban. They found the suicide reduction was limited to Washington, D.C.—where handguns were banned—and was not observed in the suburbs—where no changes were instituted to gun laws. The decline in suicide in Washington, in other words, was not part of a general reduction in suicide risk in the metropolitan area. Suicides in Washington, D.C., that were not gun-related, moreover, did not show a decline after the handgun ban. The entire reduction in suicide was because there were fewer gun suicides. If you looked at a twenty-year period—with the gun ban right in the middle of that period—there were more than thirty-one suicides per year in Washington before the ban, and only twenty-four suicides per year after the ban. The researchers also found, contra the intuitions of gun enthusiasts, that the ban was also associated with a steep decline in the homicide rate. The decline in homicide was also entirely due to a reduction in shooting deaths, and the decline was limited to Washington and not its suburbs. The District of Columbia, by the way, has one of the lowest suicide rates in the country; if you were to cut suicide by a quarter in places such as Alabama, Alaska, Colorado, Montana, Nevada, and New Mexico, which have much higher suicide rates and many more people than Washington, D.C., you could significantly reduce the scale of suicide in the United States.

If you were a public health official and someone told you there was a way to curb a malaria epidemic by 23 percent, you would be ecstatic. But lawmakers usually don't think like public health officials. They trust their intuitions, and their intuitions tell them that owning guns makes people safer. In 2008, led by Supreme Court Justice Antonin Scalia, the highest court in the United States reversed the handgun ban in Washington, D.C., on the grounds that it was unconstitutional: "We hold that the District's ban on handgun possession in the home violates the Second Amendment, as does its prohibition against rendering any lawful firearm in the home operable for the purpose of immediate self-defense." The Second Amendment, which guarantees citizens the right to bear arms, Scalia added, "elevates above all other interests the right of law-abiding, responsible citizens to use arms in defense of hearth and home." In a poll published in *The Washington Post*, 76 percent of people agreed with the Supreme Court decision.

The idea that a gun can protect you is such an intuitively appealing idea. A robber breaks into your home; you grab a gun from your nightstand and shoot the intruder. How many times have we seen movies where brave people stand guard outside their homes, rifles in hand? Advocates for gun ownership are only following their intuitions. The Second Amendment, in fact, enshrines our collective intuition about guns and self-defense into the Constitution. We believe we are safer when we have weapons to defend ourselves. What the framers of the Second Amendment did not foresee is that the long-barreled muskets of the eighteenth century—which were difficult to use to commit suicide—would one day be replaced by handguns, and the greater threat to the lives of Americans would come not from murderous strangers or an authoritarian government but from suicide, accidental shootings, and family members using handguns to kill one another.

We certainly feel more *control* when we have a gun in our possession, and it is easy to confuse the feeling of control with safety. Indeed, this is an unconscious bias in the hidden brain. Over millennia, evolution caused animals, including humans, to experience anxiety in situations where they lacked control—because those situations were more dangerous than situations in which the animal did have control. The unconscious rule of thumb that links control with safety breaks down in modern life, however. People feel safer barreling down a highway at seventy miles an hour—without seat belts—than they do sitting in a passenger plane going through turbulence. The fact that we are in control of the car gives us the illusion of safety, even though all the empirical evidence shows we are safer in the plane.

Suicide rates in states with high levels of gun ownership are much higher than in states that have low levels of gun ownership. Alabama, Idaho, Colorado, Utah, Montana, Wyoming, and New Mexico have twice the rate of suicide of Rhode Island, Massachusetts, New Jersey, Connecticut, Hawaii, and New York. The United States as a whole has a very high suicide rate compared to other industrialized countries. Researchers working for the federal government once examined the suicide rate among children in the United States and twenty-five other industrialized countries over a single year. The suicide rate among American children was more than twice the average suicide rate among children in the other twenty-five countries. The homicide rate among children in the United States was five times higher. Guns were responsible for much of this. If you measured only gun-related homicide and suicide, American children were eleven times more likely than children in the other twenty-five countries to commit suicide by shooting themselves, were nine times more likely to be killed in accidental shootings, and were sixteen times more likely to be murdered. There were 1107 children shot to death in all the countries; 957 of these victims—86 percent—were children in the United States.

The researchers Arthur Kellermann and Donald Reay once examined all gun-related deaths over a lengthy period of time in King County in the state of Washington. They were trying to find evidence for the common intuition that gun owners are safer because they can protect themselves and their families should someone break into their homes. Kellermann and Reay identified nine deaths during the period of the study where people shot and killed an intruder. These are the stories that gun advocates endlessly relate to one another. In the same period, guns in people's homes were implicated in twelve accidental deaths and forty-one homicides—usually family members shooting one another. The number of suicides? Three hundred and thirty-three.

The gun lobby has often questioned the accuracy of these studies and reports. Rather than seek more accurate answers, however, it has leaned on Congress and successive administrations to cut off funding for research into firearm-related violence. After the Centers for Disease Control and Prevention study showing high rates of gun-related suicide and homicide among American children was published, Congress slashed funding for CDC firearm-injury research. Much of the suicide and homicide data is years old today because the research has effectively been choked off.

"Guns do not cause violence," said Kellermann, an Emory University researcher. He is a Southerner who grew up around guns, and he understands and appreciates gun culture. "The trigger does not pull the finger. . . . However, guns amplify the consequences of violence, and that amplification might be to an extent you cannot reverse. You can treat an overdose patient and stop the bleeding if they cut themselves, but guns have one of the highest completion rates for suicide. It is heartbreaking."

If you visit the website of the National Rifle Association, you will find that it is devoted to the idea that people have a right to defend themselves against criminals. What is never mentioned is the risk that gun owners pose to *themselves*. When we think about it intuitively—when we let our hidden brain do the thinking for us—the risk of suicide, accidents, and domestic violence feels remote compared to the risk of homicide. If we are smart people, if we are responsible gun owners, if we are not mentally unstable or defective, surely the suicide statistics will not apply to us? That is the way most of the *thirty thousand* people who kill themselves every year in America think, too. Stop for a moment and think about that number—more than ten times the number of Americans who died in the September 11 terrorist attacks kill themselves *every year* in the United States. It's early 2009 as I write these words. At least two hundred thousand more Americans have died from suicide than from terrorism since September 10, 2001. Which would you say poses a greater risk to the average American? If you are taking about ninety seconds to read each page of this book, someone in the United States will likely have committed suicide *since you started reading this chapter*.

"If you bought a gun today, I could tell you the risk of suicide to you and your family members is going to be two- to tenfold higher over the next twenty years," epidemiologist Matthew Miller at Harvard told me. "There are not many things you can do to increase your risk of dying tenfold."

I asked Michele Shinnick what she made of John Violanti's research and his idea that cops should check their guns at the station when they left work. She was silent for a long moment. Then she said she doubted it would work. Ed Shinnick knew and loved guns; he owned five weapons. He owned his own service revolver. If departments were to take away the guns of police officers when they left work, Michele Shinnick said, cops would buy weapons for their personal protection.

"Do I wish he did not have a gun?" she asked. "Sure, but I think if he was determined, he would have done it anyway."

The empirical research into suicide, however, calls into question the intuitively popular notion that people who are intent on suicide will always find ways to kill themselves. The statistics speak for themselves. About four hundred thousand people attempt suicide each year in the United States. The vast majority of those who survive do not go on to kill themselves. Suicide is primarily an act of impulse, which is why the suicide rate in Washington, D.C., fell by a quarter when people were restrained from owning handguns. The impulse to end your life rarely spans months and years. It usually lasts hours, maybe a day or two, a week at most. Within that narrow window, people with lethal means at their disposal are at far higher risk than people who lack the "vector" of destruction. Ed Shinnick was a great example of a stable, responsible, highly trained gun owner. All the weapons in his home were locked, and the guns were always placed in a safe that was also locked. He never drank. He was an upstanding, religious family man. Guns made Ed Shinnick feel safe. He was ready to confront any assassin—except the one in the mirror.

This chapter has focused so far on the subject of risk, which is all about small numbers. Our inability to intuitively tell the difference between something that has a one in a thousand chance of occurring and something that has a one in two thousand chance of occurring explains why we make errors in thinking about homicide and suicide. Both risks are rare—they involve tiny numbers. The difference between them is abstract: We do not feel it in our gut. The risk for suicide is twice as large as the risk for homicide in the United States, but it doesn't feel that way. Homicide scares us, and suicide does not, because in the absence of being able to grasp a concrete difference between a one in a thousand risk and a one in two thousand risk, we fall back on our hidden brains to do our thinking for us.

Our unconscious minds are exquisitely tuned to the unexpected, violent attack. We are always on the lookout for strange and exotic threats. In our evolutionary history, this made sense. If a new predator arrived on the scene, or an old predator suddenly came up with a clever new ambush, it required only a single example of the new threat to reshape our behavior. Our brains were designed in the crucible of a violent past, where the greatest threats to our ancestors came from predators, injuries, and traps. This might be why we all have primal fears. The creak on the stair in the middle of the night, the airplane crash, the psychopath loose on the streets. There might well be deep evolutionary reasons for these fears; it made sense, millennia ago, to fear situations where we had no control and situations that involved malevolent attackers.

In our modern world, however, the things we really ought to fear are almost entirely of our *own* doing. Failing to climb the stairs and get enough exercise kills far more people than any number of murderers climbing those stairs. You are at far greater risk of taking your own life than being killed by a terrorist. If you were to go strictly by the numbers, that cigarette in your hand ought to have you screaming louder than a chance encounter with Hannibal Lecter. But we don't go by the numbers, because we are not very good at thinking about the relative sizes of small numbers. Our unconscious minds fall back on intuitions that bias us into fearing the kind of risks that posed the greatest danger to our ancestors—violent, external threats. This may be why terrorism, homicide, and airplane crashes scare us more than heart disease, suicide, and lung cancer.

Unconscious biases in the hidden brain explain why we fear things that are unlikely and why we are blasé about things that can do us harm. I know this firsthand. My very first front-page article as a journalist was about the risks of riding motorcycles without helmets. I have close relatives who have died in traffic accidents. Eight years after that first article, I went on a road trip in India with some friends. On a motorcycle. Without a helmet. If you ask me why I did it, I will give you the same answers as thousands of people who do stupid things every day: I don't know. The risk seemed small. All my friends were riding on bikes without helmets. I thought I was a skilled rider. There are an infinite number of ways to rationalize unconscious bias.

As I was leaning into a turn at about forty miles an hour, a patch of gravel came up suddenly. I knew I was in trouble. Time slowed down. I skidded. I will never forget the awful feeling of traveling sideways, my wheels gliding beneath me like skates. I can feel it now. And then, in a moment, it was over. The wheels found traction, I pulled out of the skid, and it was as if nothing had happened.

The dumb algorithms in our hidden brain are not programmed to trigger panic when it comes to the risks we pose ourselves, which is why I didn't feel paralyzing fear when I chose to ride a motorbike without a helmet, and why millions of gun owners feel safer with loaded guns on their nightstands. Unconscious bias explains why so many of our fears—and national policies—are completely detached from reality. Two years after the September 11 terrorist attacks, a research study found that if Americans who thought they would be personally killed by terrorism were actually killed by terrorists, there would have to be the equivalent of a September 11–scale attack *every single day* in the United States. Americans did not misperceive the risk of terrorism because they enjoyed scaring themselves. No, the hidden brain biased us into paying exaggerated attention to terrorism because the hidden brain is programmed to be disproportionately vigilant to threats that are new, terrifying, and malevolent. We have carried our Stone Age brain into the Internet Age. It is Stone Age thinking that prompts us to spend so much of our national budget fighting terrorism and so little on the everyday diseases and threats that kill many, many more Americans—and that are certain to kill many, many more Americans in the years to come.

Small numbers aren't the only challenge that the brain finds difficult to handle. We are not very good with large numbers, either. This, too, has extraordinary consequences—in the realm of moral judgment.

The *Insiko 1907* was a tramp tanker that roamed the Pacific Ocean. Its twelve-man Taiwanese crew hunted the seas for fishing fleets in need of fuel; the *Insiko* had a cargo of tens of thousands of gallons of diesel. It was supposed to be an Indonesian ship, except that it was not registered in Indonesia because its owner, who lived in China, did not bother with taxes. In terms of international law, the *Insiko 1907* was stateless, a two-hundred-sixty-foot microscopic speck on the largest ocean on earth. On March 13, 2002, a fire broke out in the *Insiko*'s engine room. It killed a crew member and singed the ship's chief engineer. The fire spread quickly, and set aflame some oil in the bilge. The fire moved so fast that crew members did not have time to radio for help. Eleven survivors and the captain's puppy, who was along for the voyage, retreated to the tanker's forecastle. They dragged supplies of food and water with them. From their perch, they watched the fire burn for twenty days and twenty nights. The ship was about eight hundred miles south of Hawaii's Big Island, and adrift. Its crew could not call on anyone for help, and no one who could help knew of the *Insiko*'s existence, let alone its problems.

Drawn by wind and currents, the *Insiko* eventually got within two hundred twenty miles of Hawaii, where it was spotted by a cruise ship called the *Norwegian Star* on April 2. The cruise ship diverted course, rescued the Taiwanese crew, and radioed the United States Coast Guard. But as the *Norwegian Star* pulled away from the *Insiko* and steamed toward Hawaii, a few passengers on the cruise ship heard the sound of barking. The captain's puppy had been left behind on the tanker.

It is not entirely clear why the cruise ship did not rescue the Jack Russell mixed terrier, or why the Taiwanese crew did not insist on it. Some accounts suggest that cruise ship officers refused to take the dog because they were concerned they would run afoul of Hawaii's strict animal quarantine laws, and the Taiwanese captain, who had just been through a terrible ordeal, did not put his foot down. There may have been communication problems.

Whatever the reason, the burned-out tanker and its lonely inhabitant were abandoned on the terrible immensity of the Pacific. The *Norwegian Star* made a stop at Maui. A passenger who heard the barking dog called the Hawaiian Humane Society in Honolulu. The animal welfare group routinely rescued abandoned animals—675 animals were rescued the previous year—but recovering a dog on a tanker adrift in the Pacific was something new.

Pamela Burns, president of the Hawaiian Humane Society, was in Florida when she got a call about the dog. She decided the society should look into a rescue. The U.S. Coast Guard said it could not use taxpayer dollars to save the dog; the tanker was in international waters and outside the purview of the United States government. Officials told the Humane Society that rescuing the dog might cost anywhere from sixty to eighty thousand dollars. The Chinese owner of the *Insiko* was not planning to recover the ship, let alone the dog. The Humane Society alerted fishing boats about the lost tanker. Media reports began appearing about the terrier, whose name was Hokget.

Something about a lost puppy on an abandoned ship on the Pacific gripped people's imaginations. Money poured into the Humane Society to fund a rescue. One check was for five thousand dollars. People got in touch from as far away as New York and even England. In the end, donations came from thirty-nine states, the District of Columbia, and four foreign countries.

"It was just about a dog," Burns told me. "It was a fabulous example of [how] they are our best friend and they deserve good. This was an opportunity for people to feel good about rescuing a dog. People poured out their support. A handful of people were incensed. These people said, 'You should be giving money to the homeless.' "

But Burns felt the great thing about America was that people were free to give money to whatever cause they cared about, and people cared about Hokget.

The problem with a rescue was that no one knew where the *Insiko* was. The coast guard estimated it could be anywhere in an area measuring 360,000 square miles. The Humane Society paid forty-eight thousand dollars to a private company called American Marine Corporation to look for the *Insiko*. Two Humane Society officers boarded a salvage tugboat, the *American Quest,* and set off into the Pacific.

Air, sea, and high-tech surveillance equipment were all pressed into service. With each passing day, the calls from around the world intensified: Had Hokget been found? In six-hour shifts, Humane Society officers and the tugboat crew studied radar screens, hoping to get a glimpse of the tanker. Pressure was mounting on U.S. officials to do something. Under the guise of exercises, the U.S. Navy began quietly hunting for the *Insiko*—the tramp tanker was deemed a search target for a maintenance and training mission.

By April 7, the expensive search had turned up nothing. The *Insiko* had either sunk or drifted outside the coast guard's search box. The letters and checks continued to pour in.

"This check is in memory of the little dog lost at sea."

"Thank you for pulling my heartstrings and for reminding me of all the hope there is left in this world."

"This story is also great for the children. They learn to respect life."

On April 9, a window of hope opened. A Japanese fishing boat, the *Victoria City,* told the coast guard it had seen something that looked like the *Insiko*. The coast guard relayed the message to the Humane Society, which got word out to fishing fleets in the area to keep an eye out for the tanker. The *Insiko* had drifted far outside the coast guard's projections. It was still in international waters, but far to the west of the search box where rescuers had been hunting. The *Insiko* seemed roughly headed in the direction of Johnston Atoll, an unincorporated and uninhabited U.S. territory—and the coast guard finally decided this was a good enough reason to intervene. The coast guard dispatched a C-130 aircraft with a high-tech forward-looking radar. After searching another fifty thousand square miles of ocean, the coast guard found the *Insiko*. A photo taken with a telephoto lens showed a brown and white blur running across the deck of the tanker—Hokget was still alive. The C-130 was not equipped for a rescue, so the crew dropped their own lunches onto the tanker for the dog—pizza, granola bars, and oranges. Media interest in the terrier surged. The captain of the *Insiko* declared he would love to have his dog back; he said he had picked her up in Indonesia and named her after the Mandarin word for "fortune."

Two fishing vessels eventually reached the *Insiko*. For two days, fishermen tried to rescue the dog. The puppy took one look at them and fled below-decks in the direction of the engine room. The rescuers tried to tempt the terrier with peanut butter. They called out in multiple languages. It wasn't possible to chase Hokget into the engine room. The fire had rendered much of the *Insiko* dangerous—it was still carrying thousands of gallons of fuel, and no one knew the extent of the damage. The fishermen eventually gave up and let the *Insiko* go its aimless way.

Rusty Nall, vice president of American Marine Corporation, the private company contracted by the Humane Society to rescue Hokget, was in regular touch with coast guard officials and fishing fleets. When he heard the dog had not been seen after it ran below-decks, his heart sank. The engine room had a ten-foot drop. Had Hokget been inadvertently injured or killed? Would the long vigil turn out to be futile? Nall felt like giving up, except that when he went home each night, his nine-year-old daughter, Morgan, would ask, "Did you find the doggie, Daddy?" Nall would come back to work the next day and press on.

There was talk of dispatching the U.S. Navy to sink the *Insiko* as a way of ensuring that any release of hazardous materials would occur hundreds of miles from shore. This, of course, would kill the dog—assuming it was still alive. Facing intense public pressure to save Hokget, government officials concluded that asking the U.S. Navy to sink the tanker—750 miles from Hawaii, nearly 2,500 miles from the U.S. mainland, and drifting *away* from the United States—posed unacceptable environmental risks. The coast guard decided to access U.S. taxpayer funds to recover the *Insiko*. It wasn't officially called an animal rescue effort. The rescue was authorized under the Oil Spill Liability Trust Fund, based on the argument that if the aimless *Insiko* somehow managed to follow a westward course for 250 straight miles, it might run aground on Johnston Atoll and harm marine life.

The environmental concern was a lovely touch, given that the United States used Johnston Atoll for a good part of the twentieth century as a nuclear weapons test site and a dumping ground for chemical weapons from various wars. Nerve agents, blister agents, sarin, and plutonium contamination were Johnston Atoll's environmental legacy, but diesel was deemed too deadly.

The *American Quest* tugboat was called up again—this time funded by taxpayers—to rescue Hokget and bring the *Insiko* back to Honolulu.

Throughout the drama of the previous weeks, the Humane Society had called the dog Forgea, because it had been told the Mandarin name for the dog was "For-gay." That was the name that the fishermen had used when they'd tried to lure the dog with peanut butter. Now the Humane Society learned the dog's name was actually Hokget, according to the correct pronunciation in the dialect Hokkien, the language of the tanker's captain. Armed with this new information and a dog trap, the *American Quest* set off. In case the terrier did not come voluntarily, the rescuers also took along treats and a ham bone.

On April 26, nearly one and a half months after the puppy's ordeal began, the *American Quest* found the *Insiko* and boarded the tanker. The forty-pound female pup was still alive, and hiding in a pile of tires. It was a hot day, so Brian Murray, the *American Quest*'s salvage supervisor, went in and simply grabbed the terrier by the scruff of her neck. The puppy was terrified and shook for two hours. Her rescuers fed her, bathed her, and applied lotion to her nose, which was sunburned.

Hokget arrived in Honolulu on May 2 (with the *Insiko* hauled in tow so her diesel could be salvaged) and was greeted by crowds of spectators, a press conference, banners welcoming her to America, and a pretty red Hawaiian lei. A local radio station played "Who Let the Dogs Out?" The local, national, and international media were all in prominent attendance. After serving a period in quarantine, Hokget was adopted by the family of Michael Kuo of Honolulu. She put on weight and was signed up for dog classes.

The story of Hokget's rescue is comical, but it is also touching. Human beings from around the world came together to save a dog. The vast majority of people who sent money to the Humane Society knew they would never personally see Hokget, never have their hands licked in gratitude. Saving the dog, as Pamela Burns suggested to me, was an act of pure altruism, and a marker of the remarkable capacity human beings have to empathize with the plight of others.

There are a series of disturbing questions, however. Eight years before Hokget was rescued, the same world that showed extraordinary compassion in the rescue of a dog sat on its hands as a million human beings were killed in Rwanda. Shortly after the dog rescue, as a genocide in Darfur unfolded with terrible accounts of mass rape and murder, ABC News devoted eighteen minutes over the entire course of 2004 to tell Americans in nightly newscasts what was happening. ABC, by the way, led the way among the major networks. NBC devoted five minutes and CBS three minutes in 2004 to Darfur.

The twentieth century reveals a shockingly long list of similar horrors that have been ignored by the world as they unfolded: two million Armenians in 1915, six million Jews in the Holocaust. John Prendergast of the Enough project, an advocacy group committed to ending genocide, told me that more than five million people have died as a result of war, famine, and disease in the Congo over the past decade. Why have successive generations of Americans—a people with extraordinary powers of compassion—done so little to halt suffering on such a large scale? Why have successive American presidents placed genocide so low on their list of priorities? It isn't because of a lack of awareness. When President George W. Bush was sworn into office in January 2001, the first words he heard as president were about an unfolding crisis in southern Sudan, where more than two million people eventually died. The Reverend Franklin Graham, who was leading a prayer at the Bush inauguration, whispered, "Mr. President, I hope you do something about southern Sudan."

There are many explanations for the discrepancy between our response to Hokget and our response to genocide. Some argue that Americans care little about foreign lives—but then what should we make about their willingness to spend thousands of dollars to rescue a dog, a foreign dog on a stateless ship in international waters? Well, perhaps Americans care more about pets than people? But that does not stand up to scrutiny, either. Hokget's rescue was remarkable, but there are countless stories about similar acts of compassion and generosity that people show toward their fellow human beings every day. No, there is something about genocide, about mass death in particular, that seems to trigger inaction.

I believe our inability to wrap our minds around large numbers is responsible for our apathy toward mass suffering. We are unconsciously biased in our moral judgment, in much the same way we are biased when we think about risk. Just as we are blasé about heart disease and lackadaisical about suicide, but terrified about psychopaths and terrorists, so also we make systematic errors in thinking about moral questions—especially those involving large numbers of people.

The philosopher Peter Singer once devised a dilemma that highlights a central contradiction in our moral reasoning. If you see a child drowning in a pond, and you know you can save the child without any risk to your own life—but you would ruin a fine pair of shoes worth two hundred dollars if you jumped into the water—would you save the child or save your shoes? Most people react incredulously to the question; obviously, a child's life is worth more than a pair of shoes. If this is the case, Singer asked, why do large numbers of people hesitate to write a check for two hundred dollars to a reputable charity that could save the life of a child halfway around the world—when there are millions of such children who need our help? Even when people are absolutely certain their money will not be wasted and will be used to save a child's life, fewer people are willing to write the check than to leap into the pond.

Our moral responsibilities feel different in these situations even though Singer is absolutely right in arguing they are equivalent challenges; one feels immediate and visceral, the other distant and abstract. We feel personally responsible for one child, whereas the other is one of millions who need help. Our responsibility feels diffused when it comes to children in distant places—there are many people who could write that check. But distance and diffusion of responsibility do not explain why we step forward in some cases—why did so many people come forward to save Hokget? Why did they write checks for a dog they would never meet? Why did they feel a single abandoned dog on a stateless ship was *their* problem?

I want to offer a disturbing idea. The reason human beings seem to care so little about mass suffering and death is precisely *because* the suffering is happening on a mass scale. The brain is simply not very good at grasping the implications of mass suffering. Americans would be far more likely to step forward if only a few people were suffering, or a single person were in pain. Hokget did not draw our sympathies because we care more about dogs than people; she drew our sympathies because she was a *single* dog lost on the biggest ocean in the world. If the hidden brain biases our perceptions about risk toward exotic threats, it shapes our compassion into a telescope. We are best able to respond when we are focused on a single victim.

We don't feel twenty times sadder when we hear that twenty people have died in a disaster than when we hear that one person has died, even though the magnitude of the tragedy *is* twenty times larger. We feel outrage at a murderer who kills someone, but we don't feel ten times the outrage if the murderer turns out to be a serial killer. We certainly don't feel one hundred times the outrage if he turns out to be a mass-murdering psychopath who kills a hundred people. We do not viscerally feel that a Hitler, who is responsible for the deaths of millions, is millions of times worse than the murderer who kills one person. We can certainly reach such a conclusion abstractly, in our conscious minds, but we cannot *feel it viscerally,* because that is the domain of the hidden brain, and the hidden brain is simply not calibrated to deal with the difference between a single death and a million deaths.

But the paradox does not end there. Even if ten deaths do not make us feel ten times as sad as a single death, shouldn't we feel five times as sad, or even at least twice as sad? There is disturbing evidence that shows that in many situations, not only do we not care twice as much about ten deaths as we do about one, but we may actually care *less*. I strongly suspect that if the *Insiko* had been carrying a hundred dogs, many people would have cared less about their fate than they did about Hokget. A hundred dogs do not have a single face, a single name, a single life story around which we can wrap our imaginations—and our compassion.

I found it ironic when Pamela Burns of the Hawaiian Humane Society told me that the thing she could not understand is how people spend fifty thousand dollars getting a kidney transplant for their cat when hundreds of healthy animals at shelters around the country are being euthanized. But when you consider the problem we have with large numbers, this makes sense. We spend our money to save one life and not ten lives or a hundred, because our internal telescope unconsciously biases us to care more about one life than a hundred.

The evidence for what I am going to call the telescope effect comes from a series of fascinating experiments. At the University of Oregon, the psychologist Paul Slovic asked volunteers shortly after the Rwandan genocide to imagine they were officials in charge of a humanitarian rescue effort. They could spend their money saving forty-five hundred lives at a refugee camp, but there were also many other pressing needs for the money. Without the volunteers being aware of it, Slovic divided them into two groups. Both groups were told their money could save forty-five hundred lives, but one group was told the refugee camp had eleven thousand people, whereas the other group was told the refugee camp had one hundred thousand people. Slovic found that people were much more reluctant to spend the money on the large camp than they were to spend the money on the small camp.

Intrigued, Slovic pressed further. He asked different groups of volunteers to imagine they were running a philanthropic foundation. Would they rather spend ten million dollars to save 10,000 lives from a disease that caused 15,000 deaths a year, or save 20,000 lives from a disease that killed 290,000 people a year? Overwhelmingly, volunteers preferred to spend money saving the ten thousand lives rather than the twenty thousand lives. Rather than tailor their investments to saving the largest number of lives, people sought to save the largest *proportion* of lives among the different groups of victims. An investment directed toward disease A could save two-thirds of the victims, whereas an investment directed at disease B could save "only" seven percent of the victims.

We respond to mass suffering in much the same way we respond to most things in our lives. We fall back on rules of thumb, on feelings, on intuitions. People who choose to spend money saving ten thousand lives rather than twenty thousand lives are not bad people. Rather, like those who spend thousands of dollars rescuing a single dog rather than directing the same amount of money to save a dozen dogs, they are merely allowing their hidden brain to guide them.

I have often wondered why the hidden brain displays a telescope effect when it comes to compassion. Evolutionary psychology tends to be an armchair sport, so please take my explanation for the paradox as one of several possible answers. The telescope effect may have arisen because evolution has built a powerful bias into us to preferentially love our kith and kin. It is absurd that we spend two hundred dollars on a birthday party for our son or our daughter when we could send the same money to a charity and save the life of a child halfway around the world. How can one child's birthday party mean more to us than another child's life? When we put it in those terms, we sound like terrible human beings. The paradox, as with the rescue of Hokget, is that our impulse springs from love, not callousness. Evolution has built a fierce loyalty toward our children into the deepest strands of our psyche. Without the unthinking telescope effect in the unconscious mind, parents would not devote the immense time and effort it takes to raise children; generations of our ancestors would not have braved danger and cold, predators and hunger, to protect their young. The fact that you and I exist testifies to the utility of having a telescope in the brain that caused our ancestors to care intensely about the good of the few rather than the good of the many.

This telescope is activated when we hear a single cry for help—the child drowning in the pond, the puppy abandoned on an ocean. When we think of human suffering on a mass scale, our telescope does not work, because it has not been designed to work in such situations.

What makes evolutionary sense rarely makes moral sense. (One paradox of evolution is that ruthless natural selection has produced a species that recoils at the ruthlessness of natural selection.) Humans are the first and only species that is even aware of large-scale suffering taking place in distant lands; the moral telescope in our brain has not had a chance to evolve and catch up with our technological advances. When we are told about a faraway genocide, we can apply only our conscious mind to the challenge. We can reason, but we cannot feel the visceral compassion that is automatically triggered by the child who is drowning right before us. Our conscious minds can tell us that it is absurd to spend a boatload of money to save one life when the same money could be used to save ten—just as it can tell us it is absurd to be more worried about homicide than suicide. But in moral decision-making, as in many other domains of life where we are unaware of how unconscious biases influence us, it is the hidden brain that usually carries the day.

Slovic once told volunteers about a seven-year-old girl in Mali who was starving and in desperate need of help. Volunteers in the experiment were given a certain amount of money and asked how much they were willing to spend to help the little girl. On average, people gave half their money to help the girl. Slovic then asked another group of volunteers the same question, except instead of the little girl, the volunteers were told about the problem of famine in Africa, and that there were millions of people in dire need of help. The volunteers gave half as much money as the volunteers in the first group. In another study in Israel, Slovic and his colleagues found that people were willing to donate more money to help save the life of a single child with cancer than they were to help eight children with cancer.

Slovic took the experiment that showcased the little girl in Africa a step further. He told another group of volunteers about a little boy in Mali. One group of volunteers was asked whether they would give money to the little girl; another was asked whether they would donate money to the little boy. A third group of volunteers was told about both the boy and the girl and asked how much they were willing to give. People gave the same amount of money when told about either the boy or the girl. But when the children were presented together, the volunteers gave less.

Journalists sometimes talk about compassion fatigue, the inability of people to respond to suffering when the scale or length of the suffering exceeds some astronomical number. But Slovic's work suggests that compassion fatigue starts when the number of victims in need of help rises from one to two.

"The feelings of sadness dropped," Slovic said about the volunteers who were told about the two children in need of help. He added, "You can't lock on to two people in need of help as closely as you can lock on to one person. You can't make an emotional connection as strongly to two as to one. If empathy is putting yourself in someone else's shoes, think of putting yourself in two people's shoes. It does not work. It falls apart."

When we rely on the hidden brain to guide our moral decision-making, we spend millions on dramatic rescues of a few lives, and spend next to nothing on saving the lives of millions. There is no use complaining about the hidden brain, or wishing it away. The telescope effect in our moral judgment is part of our nature. There is nothing we can do about it. But there is something we can do about our *actions*. We can choose to allow our actions to be guided by reason rather than instinct, choose to set up national and international institutions that respond instantly to humanitarian crises, rather than wait for our heartstrings to be pulled by stories of individual tragedy. If we rely on our moral telescopes, there will be people in a hundred years who ask how the world could have sat on its hands through so many genocides in the twenty-first century.

Making the unconscious conscious is difficult because the central obstacle lies within ourselves. But putting reason ahead of instinct and intuition is also what sets us apart from every other species that has ever lived. Understanding the hidden brain and building safeguards to protect us against its vagaries can help us be more successful in our everyday lives. It can aid us in our battle against threats and help us spend our money more wisely. But it can also do something more important than any of those things: It can make us better people.

For all the ways this book has shown how the rational mind is unequal to the machinations of the hidden brain, this is also a book that argues that reason is our only bulwark against bias. Our hidden brain will always make some criminals seem more dangerous, and some presidential candidates seem less trustworthy, because of the color of their skin. Terrorism, psychopaths, and homicide will always seem scarier to us than obesity, smoking, and suicide. The heartbreaking story about the single puppy lost at sea will make us cry more quickly than a dry account of a million children killed by malaria. In every one of these cases, reason is our only rock against the tides of unconscious bias. It is our lighthouse and our life jacket. It is—or should be—our voice of conscience.

Acknowledgments

This book is filled with ideas that are not my own: I have drawn on the work and insights of hundreds of researchers, research studies, books, and reports. Scientists across the United States and the world have my grateful thanks for the experimental data and research that form the backbone of this book. In many cases I have taken scientific ideas and applied them to everyday problems that cannot be studied in laboratories. Dozens of people have helped me do this by sharing personal stories of triumph and tragedy. I am very grateful to them.

It is impossible to mention every researcher and source who informed my reporting, but I would like to note my immense debt to Mahzarin Banaji, the Harvard University psychologist who first inspired me to study the effects of unconscious bias in everyday life. Among many others I am very grateful to Brian Nosek and Anthony Greenwald; Frances Aboud and John Bargh; Abraham Tesser, John Trojanowski, and Virginia Lee; Ben Barres and Joan Roughgarden; Brian and Wendy NcNamara and Evelyn Sommers; Tiffany Alexander, Will DeRiso, and Benigno Aguirre; Jennifer Eberhardt, Robert Dunham, and Ernest Porter; Rosann Barker, John Powell, Drew Westen, Jerry Kang, Camille Charles, Todd Rogers, and Celinda Lake; Ariel Merari, Masami Takahashi, Scott Atran, Rebecca Moore, Fielding McGehee, Vernon Gosney, and Deborah and Larry Layton; Michele Shinnick, Arthur Kellermann, Matthew Miller, John Violanti, Pamela Burns, and Paul Slovic. There are many people who contributed to my reporting who are not mentioned in the pages of this book. They include Eric Ferrero, Nick Brustin, Debi Cornwall, and Sam Millsap; Baba Shiv and Debu Purohit; Kelly Connelly and the Baycrest Center for Geriatric Care; Eric Finzi and Elizabeth Sheldon; Kevin Simowski, Andrew Cullen, and John Duffy; Scott Plous, Ludovic Blain, Ismail White, and Marty Marks; Sandra Castro and Billy Nolas, Pam Willenz, Cherie Castellano, and the California Historical Society. Special thanks go to Scott Fappiano, John D. Cerqueira, and the great guitarist Les Paul.

My agent Laurie Liss of Sterling Lord Literistic spurred me to write the book proposal that led to *The Hidden Brain,* and guided me through countless revisions. This book would not exist without her. Throughout the reporting and writing of this book, Laurie offered me hours of counsel—literary and personal—for which I am deeply grateful.

I am honored to have had Chris Jackson of Spiegel & Grau edit this book. Every conversation I had with Chris replenished my reserves of curiosity and energy, those twin engines that propel all writers. I am indebted to him—and to Julie Grau and Cindy Spiegel—for their deep commitment to this book and its ideas.

Many colleagues taught me how to be a good reporter—and gave me breaks when I needed them. I am so grateful to Arlene Morgan and Donald Drake for years of mentoring and friendship, and to Leonard Downie Jr., Phil Bennett, Dorothy Brown, Mark Bowden, Ted Glasser, Marion Lewenstein, Dale Maharidge, Judy Serrin, Reggie Stuart, and Julia Vitullo-Martin. A Neiman Fellowship at Harvard University and a fellowship at the Peter Jennings Project for Journalists and the Constitution helped this book in crucial ways. My warm thanks to Bob Giles, Jane Eisner, and Kayce Freed Jennings. Many journalism organizations provided me with comrades and recognition—among them, I am very grateful to the Asian American Journalist Association and the South Asian Journalists Association.

The Washington Post makes an appearance on the very first line of the book; its influence runs to the very last. Donald Graham, Katharine Weymouth, and the extended Graham family have built an institution of tremendous depth and integrity, and editors Marcus

Brauchli, Liz Spayd, and Raju Narisetti have continued a proud tradition of excellence. Many editors at the *Post* have guided me over the years. Among them, I am especially grateful to Steve Coll, Susan Glasser, Steve Holmes, Nils Bruzelius, Maralee Schwartz, Tom Shroder, Kevin Merida, and Peter Perl. I am particularly grateful to Rob Stein and Sydney Trent, for seeing abilities in me that I did not know I possessed.

Countless friends aided me as I wrote this book. Among them are Brian Lopp, Sara Borwick, Sandra Marquardt, Hans Kristensen, Paul Joseph, and Karen Williams; Alissa Trotz, Aparna Devare, Salil Joshi, Molly Hindman, Karan Singh, Maya Bhullar, Yael Intrator, and Sanjay D'Souza. I am especially indebted to Kay Intrator, Ashwin Joshi, Kiran Mirchandani, and Ena Dua for their endless love and generosity.

I owe so much of this book to my parents, Vatsala Vedantam and Vedantam L. Sastry, who know a thing or two about fighting bias and unfairness. Gayatri Vedantam is very likely the finest sister in the world. My sincere thanks to Sudheer Tambe, Abhijeet Tambe, and V. K. Viswanathan for never behaving like in-laws.

Through the long journey of this book, my daughter Anya filled my world with sunshine and revealed to me my own reserves of strength and kindness. My wife, Ashwini Tambe, dealt patiently with my endless distractions and insane work hours, and provided me with crucial advice when I needed it most. I will always be in their debt.

Notes

Chapter 1: The Myth of Intention

18 the *vicinity* of an overweight person Michelle R. Hebl and Laura M. Mannix, "The Weight of Obesity in Evaluating Others: A Mere Proximity Effect," *Personality and Social Psychology Bulletin,* Vol. 29 (2003), p. 28.

19 more competent based only on appearance Shankar Vedantam, "Look and Act Like a Winner, and You Just Might Be One," *Department of Human Behavior, The Washington Post,* November 6, 2006, p. 2.

Chapter 2: The Ubiquitous Shadow

26 people were far more honest Melissa Bateson, Daniel Nettle, and Gilbert Roberts, "Cues of Being Watched Enhance Cooperation in a Real-world Setting," *Biology Letters,* Published Online, doi:10.1098/rsbl.2006.0509.

26 more optimism about their lives David Hirshleifer and Tyler Shumway, "Good Day Sunshine: Stock Returns and the Weather," *The Journal of Finance,* Vol. 58, No. 3 (June 2003), pp. 1009–1032.

27 Figure 1. Pounds paid per litre Bateson, Nettle, and Roberts, "Cues of Being Watched Enhance Cooperation in a Real-world Setting," Reprinted with permission.

29 overvalue companies with easy names Adam L. Alter and Daniel M. Oppenheimer, "Predicting Short-term Stock Fluctuations by Using Processing Fluency," *Proceedings of the National Academy of Sciences,* Vol. 103, No. 24 (June 13, 2006), pp. 9369–9372.

31 tips that were *140 percent larger* Rick B. van Baaren, Rob W. Holland, Bregje Steenaert, and Ad van Knippenberg, "Mimicry for Money: Behavioral Consequences of Imitation," Journal of Experimental Social Psychology, Vol. 39 (2003), pp. 393–398.

32 shaking their feet in response Tanya L. Chartrand and John. A. Bargh,

"The Chameleon Effect: The Perception-Behavior Link and Social Interaction," *Journal of Personality and Social Psychology,* Vol. 76, No. 6 (1999), pp. 893–910.

33 **constantly adapting to different contexts** Shankar Vedantam, "For Political Candidates, Saying Can Become Believing," *Department of Human Behavior, The Washington Post,* February 25, 2008, p. A03.

34 **"calls us fire and ice"** Shankar Vedantam, "Scientific Couple Devoted to Each Other and Alzheimer's Work," *The Philadelphia Inquirer,* October 26, 1998.

39 **help strangers and undermine their lovers** Abraham Tesser and Jonathan Smith, "Some Effects of Task Relevance and Friendship on Helping: You Don't Always Help the One You Like," *Journal of Experimental Social Psychology,* Vol. 16 (1980), pp. 582–590.

39 **success of the son** Abraham Tesser, "Self-esteem Maintenance in Family Dynamics," *Journal of Personality and Social Psychology,* Vol. 39, No. 1 (1980), pp. 77–91.

Chapter 3: Tracking the Hidden Brain

52 **sixteen patients with frontotemporal dementia** Mario F. Mendez, Andrew K. Chen, Jill S. Shapira, and Bruce L. Miller, "Acquired Sociopathy and Frontotemporal Dementia," *Dementia and Geriatric Cognitive Disorders,* Vol. 20 (2005), pp. 99–104.

53 **researchers posed a series of dilemmas** Michael Koenigs, Liane Young, Ralph Adolphs, Daniel Tranel, Fiery Cushman, Marc Hauser, and Antonio Damasio, "Damage to the Prefrontal Cortex Increases Utilitarian Moral Judgements," *Nature,* Vol. 446 (2007), pp. 908–911.

55 **ancient rules developed** Shankar Vedantam, "If It Feels Good to Be Good, It Might Be Only Natural," *The Washington Post,* May 28, 2007, p. A01.

56 **Decreases in gray matter** Jason Tregellas, "Connecting Brain Structure and Function in Schizophrenia," *The American Journal of Psychiatry,* Vol. 166 (February 2009), pp. 134–136.

56 **Being able to read expressions** Jeremy Hall, Jonathan M. Harris, Reiner Sprengelmeyer, Anke Sprengelmeyer, Andrew W. Young, Isabel M. Santos, Eve C. Johnstone, and Stephen M. Lawrie, "Social Cognition and Face Processing in Schizophrenia," *The British Journal of Psychiatry,* Vol. 185 (2004), pp. 169–170.

Chapter 4: The Infant's Stare, Macaca, and Racist Seniors

61 **newborns who were just a day** Carlo Umilta, Francesca Simion, and Eloisa Valenza, "Newborn's Preference for Faces," *European Psychologist,* Vol. 1, No. 3 (September 1996), pp. 200–205.

61 **preferential attachment to her mother's face** I.W.R. Bushnell, "Mother's

Face Recognition in Newborn Infants: Learning and Memory," *Infant and Child Development,* Vol. 10 (2001), pp. 67–74.

62 **scientists have found an area** Nancy Kanwisher, Damian Stanley, and Alison Harris, "The Fusiform Face Area Is Selective for Faces, Not Animals," *NeuroReport,* Vol. 10, No. 1 (January 18, 1999), pp. 183–87.

62 **dictator's face imprinted on the moon** "Iraqi Bloggers React to Execution," BBC News, http://news.bbc.co.uk/2/hi/talking_point/6228785.stm, January 11, 2007.

62 **the form of a human smile** Pankaj Aggarwal and Ann L. McGill, "Is That Car Smiling at Me? Schema Congruity As a Basis for Evaluating Anthropomorphized Products," *Journal of Consumer Research,* Vol. 34 (December 2007), pp. 468–479.

63 **Experiments show that our unthinking tendency** Gerald J. Gorn, Yuwei Jiang, and Gita Venkataramani Johar, "Babyfaces, Trait Inferences, and Company Evaluations in a Public Relations Crisis," *Journal of Consumer Research,* Vol. 35, No. 1 (June 2008), pp. 36–49.

65 **officer had treated McKinney with "disrespect"** "McKinney Decries 'Inappropriate Touching' by Capitol Police," FOX News, www.foxnews.com/story/0,2933,189940,00.html, April 1, 2006.

66 **Ignoring the role of race** Christian A. Meissner and John C. Brigham, "Thirty Years of Investigating the Own-Race Bias in Memory for Faces: A Meta-Analytic Review," *Psychology, Public Policy, and Law,* Vol. 7, No. 1 (2001), pp. 3–35.

67 **"good," "kind," and "clean"** Frances E. Aboud, "The Formation of In-Group Favoritism and Out-Group Prejudice in Young Children: Are They Distinct Attitudes?" *Developmental Psychology,* Vol. 39, No. 1 (2003), pp. 48–60.

67 **similar studies going back many years** Frances E. Aboud, Morton J. Mendelson, and Kelly T. Purdy, "Cross-Race Peer Relations and Friendship Quality," *International Journal of Behavioral Development,* Vol. 27, No. 2 (2003), pp. 165–173.

68 **assessed the racial views of children** Frances Aboud and Anna-Beth Doyle, "Parental and Peer Influences on Children's Racial Attitudes," *International Journal of Intercultural Relations,* Vol. 20, No. 3–4 (1996), pp. 371–383. Aboud did not conduct her studies in the chronological order in which I have described them in this chapter. Like all journeys of scientific discovery, Aboud's path was winding and doubled back on itself. To solve a particular problem, for example, she sometimes went back to a study she'd conducted earlier in her career. In the interest of explaining her ideas clearly, I have described these experiments in a sequence that allows ideas to unfold in a relatively linear manner. I want to make clear that this is a writer's liberty; scientific discoveries invariably unfold in chaotic steps with numerous roadblocks and dead ends.

68 **a regular diet of hate speech** Ibid.

69 **playing on a river** The story was modified from the children's book *Three at Sea* by Timothy Bush.

73 **may feel white dolls are prettier** Psychologists Kenneth and Mamie Clark conducted groundbreaking experiments in the 1940s showing that black children believed white dolls were good and black dolls were bad. A remarkable replication of the experiment in 2005 can be viewed at http://mediathatmattersfest.org/films/a_girl_like_me.

74 **straight people *and* gay people** Shankar Vedantam, "See No Bias," *The Washington Post Magazine,* January 23, 2005, p. 12.

76 **far fewer interracial friendships** Maureen T. Hallinan and Ruy A. Teixeira, "Students' Interracial Friendships: Individual Characteristics, Structural Effects, and Racial Differences," *American Journal of Education,* Vol. 95, No. 4. (1987), pp. 563–583.

76 **the same phenomenon has been documented** Frances E. Aboud and Janani Sankar, "Friendship and Identity in a Language-Integrated School," *International Journal of Behavioral Development,* Vol. 31, No. 5 (2007), pp. 445–453.

76 **a close friend from another race** Aboud, Mendelson, and Purdy, "Cross-Race Peer Relations and Friendship Quality."

76 **When a prejudiced child was placed** Frances Aboud and Anna-Beth Doyle, "Does Talk of Race Foster Prejudice or Tolerance in Children?" Unpublished Manuscript, 1996.

82 **six-year-olds, ten-year-olds** Andrew Scott Baron and Mahzarin Banaji, "The Development of Implicit Attitudes," *Psychological Science,* Vo. 17, No. 1 (2006), pp. 53–58.

83 **"It's contrary to what I believe"** *Meet the Press,* September 17, 1006.

86 **her ability to exert "executive control"** William von Hippel, "Aging, Executive Functioning, and Social Control," *Current Directions in Psychological Science,* Vol. 16, No. 5 (2007), pp. 240–244.

86 **If people need executive control** Matthew T. Gailliot, B. Michelle Peruche, E. Ashby Plant, and Roy F. Baumeister, "Stereotypes and Prejudice in the Blood: Sucrose Drinks Reduce Prejudice and Stereotyping," *Journal of Experimental Social Psychology,* Vol. 45 (2009), pp. 288–290.

Chapter 5: The Invisible Current

93 **the role that sexism plays** Shankar Vedantam, "The Myth of the Iron Lady," *Department of Human Behavior, The Washington Post,* November 12, 2007, p. A03.

94 **Andrea seemed less likeable** Madeline E. Heilman and Tyler G. Okimoto, "Why Are Women Penalized for Success at Male Tasks? The Implied Communality Deficit," *Journal of Applied Psychology,* Vol. 92, No. 1 (2007), pp. 81–92.

94 **the ever popular "bitch"** Katharine Q. Seelye and Julie Bosman, "Media

Charged with Sexism in Clinton Coverage," *The New York Times,* June 13, 2008.

95 **"attacks were being made"** Ibid.

96 **earn about seventy-seven cents** Shankar Vedantam, "Salary, Gender and the Social Cost of Haggling," *The Washington Post,* July 30, 2007, p. A07.

96 **women who work full-time** Ibid.

99 **followed the lives of twenty-nine transmen** Kristen Schilt, "Just One of the Guys? How Transmen Make Gender Visible at Work," *Gender & Society,* Vol. 20, No. 4 (August 2006), pp. 465–489.

99 **"I swear they let the guys"** Ibid.

100 **thirty-four-year-old "stealth" transman** Ibid.

100 **"from one day to the next"** Ibid.

100 **salaries of forty-three transgendered people** Kristen Schilt and Matthew Wiswall, "Before and After: Gender Transitions, Human Capital, and Workplace Experiences," *The B. E. Journal of Economic Analysis & Policy,* Vol. 8, No. 1 (2008), Article 39, pp. 1–26.

100 **"While transgender people have"** Ibid.

103 **fewer women professors** Ben A. Barres, "Does Gender Matter?" *Nature,* Vol. 442, July 13, 2006, pp. 133–136.

104 **all male-female human relationships** Joan Roughgarden, Meeko Oishi, and Erol Akcay, "Reproductive Social Behavior: Cooperative Games to Replace Sexual Selection," *Science,* Vol. 311, February 17, 2006, pp. 965–969.

104 **Sex was also about building alliances** Joan Roughgarden published a book in April 2009 detailing her theory of social selection. It is titled *The Genial Gene: Deconstructing Darwinian Selfishness.*

Chapter 6: The Siren's Call

113 **thirty-three-year-old woman** Some of this information is based on interviews I conducted with Kevin Simowski, who was a member of the prosecution team that helped convict Martell Welch, and with Tiffany Alexander, an eyewitness on the Belle Isle bridge.

115 **Behind Tiffany, other cars stopped** I drew on personal interviews and several news accounts to piece together the events that led to Deletha Word's death. The articles include an August 24, 1995, account in the *Detroit Free Press* titled "Belle Isle Attack Witness Recalls No Cheering"; a September 2, 1995, article in *The New York Times* titled "Witnesses Recall Beaten Woman's Final Leap"; and a *Time* magazine article on September 11, 1995, titled "Death in a Crowded Place."

119 **account of the event pieced together** John Duffy and Mary S. Schaeffer, *Triumph Over Tragedy: September 11 and the Rebirth of a Business,* Hoboken, N.J.: Wiley, 2002.

120 **from their perch in the sky** For a masterful account of what happened in the World Trade Center on September 11—told from the point of view of its

victims scattered across the towers and on various floors—please read *102 Minutes: The Untold Story of the Fight to Survive Inside the Twin Towers*, a book by Jim Dwyer and Kevin Flynn (New York: Times Books, 2004). The book grew out of an account published in *The New York Times* on May 26, 2002, headlined, "102 MINUTES: Last Words at the Trade Center; Fighting to Live as the Towers Died" by Dwyer, Flynn, Eric Lipton, James Glanz, and Ford Fessenden, Alain Delaqueriere and Tom Torok.

124 **Beningo Aguirre published an extraordinary paper** B. E. Aguirre, Dennis Wenger, and Gabriela Vigo, "A Test of the Emergent Norm Theory of Collective Behavior," *Sociological Forum,* Vol. 13, No. 2 (1998), pp. 301–320.

130 **Actors in elevators "accidentally" dropped** Bibb Latané and James M. Dabbs, Jr., "Sex, Group-Size and Helping in Three Cities," *Sociometry,* Vol. 38, No. 2 (1975), pp. 180–194.

Chapter 7: The Tunnel

141 **Ariel Merari once wondered** Ariel Merari explained his research to me during interviews. He also shared drafts of papers and other materials. Some of Merari's work was published in the book *Root Causes of Terrorism: Myths, Reality and Ways Forward,* edited by Tore Bjørgo (New York: Routledge, 2005).

145 ***In My Father's House*** Min S. Yee and Thomas N. Layton, *In My Father's House: The Story of the Layton Family and the Reverend Jim Jones,* New York: Holt, Rinehart, and Winston, 1981.

155 **Berman and Laitin convincingly argue** Eli Berman and David D. Laitin, "Religion, Terrorism and Public Goods: Testing the Club Model," Journal of Public Economics, Vol. 92 (2008), pp. 1942–1967.

Chapter 8: Shades of Justice

170 **asked authorities to keep black "outsiders"** Henry Goldman, "Jury Rules That Killer Should Die," *The Philadelphia Inquirer,* February 28, 1986, p. B03.

172 **"Mr. Gentile, I'd just like"** *Commonwealth v. Ernest Porter,* Court of Common Pleas, First Judicial District of Pennsylvania, Trial Transcripts, February 20–27, 1986.

173 **On a Thursday morning that November** *Commonwealth v. Arthur Hawthorne,* Court of Common Pleas, First Judicial District of Pennsylvania, Trial Transcripts, Docket No. CP-51-CR-0104701-1993.

173 **"Get her in here!"** Ibid.

174 **"What did you do that for?"** Ibid.

175 **"It was fucked up"** Ibid.

175 **"Shut up. You talk too much."** Ibid.

176 **some violent crimes produce death sentences** Jennifer L. Eberhardt, Paul G. Davies, Valerie J. Purdie-Vaughns, and Sheri Lynn Johnson, "Look-

ing Deathworthy: Perceived Stereotypicality of Black Defendants Predicts Capital-Sentencing Outcomes," *Psychological Science*, Vol. 17, No. 5 (2006), pp. 383–386.

178 **"Those who bring a criminal purpose"** Kurt Heine, "You Deserve the Electric Chair, Justices Tell 3 Murderers," *Philadelphia Daily News*, February 9, 1990, p. 8.

178 **less likely than their counterparts** Charles S. Lanier and James R. Acker, "Capital Punishment, the Moratorium Movement, and Empirical Questions," *Psychology, Public Policy, and Law*, Vol. 10, No. 4 (2004), pp. 577–617.

179 **A variety of reports suggest** Eugene Robinson, "(White) Women We Love," *The Washington Post*, June 10, 2005, p. A23.

181 **Sabo sentenced more people to die** Richard Willing, "'King of Death Row' Forced from Bench: Pa. Jurist Who Has Sentenced 31 to Die Is Ordered to Retire," *USA Today*, December 31, 1997, p. 3A.

183 **"Were you able to see positively"** *Commonwealth v. Ernest Porter.*

184 **"On April 30, 1985, my Philadelphia"** *Commonwealth of Pennsylvania (Respondent) v. Ernest Porter (Petitioner)*, Court of Common Pleas, Philadelphia County, Petitioner's Response to Commonwealth's Letter Brief, March 22, 2007.

Chapter 9: Disarming the Bomb

188 **Greenwald guessed if he gave people** Vedantam, "See No Bias."

190 **Many Americans are quicker to associate** Thierry Devos and Mahzarin Banaji, "America = White?" *Journal of Personality and Social Psychology*, Vol. 88, No. 3 (2005), pp. 447–466.

191 **unconsciously associated Obama with being American** Thierry Devos, Debbie S. Ma, and Travis Gaffud, "Is Barack Obama American Enough to Be the Next President? The Role of Ethnicity and National Identity in American Politics," http://www-rohan.sdsu.edu/~tdevos/thd/Devos_spsp2008.pdf.

196 **A large majority of Americans** Vedantam, "See No Bias."

198 **Obama won only 43 percent** Adam Nossiter, "For South, a Waning Hold on National Politics," *The New York Times*, November 10, 2008.

200 **"Higher welfare payments do not assist"** www.heritage.org/Research/welfare/BG1063.cfm.

201 **attitudes toward the black welfare mom** Martin Gilens, "Race Coding and White Opposition to Welfare," *American Political Science Review*, Vol. 90, No. 3 (1996), pp. 593–604.

203 **woman had been severely injured** Vedantam, "See No Bias."

204 **more than 60 percent of respondents** James H. Kuklinski, Paul J. Quirk, Jennifer Jerit, David Schwieder, and Robert F. Rich, "Misinformation and the Currency of Democratic Citizenship," *The Journal of Politics*, Vol. 62, No. 3 (Aug. 2000), pp. 790–816.

206 **There is experimental evidence** Franklin D. Gilliam, Jr., Shanto Iyengar,

Adam Simon, and Oliver Wright, "Crime in Black and White: The Violent, Scary World of Local News," *The Harvard International Journal of Press/Politics,* Vol. 1, No. 6 (1996), pp. 6–23.

208 **existing stereotypes and biased media coverage**   Gilens, "Race Coding and White Opposition to Welfare."

208 **Richard L. Trumka, told colleagues**   A transcript of Trumka's speech is at www.aflcio.org/mediacenter/prsptm/sp07012008.cfm, but the remarks as delivered were slightly different: www.youtube.com/watch?v=7QIGJTHdH50.

209 **a quarter of the land area**   Pennsylvania Congressional Districts, www .dos.state.pa.us/bcel/LIB/bcel/20/9/2000_stw_congress.pdf, 2002.

210 **"Barack HUSSEIN Obama"**   Type the keywords "Palin rally," "Johnstown," and "Oct 11" into the YouTube search box at www.youtube.com for a number of videos.

215 **when some Republican party leaders**   Peter Wallsten, "Frank Talk of Obama and Race in Virginia," *Los Angeles Times,* October 5, 2008, p. A01.

216 **"Obama's support among working, hard-working Americans"**   Kathy Kiely and Jill Lawrence, "Clinton Makes Case for Wide Appeal," *USA Today,* www.usatoday.com/news/politics/election2008/2008-05-07-clintoninter view_N.htm, May 7, 2008.

218 **comments made by John C. Hagee**   Michael Luo, "McCain Rejects Hagee Backing as Nazi Remarks Surface," *The New York Times,* http://thecau cus.blogs.nytimes.com/2008/05/22/mccain-rejects-hagee-backing-as-nazi -remarks-surface/?scp=2&sq=mccain%20and%20pastor&st=cse, May 22, 2008.

218 **"strike . . . the United States of America"**   Pastor Larry Kroon, "Sin Is Personal to God," Wasilla Bible Church, www.wasillabible.org/sermon _files/2008_Transcripts/Sin%20is%20Personal%20to%20God.doc, July 20, 2008.

218 **"In the fine, new American tradition"**   David Waters, "Palin's Pastor Problem," *On Faith, The Washington Post,* http://newsweek.washingtonpost .com/onfaith/undergod/2008/09/palins_new_pastor_problem.html, September 26, 2008.

219 **"things I don't always agree with"**   Brian Ross and Rehab El-Buri, "Obama's Pastor: God Damn America, U.S. to Blame for 9/11," http://abc news.go.com/blotter/story?id=4443788, March 13, 2008.

219 **the black infant mortality rate**   Philip J. Mazzocco, Timothy C. Brock, Gregory J. Brock, Kristina R. Olson, and Mahzarin R. Banaji, "The Cost of Being Black: White Americans' Perceptions and the Question of Reparations," *Du Bois Review,* Vol. 3, No. 2 (2006), pp. 261–297.

220 **worse two hundred years ago**   Richard P. Eibach and Joyce Ehrlinger, " 'Keep Your Eyes on the Prize': Reference Points and Racial Differences in Assessing Progress Toward Equality," *Personality and Social Psychology Bulletin,* Vol. 32 (2006), p. 66.

Chapter 10: The Telescope Effect

233 **his service revolver to his head** John Violanti, "Analysis of Risk Factors for Police Suicides and Homicides," Research in Progress, 2008.

234 **the relative risk of suicide** Ibid. Violanti examined death certificates in Alaska, Colorado, Georgia, Hawaii, Idaho, Indiana, Kansas, Kentucky, Maine, Missouri, Nebraska, Nevada, New Hampshire, New Jersey, New Mexico, New York, North Carolina, Ohio, Oklahoma, Pennsylvania, Rhode Island, South Carolina, Tennessee, Utah, Vermont, Washington, West Virginia, and Wisconsin.

236 **gun suicides account for more than** Shankar Vedantam, "Packing Protection or Packing Suicide Risk?" *Department of Human Behavior, The Washington Post,* July 7, 2008, p. A02.

236 **a reduced number of handgun suicides** Colin Loftin, David McDowall, Brian Wiersema, and Talbert J. Cottey, "Effects of Restrictive Licensing of Handguns on Homicide and Suicide in the District of Columbia," *The New England Journal of Medicine,* Vol. 325 (December 5, 1991), pp. 1615–1620.

237 **"for the purpose of immediate self-defense"** Robert Barnes, "Justices Reject D.C. Ban on Handgun Ownership," *The Washington Post,* June 27, 2008, p. A01.

238 **high levels of gun ownership** National Center for Health Statistics, Centers for Disease Control and Prevention, http://www.cdc.gov/nchs/. Information was gathered from various tables and reports.

238 **957 of these victims—86 percent** "Rates of Homicide, Suicide, and Firearm-Related Death Among Children—26 Industrialized Countries," www.cdc.gov/MMWR/preview/mmwrhtml/00046149.htm, February 7, 1997.

238 **guns in people's homes were implicated** Arthur L. Kellermann and Philip J. Cook, "Armed and Dangerous, Guns in American Homes," in *Lethal Imagination: Violence and Brutality in American History,* ed. Michael Bellesiles, New York: New York University Press, 1999, pp. 425–439.

239 **Congress slashed funding for CDC** William Kistner, "Firearm Injuries: The Gun Battle over Science," Frontline, www.pbs.org/wgbh/pages/front line/shows/guns/procon/injuries.html, May 1997.

239 **"highest completion rates for suicide"** Shankar Vedantam, "The Assassin in the Mirror," *Department of Human Behavior, The Washington Post,* July 7, 2008, p. A02.

239 **ninety seconds to read each page** www.cdc.gov/ncipc/dvp/suicide/Suicide DataSheet.pdf. There is one suicide every sixteen minutes, on average, in the United States.

242 **would be personally killed by terrorism** Jennifer S. Lerner, Roxana M. Gonzalez, Deborah A. Small, and Baruch Fischhoff, "Effects of Fear and Anger on Perceived Risks of Terrorism: A National Field Experiment," *Psychological Science,* Vol. 14, No. 2 (2003), pp. 144–150.

243 **no one who could help** Chris Lee and George Butler, "Complex Response to Tankship *Insiko 1907*," *Proceedings of the Marine Safety Council*, Vol. 60, No. 1 (January–March 2003), pp. 49–51.

246 **rescuers tried to tempt the terrier** "Costly Effort to Rescue Dog Gives Some Pause," *Los Angeles Times*, April 26, 2002, p. A34.

248 **ABC News devoted eighteen minutes** Paul Slovic, " 'If I Look at the Mass, I Will Never Act': Psychic Numbing and Genocide," *Judgment and Decision Making*, Vol. 2, No. 2 (April 2007), pp. 79–95.

249 **The philosopher Peter Singer once devised** Peter Singer has mentioned the story about the drowning child in a number of publications, including his 2009 book, *The Life You Can Save*, Random House, Inc.

ABOUT THE AUTHOR

SHANKAR VEDANTAM is a national science writer at *The Washington Post*. Between 2006 and 2009, Vedantam authored the weekly Department of Human Behavior column in *The Washington Post*. He is the winner of several journalism awards. Vedantam is a 2009–2010 Nieman Fellow at Harvard University and currently lives in Cambridge, Massachusetts, with his wife and daughter.

ABOUT THE TYPE

This book was set in Sabon, a typeface designed by the well-known German typographer Jan Tschichold (1902–1974). Sabon's design is based upon the original letter forms of Claude Garmond and was created specifically to be used for three sources: foundry type for hand composition, Linotype, and Monotype. Tschichold named his typeface for the famous Frankfurt typefounder Jacques Sabon, who died in 1580.